HARDWIRING
HAPPINESS

Dr Ri... is a neuropsychologist, and an authority on self-d... plasticity... nder of the Wellspring I...
for N... Con...ative Wisdom... an Affi...ate of the... Science... has been invite... Oxford, Stanford and other universities, and ta... in meditation centers worldwide.

He is the author of *Buddha's Brain: the practical ... ...ce of happiness, love and wisdom* (written with Rick Mendius, and tran...ed into 24 languages), *Just One Thing* and *Mother Nurture*. His work has been featured widely, including by the BBC, CBC, NPR and *O* magazine, and his articles have appeared in *Tricycle* magazine, *Insight Journal* and *Inquiring Mind*. He edits the Wise Brain Bulletin, and his weekly e-newsletter – Just One Thing – has more than 80,000 subscribers. He also appears on the Huffington Post, Psychology Today and other major websites.

For more information, please see www.RickHanson.net

Praise for *Hardwiring Happiness*

"Rick Hanson is a master of his craft, showing us a wise path for daily living in this book. Based on the latest findings in neuroscience, this book reveals that if we understand the brain a little, we can take care of our lives a lot, and make a real difference to our well-being. Here is a book to savour, to practise, and take to heart."

— Mark Williams, PhD, professor, University of Oxford, and
author of *Mindfulness: Finding Peace in a Frantic World*

"The cultivation of happiness is one of the most important skills anyone can ever learn. Luckily, it's not hard when we know the way to water and nourish these wholesome seeds, which are already there in our consciousness. This book offers simple, accessible, practical steps for touching the peace and joy that are every person's birthright."

—Thich Nhat Hahn, author of *Being Peace* and
Understanding Our Mind

"This book is as clear and inspired as it gets as far as explaining how to use this orb on top of our necks as means to a better life and, dare I say, happiness. It worked for me."

—Ruby Wax, author of *Sane New World: Taming The Mind*

"Truly helpful and wise, this book nourishes your practical goodness and feeds the vitality of your human spirit. Following these practices will transform your life."

—Jack Kornfield, PhD, author of *A Path with Heart*

"In this remarkable book, one of the world's leading authorities on mind training takes these insights and shows us ways we can cultivate the helpful and good within us. In a beautifully written and accessible way, Rick Hanson offers us an inspiring gift of wise insights and compassionate and uplifting practices that will be of enormous benefit to all who read this book. A book of hope and joyfulness."

—Paul Gilbert, PhD, OBE, author of *The Compassionate Mind:
A New Approach to Life's Challenges*

"*Hardwiring Happiness* teaches us the life-affirming skills of inverting our evolutionary bias to hold on to the negative in our lives and instead soak in and savor the positive. What better gift can we give ourselves or our loved ones than an effective strategy to increase joy through brain-based steps that are both accessible and pleasurable? Bravo!"

—Daniel J. Siegel, MD, clinical professor, UCLA School of Medicine, and author of *Mindsight*, *The Mindful Brain*, and *Brainstorm*

"I have learned more about positive psychology from Rick Hanson than from any other scientist. Read this book, take in the good, and change your brain so that you can become the person you were destined to be."

—Robert A. Emmons, PhD, editor-in-chief of *The Journal of Positive Psychology*, and author of *Gratitude Works!* and *Thanks!*

"Learning to take in the good is like fully and mindfully breathing in life: it allows us to access our inner strengths, creativity, vitality, and love. In his brilliant new book, Rick Hanson gives us the fascinating science behind attending to positive experiences, and offers powerful and doable ways to awaken the deep and lasting well-being we yearn for."

—Tara Brach, PhD, author of *Radical Acceptance* and *True Refuge*

"Dr. Hanson has laid out an amazingly clear, easy, and practical pathway to happiness."

—Kristin Neff, PhD, associate professor, University of Texas at Austin, and author of *Self-Compassion*

"A fascinating exploration of the new science of happiness and how we can learn to shape our own brains."

—Roman Krznaric, PhD, author of *The Wonderbox*

"Rick Hanson is brilliant not only at making complex scientific information about the brain simple. For anyone wanting to decode the black box of the brain and take advantage of its potential, this is the book to read."

—Harville Hendrix, PhD, coauthor of *Making Marriage Simple*

"With current neuroscience to back him up, Rick Hanson has given us an incredible gift. The practices within this book don't take much time at all, yet have the potential to yield true and lasting change."

—Sharon Salzberg, author of *Lovingkindness* and *Real Happiness: The Power of Meditation*

"Dr. Hanson offers a remarkably simple, yet transformative, approach to cultivating happiness. He provides clear instructions for bringing these insights into challenging areas such as parenting, procrastination, healing trauma, and transforming relationships. This book is a gift, one you will want to read over and over and share with your friends."

—Christopher Germer, PhD, clinical instructor, Harvard Medical School, author of *The Mindful Path to Self-Compassion*, and coeditor of *Mindfulness and Psychotherapy*

"Seamlessly weaving together insights from modern neuroscience, positive psychology, evolutionary biology, and years of clinical practice, Dr. Hanson provides a wealth of practical tools anyone can use to feel less anxious, frustrated, and distressed in everyday life. With humor, warmth, and humility, this book combines new research and ancient wisdom to give us easy-to-follow, step-by-step instructions to counteract our hardwired tendency for psychological distress and live richer, happier, more loving and fulfilled lives."

—Ronald D. Siegel, PsyD, assistant clinical professor of psychology, Harvard Medical School, and author of *The Mindfulness Solution: Everyday Practices for Everyday Problems*

"Dr. Hanson shows us, in compelling prose sprinkled with humor, how we can learn to 're-wire' our brain, so that we can respond to the world in a receptive mode, one resting in peace, contentment, and love. I can't imagine a better prescription for our troubled world!"

—Robert D. Truog, MD, professor of medical ethics, anesthesiology, and pediatrics; director of clinical ethics, Harvard Medical School

"In a lively and lovely voice, Rick Hanson offers an inspiring, easily accessible guidebook to living happily."

—Sylvia Boorstein, PhD, author of *Happiness Is an Inside Job*

"In *Hardwiring Happiness,* Dr. Rick Hanson has given us an instruction manual for creating new brain patterns. This ability, once mastered, can change your life. And he does it all with a gentle humor and kindness that shines throughout the book."

—Bill O'Hanlon, author of *The Change Your Life Book* and *Do One Thing Different*

"This book is a gem. I recommend keeping it on your bedside table and making it the first thing you read each day."

—Cassandra Vieten, PhD, president, Institute of Noetic Sciences, and coauthor of *Living Deeply*

"Unique in the growing field of neuroscience, Rick Hanson not only explains how the brain works, he gives us the tools to fix it. This book is a toolbox for transformation."

—Wes Nisker, author of *Buddha's Nature*

HARDWIRING
HAPPINESS

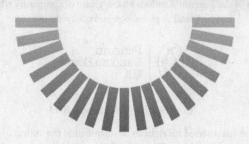

How to reshape
your brain and your life

RICK HANSON

RIDER

LONDON · SYDNEY · AUCKLAND · JOHANNESBURG

5 7 9 10 8 6

Rider, an imprint of Ebury Publishing,
20 Vauxhall Bridge Road,
London SW1V 2SA

Rider is part of the Penguin Random House group of companies whose addresses
can be found at global.penguinrandomhouse.com

Copyright © Rick Hanson 2013

Rick Hanson has asserted his right to be identified as the author of this Work in
accordance with the Copyright, Designs and Patents Act 1988

This edition published in 2014

First published by Rider in 2013
First published in the United States by Harmony, an imprint of the
Crown Publishing Group, in 2013

www.eburypublishing.co.uk

A CIP catalogue record for this book is available from the British Library

ISBN 9781846043574

Penguin Random House is committed to a sustainable future for
our business, our readers and our planet. This book is made from
Forest Stewardship Council® certified paper.

Printed and bound in Great Britain by Clays Ltd, St Ives plc

For Laurel and Forrest

Think not lightly of good, saying, "It will not come to me."

Drop by drop is the water pot filled.

Likewise, the wise one, gathering it little by little,

fills oneself with good.

—DHAMMAPADA 9.122

Contents

Acknowledgments

The practice of taking in the good is a natural one. Who has not spent a dozen seconds enjoying and absorbing a positive experience? Nonetheless, like other common practices such as gratitude and forgiveness, this one has not received much attention until recently. It's been a pleasure to explore the research on savoring by Fred Bryant, Nancy Fagley, Joseph Veroff, Jordi Quoidbach, Erica Chadwick, and others, and the work on coherence therapy by Bruce Ecker, Laurel Hulley, Brian Toomey, Robin Ticic, and colleagues. More generally, I've drawn on the century of scholarship in humanistic and positive psychology, from sources that include Abraham Maslow, Roger Walsh, Martin Seligman, Chris Peterson, Nansook Park, Shauna Shapiro, Barbara Fredrickson, Sonja Lyubomirsky, Michele Tugade, Todd Kashdan, Dacher Keltner, Robert Emmons, Michael McCullough, and Wil Cunningham. I did not invent taking in the good. I've tried to understand its importance in light of our evolved negativity bias and to develop systematic ways to turn transient positive experiences into long-lasting neural structures.

I've been blessed with many benefactors. There are too many to name all of them here, but at least I can honor some of them, including James Baraz, Tara Brach, Jack Kornfield, Joseph Goldstein, Dacher Keltner and everyone at the Greater

Good Science Center of UC Berkeley, Gil Fronsdal, Phillip Moffit, Wes Nisker, Mark Williams, Dan Siegel, Tom Bowlin, Richard Davidson, Andy Olendzki and Mu Soeng at the Barre Center for Buddhist Studies, Saybrook University, Spirit Rock Meditation Center, the Mind and Life Institute, Peter Bauman, the members of the San Rafael Meditation Gathering, Terry Patten, Daniel Ellenberg, Rick Mendius, Tami Simon and everyone at Sounds True, Marci Shimoff, Suzanna Gratz, Julie Benett and everyone at New Harbinger Publications, Andy Dreitcer, Michael Hagerty, and Linda Graham.

Michelle Keane has been an extraordinary business manager and friend even while bearing and rearing a beautiful baby girl. Marion Reynolds has been both caring and competent with my late night administrative needs. Janelle Caponigro has brought tremendous skill to the research on my course on taking in the good. Kerri McGowan created order from chaos under extreme time pressure with the Reference Notes and Bibliography. Vesela Simic did a wonderful job with the stories in the book, and Michael Taft saved my bacon with his skillful editing, writing, and advice. Under intense time pressure, Laurel Hanson, Stacia Trask, Daniel Ellenberg, Linda Graham, and Risa Kaparo read the manuscript carefully and made many helpful suggestions; special thanks to Laurel for the word, "Link," for the fourth step of taking in the good. My agent, Amy Rennert, has both a huge heart and complete mastery of her craft; Michael Jordan is the Amy Rennert of basketball players. My editor at Crown, Heather Jackson, has been a wonderful combination of encouragement, warmth, and pencil-sharp feedback; the team at Crown, including Jillian Sanders, Lisa Erickson, Meredith McGinnis, Sigi Nacson, and Rick Willett, have been a pleasure to work with.

My father, William; sister Lynne and her husband, Jim;

and brother Keith and his wife, Jenny, are friends as well as family. And of course there are my wife, son, and daughter—Jan, Forrest, and Laurel—who make me happy every time I see them; thank you for loving me.

To all of you, it has meant so much to me to be able to take in at least a little of the good you've so generously offered, and I thank you for this from the bottom of my heart.

Introduction

If you're like me and many people, you go through each day zipping from one thing to another. But along the way, when's the last time you stopped for ten seconds to feel and take in one of the positive moments that happen in even the most hectic day? If you don't take those extra seconds to enjoy and stay with the experience, it passes through you like wind through the trees, momentarily pleasant but with no lasting value.

This book is about one simple thing: the hidden power of everyday positive experiences to change your brain—and therefore your life—for the better. I'll show you how to turn good moments into a great brain, full of confidence, ease, comfort, self-worth, and feeling cared about. These are not million-dollar moments. They're simply the cozy feeling of a favorite sweater, pleasure in a cup of coffee, warmth from a friend, satisfaction after finishing a task, or love from your mate.

A few times a day, a dozen seconds at a time, you'll learn how to *take in the good*, which will naturally grow more joy, calm, and strength inside you. But this practice and the science behind it are neither positive thinking nor another program for manufacturing positive experiences, both of which are usually wasted on the brain. This is about transforming fleeting experiences into lasting improvements in your neural net worth.

The inner strengths we need for well-being, coping, and success are built from brain structure—but to help our ancestors survive, the brain evolved a negativity bias that makes it like Velcro for bad experiences but Teflon for good ones. To solve this problem and build inner strengths into your brain, you'll learn which positive experiences can meet your three essential needs for *safety*, *satisfaction*, and *connection*. As you build up inner peace, contentment, and love, you won't need to chase after pleasant events or struggle with unpleasant ones. You'll increasingly enjoy a sense of wellness that's unconditional, not based on external conditions.

Your brain is the most important organ in your body, and what happens in it determines what you think and feel, say and do. Many studies show that your experiences are continually changing your brain one way or another. This book is about getting good at changing your brain for the better.

The brain is amazing, and you'll learn a lot about it. In the first three chapters, I'll give an overview of how your brain works, why you need to take charge of it, and how you can come home to your wonderful deep nature. Then in the rest of the book, I'll show you many effective ways to take in the good and become really skillful at this practice. You won't need a background in neuroscience or psychology to understand these ideas. I've distilled them down to four simple steps with the acronym **HEAL**: Have a positive experience. Enrich it. Absorb it. Link positive and negative material so that positive soothes and even replaces negative. (The fourth step is optional.) We'll explore each step thoroughly, and you'll learn many practical, down-to-earth ways, right in the middle of a busy day, to notice or create positive experiences and then weave them into your mind, your brain, and your life. At the end of each chapter, there's a section called "Taking It In" that summarizes the key points. And if you want to learn more about the science I've drawn upon or read my occasional side comments, see the Reference Notes and Bibliography in the back of the book.

I stumbled on how to take in the good while still in college, and it changed my life. Now, forty years later, in my work as a neuropsychologist I've tried to develop this practice in depth. I've taught it to thousands of people and many of them have sent me stories about how it's changed their lives as well; you'll see some of these stories in italics in the chapters to come. I am delighted to be able to share this powerful practice with you, and if you'd like to learn more about it, please see the freely offered resources at www.RickHanson.net.

As a father, husband, psychologist, meditation teacher, and business consultant, I've learned that it's what we actually *do* both inside the mind and out in the world that makes the most difference. Therefore, you'll see experiential methods for converting passing mental states into enduring neural structure; adapt my suggestions to your own needs. I hope you enjoy what you find in this book, which will help your discoveries sink into your brain and your life.

Trust yourself. Taking in the good helps you see the good in yourself, and in the world and other people.

PART ONE

Why

Chapter 1

Growing Good

Going through school, I was a year or two younger than the other kids in my grade, a shy, skinny, nerdy boy with glasses. Nothing awful happened to me, but it felt like I was watching everyone else through a wall of glass. An outsider, ignored, unwanted, put down. My troubles were small compared to those of many other people. But we all have natural needs to feel seen and valued, especially as children. When these needs aren't met, it's like living on a thin soup. You'll survive, but you won't feel fully nourished. For me, it felt like there was an empty place inside, a hole in my heart.

But while I was in college I stumbled on something that seemed remarkable then, and still seems remarkable to me now. Some small thing would be happening. It could be a few guys saying, "Come on, let's go get pizza," or a young woman smiling at me. Not a big deal. But I found that if I let the good fact become a good *experience*, not just an idea, and then stayed with it for at least a few breaths, not brushing it off or moving on fast to something else, it felt like something good was sinking into me, becoming a part of me. In effect, I was *taking in the good*—a dozen seconds at a time. It was quick, easy, and enjoyable. And I started feeling better.

In the beginning the hole in my heart seemed as big as an empty swimming pool. But taking in a few experiences each day of being included, appreciated, or cared about felt like tossing a few buckets of water into the pool. Day after day, bucket after bucket, month after month, I was gradually filling that hole in my heart. This practice lifted my mood and made me feel increasingly at ease, cheerful, and confident.

Many years later, after becoming a psychologist, I learned why doing this seemingly small practice had made such a large difference for me. I'd been weaving inner strengths into the fabric of my brain, my mind, and my life—which is what I mean by "hardwiring happiness."

Inner Strengths

I've hiked a lot and have often had to depend on what was in my pack. *Inner strengths* are the supplies you've got in your pack as you make your way down the twisting and often hard road of life. They include a positive mood, common sense, integrity, inner peace, determination, and a warm heart. Researchers have identified other strengths as well, such as self-compassion, secure attachment, emotional intelligence, learned optimism, the relaxation response, self-esteem, distress tolerance, self-regulation, resilience, and executive functions. I'm using the word *strength* broadly to include positive feelings such as calm, contentment, and caring, as well as skills, useful perspectives and inclinations, and embodied qualities such as vitality or relaxation. Unlike fleeting mental *states*, inner strengths are stable *traits*, an enduring source of well-being, wise and effective action, and contributions to others.

The idea of inner strengths might seem abstract at first. Let's bring it down to earth with some concrete examples. The alarm goes off and you'd rather snooze—so you find the will to get up. Let's say you have kids and they're squabbling and it's frustrating—so instead of yelling, you get in touch with that place inside that's firm but not angry. You're embarrassed about making a mistake at work—so you call up a sense of worth from past accomplishments. You get stressed racing around—so you find some welcome calm in several long exhalations. You feel sad about not having a partner—so you find some comfort in thinking about the friends you do have. Throughout your day, other inner strengths are operating automatically in the back of your mind, such as a sense of perspective, faith, or self-awareness.

A well-known idea in medicine and psychology is that how you feel and act—both over the course of your life and in specific relationships and situations—is determined by three factors: the *challenges* you face, the *vulnerabilities* these challenges grind on, and the *strengths* you have for meeting your challenges and protecting your vulnerabilities. For example, the challenge of a critical boss would be intensified by a person's vulnerability to anxiety, but he or she could cope by calling on inner strengths of self-soothing and feeling respected by others.

We all have vulnerabilities. Personally, I wish it were not so easy for me to become worried and self-critical. And life has no end of challenges, from minor hassles like dropped cell phone calls to old age, disease, and death. You need strengths to deal with challenges and vulnerabilities, and as either or both of these grow, so must your strengths to match them. If you want to feel less stressed, anxious, frustrated, irritable, depressed, disappointed, lonely, guilty, hurt, or inadequate, having more inner strengths will help you.

Inner strengths are fundamental to a happy, productive, and loving life. For example, research on just one strength, positive emotions, shows that these reduce reactivity and stress, help heal psychological wounds, and improve resilience, well-being, and life satisfaction. Positive emotions encourage the pursuit of opportunities, create positive cycles, and promote success. They also strengthen your immune system, protect your heart, and foster a healthier and longer life.

On average, about a third of a person's strengths are innate, built into his or her genetically based temperament, talents, mood, and personality. The other two-thirds are developed over time. *You get them by growing them.* To me this is wonderful news, since it means that we can develop the happiness and other inner strengths that foster fulfillment, love, effectiveness, wisdom, and inner peace. Finding out *how* to grow these strengths inside you could be the most important thing you ever learn. That's what this book is all about.

In the Garden

Imagine that your mind is like a garden. You could simply be with it, looking at its weeds and flowers without judging or changing anything. Second, you could pull weeds by decreasing what's negative in your mind. Third, you could grow flowers by increasing the positive in your mind. (See the box on page 7 for what I mean by *positive* and *negative*.) In essence, you can manage your mind in three primary ways: *let be, let go, let in.* This book is about the third one, the cultivation of inner strengths:

growing flowers in the garden of the mind. To help you do this most effectively, I'd like to relate it to the other two ways to approach your mind.

WHAT IS *POSITIVE*?

By *positive* and *good*, I mean what leads to happiness and benefit for oneself and others. *Negative* and *bad* mean what leads to suffering and harm. I'm being pragmatic here, not moralistic or religious.

Positive experiences usually feel good. But some experiences that feel bad have good results, so I'll refer to them as positive. For example, the pain of a hand on a hot stove, the anxiety at not finding your child at a park, and the remorse that helps us take the high road make us feel bad now to help us feel better later.

Similarly, negative experiences usually feel bad. But some experiences that feel good have bad results, and I'll call these negative. The buzz from three beers or the vengeance in gossiping about someone who wronged you may feel momentarily pleasurable, but the costs outweigh the benefits. Experiences like these make us feel good now but worse later.

Being with Your Mind

Letting your mind be, simply observing your experience, gives you relief and perspective, like stepping out of a movie screen and watching from twenty rows back. Letting the stream of consciousness run on its own helps you stop chasing what's pleasant and struggling with what's unpleasant. You can explore your experience with interest and (hopefully) kindness toward yourself, and perhaps connect with softer, more vulnerable, and possibly younger layers in your mind. In the light of an accepting, nonreactive awareness, your negative thoughts and feelings can sometimes melt away like morning mists on a sunny day.

Working with Your Mind

But just being with your mind is not enough. You also need to *work with* it, making wise efforts, pulling weeds and growing flowers. Merely witnessing stress, worries, irritability, or a blue mood will not necessarily uproot any of these. As we'll see in the next chapter, the brain evolved to learn all too well from negative experiences, and it stores them in long-lasting neural structures. Nor does being with your mind by itself grow gratitude, enthusiasm, honesty, creativity, or many other inner strengths. These mental qualities are based on underlying neural structures that don't spring into being on their own. Further, to be with your mind fully, you've got to work with it to grow inner strengths such as calm and insight that enable you to feel all your feelings and face your inner shadows even when it's hard. Otherwise, opening to your experience can feel like opening a trapdoor to Hell.

Staying Mindful

Whether you are letting be, letting go, or letting in, be *mindful,* which simply means staying present moment by moment. Mindfulness itself only witnesses, but alongside that witnessing could be active, goal-directed efforts to nudge your mind one way or another. Working with your mind is not at odds with mindfulness. In fact, you need to work with your mind to build up the inner strength of mindfulness.

Be mindful of both your outer world and your inner one, both the facts around you and how you feel about them. Mindfulness is not just *self*-awareness. While rock climbing, I've been extremely mindful of my partner belaying me and looking out for me far below!

A Natural Sequence

When something difficult or uncomfortable happens—when a storm comes to your garden—the three ways to engage your mind give you a very useful, step-by-step sequence. First, be with your experience. Observe it and accept it for what it is even if it's painful. Second, when it feels right—which could be a matter of seconds with a familiar worry or a matter of months or years with the loss of a loved one—begin letting go of whatever is negative. For example, relax your body to reduce tension. Third, again when it feels right, after you've released some or all of what was negative, replace it with something positive. For instance, you could remember what it's like to be with someone who appreciates you, and then stay with this experience for ten or twenty seconds. Besides feeling good in the moment, this third step will have lasting benefits, for when you take in positive experiences, you are not only growing flowers in your mind. You are growing new neural circuits in your *brain*. You are hardwiring happiness.

Experience-Dependent Neuroplasticity

The brain is the organ that *learns*, so it is designed to be changed by your experiences. It still amazes me but it's true: Whatever we repeatedly sense and feel and want and think is slowly but surely sculpting neural structure. As you read this, in the five cups of tofu-like tissue inside your head, nested amid a trillion support cells, 80 to 100 billion neurons are signaling one another in a network with about half a quadrillion connections, called synapses. All this incredibly fast, complex, and dynamic neural activity is continually changing your brain. Active synapses become more sensitive, new synapses start growing within minutes, busy regions get more blood since they need more oxygen and glucose to do their work, and genes inside neurons turn on or off. Meanwhile, less active connections wither away in a process sometimes called neural Darwinism: the survival of the busiest.

All mental activity—sights and sounds, thoughts and feelings, conscious and unconscious processes—is based on underlying neural activity. Much mental and therefore neural activity flows through the brain like ripples on a river, with no lasting effects on its channel. But intense, prolonged, or repeated mental/neural activity—especially if it is conscious—will leave an enduring imprint in neural structure, like a surging current reshaping a riverbed. As they say in neuroscience: *Neurons that fire together wire together*. Mental states become neural traits. Day after day, your mind is building your brain.

This is what scientists call *experience-dependent neuroplasticity*, which is a hot area of research these days. For example, London taxi drivers memorizing the city's spaghetti snarl of streets have thickened neural layers in their *hippocampus*, the region

that helps make visual-spatial memories; as if they were building a muscle, these drivers worked a part of their brain and grew
new tissue there. Moving from the cab to the cushion, mindfulness meditators have increased gray matter—which means
a thicker *cortex*—in three key regions: *prefrontal* areas behind
the forehead that control attention; the *insula,* which we use for
tuning into ourselves and others; and the hippocampus. Your
experiences don't just grow new synapses, remarkable as that is
by itself, but also somehow reach down into your genes—into
little strips of atoms in the twisted molecules of DNA inside the
nuclei of neurons—and change how they operate. For instance,
if you routinely practice relaxation, this will increase the activity of genes that calm down stress reactions, making you more
resilient.

Changing the Brain for the Better

If you step back from the details of these studies, one simple
truth stands out: Your experiences *matter.* Not just for how they
feel in the moment but for the lasting traces they leave in your
brain. Your experiences of happiness, worry, love, and anxiety
can make real changes in your neural networks. The structure-
building processes of the nervous system are turbocharged by
conscious experience, and especially by what's in the foreground
of your awareness. Your attention is like a combination spotlight
and vacuum cleaner: It highlights what it lands on and then
sucks it into your brain—for better or worse.

There's a traditional saying that the mind takes its shape
from what it rests upon. Based on what we've learned about
experience-dependent neuroplasticity, a modern version would

be to say that *the brain* takes *its* shape from what the mind rests upon. If you keep resting your mind on self-criticism, worries, grumbling about others, hurts, and stress, then your brain will be shaped into greater reactivity, vulnerability to anxiety and depressed mood, a narrow focus on threats and losses, and inclinations toward anger, sadness, and guilt. On the other hand, if you keep resting your mind on good events and conditions (someone was nice to you, there's a roof over your head), pleasant feelings, the things you do get done, physical pleasures, and your good intentions and qualities, then over time your brain will take a different shape, one with strength and resilience hardwired into it, as well as a realistically optimistic outlook, a positive mood, and a sense of worth. Looking back over the past week or so, where has your mind been mainly resting?

In effect, what you pay attention to—what you rest your mind on—is the primary shaper of your brain. While some things naturally grab a person's attention—such as a problem at work, a physical pain, or a serious worry—on the whole you have a lot of influence over where your mind rests. This means that you can deliberately prolong and even create the experiences that will shape your brain for the better.

I'll show you how to do this in detail, beginning in chapter 4. Meanwhile, feel free to start taking in the good right now. This practice, applied to a positive experience, boils down to just four words: *have it, enjoy it.* And see for yourself what happens when you do.

The Experiences That Serve You Most

Contemplating your mental garden these days, which flowers would be good to grow? Certain kinds of experiences will help you more than others will.

Negative experiences might have value for a person. For instance, working the graveyard shift in a bottling plant one summer while in college toughened me up. But negative experiences have inherent negative side effects, such as psychological discomfort or the health consequences of stress. They can also create or worsen conflicts with others. When my wife and I were tired and frazzled raising two young children, we snapped at each other more often. The costs of negative experiences routinely outweigh their benefits, and often there's no benefit at all, just pain with no gain. Since neurons that fire together wire together, staying with a negative experience past the point that's useful is like running laps in Hell: You dig the track a little deeper in your brain each time you go around it.

On the other hand, positive experiences always have gain and rarely have pain. They usually feel good in the moment. Additionally, the most direct way to grow inner strengths such as determination, a sense of perspective, positive emotions, and compassion is to have experiences of them in the first place. If you want to develop more gratitude, keep resting your mind on feeling thankful. If you want to feel more loved, look for and stay with experiences in which you feel included, seen, appreciated, liked, or cherished. The answer to the question of *how* to grow good things inside your mind is this: *Take in experiences of them.* This will weave them into your brain, building up their neural circuits, so you can take them with you wherever you go.

Besides growing specific inner strengths for yourself, taking in the good has built-in, general benefits such as being active rather than passive, treating yourself as if you matter, and strengthening your attention. Additionally, as we'll see in chapter 3, over time you can gradually sensitize your brain to positive experiences so they become inner strengths more quickly and easily.

Self-Directed Neuroplasticity

A neurologist friend of mine once described the brain as "three pounds of tapioca pudding." It looks like a gooey, unimpressive blob. But it's the master organ of the body and the primary internal source of your well-being, everyday effectiveness, psychological healing, personal growth, creativity, and success. Whether you feel angry or at ease, frustrated or fulfilled, lonely or loved depends on your neural networks. Further, how brains interact is the basis of fulfilling relationships, successful organizations, thriving nations, and ultimately, whether we live in a peaceful and sustainably prosperous world.

The science of experience-dependent neuroplasticity shows that each person has the power to change his or her brain for the better—what Jeffrey Schwartz has called *self-directed* neuroplasticity. If you don't make use of this power yourself, other forces will shape your brain for you, including pressures at work and home, technology and media, pushy people, the lingering effects of painful past experiences, and as we'll see in the next chapter, Mother Nature herself.

On the other hand, in quick, easy, and enjoyable ways right in the flow of your day, you can use the power of self-directed neuroplasticity to build up a *lasting* sense of ease, confidence, self-acceptance, kindness, feeling loved, contentment, and inner peace. In essence what you'll do with the practices in this book is simple: turn everyday good experiences into good neural structure. Putting it more technically: You will *activate* mental states and then *install* them as neural traits. When you need them, you'll be able to draw on these neural traits, which are your inner strengths, the good growing in your mind.

You'll be using your mind to change your brain to change your mind for the better. Bit by bit, synapse by synapse, you really can build happiness into your brain.

And by doing this, you'll be overcoming its negativity bias: The brain is good at learning from bad experiences, but bad at learning from good ones. As you'll see in the next chapter, if the mind is like a garden, the "soil" of your brain is more fertile for weeds than for flowers. So it's really important to plant the seeds of inner strengths by repeatedly taking in the good.

TAKING IT IN

- A person's inner strengths include peacefulness, content-ment, and love, as well as resilience, confidence, deter-mination, and insight. These strengths help you cope with the hard things in life, recover from stress, heal old pain, maintain your well-being, get things done at home and work, and be patient and caring toward others.

- Most of your inner strengths are developed over time. This book is about growing inner strengths through positive experiences, which is *hardwiring happiness*.

- Simply observing your mind is extremely useful, but you also need to decrease what's negative and increase what's positive. My focus is on increasing the positive: growing flowers in the garden of the mind. Which means changing the structures of your brain.

- All mental activity—sights and sounds, joys and sorrows—is based on underlying neural activity. Repeated mental/neural activity leaves lasting changes in neural structure: what's called experience-dependent neuroplasticity. This means you can use your mind to change your brain to change your mind for the better.

- The best way to develop greater happiness and other inner strengths is to have experiences of them, and then help these good mental states become good neural traits. This is *taking in the good*: activating a positive experience and installing it in your brain.

Chapter 2

Velcro for the Bad

More than twenty years ago, in a neuroscience class for psychologists, the professor walked in with a large bucket, put on a pair of yellow rubber gloves, and with a flourish pulled out a preserved human brain. It looked like a small, spongy, yellowish cauliflower. As the professor droned on about it, I had a weirdly dislocating experience. A thing like the one in his hand "over there" was also "in here," inside my head, trying to make sense of what he was holding. It really hit me that this unimpressive-looking thing was actually producing the sight of the bucket, the sound of the teacher, and my feelings of both "ew" and awe. Every pleasure and pain I had, every love and loss, was the result of activity within this glistening blob of flesh. My brain was the final common pathway of all the causes streaming through me to make each moment of consciousness.

People have long asked why we are glad or sad, why we help or hurt each other. Sages and scientists have explored the *mental* causes of happiness and suffering. Now, for the first time in history, we can ask ourselves: What are the underlying *neural* causes of these causes? And we can find answers in the structures and processes of the human brain as it has been shaped by *evolution.*

The brain didn't spring into being overnight. It acquired its capabilities and tendencies over hundreds of millions of years, and the factors that shaped this long, impersonal history show up in your life today in very personal ways. Suppose you got twenty things done today and made one mistake. What's likely to stick with you as you're falling asleep? Probably the mistake, even though it was just a small part of your day. As you'll see, the reason for this is found in the brain's evolution. By learning how your brain has been built over time, you'll understand yourself and others better. Plus, you'll become more effective at using and shaping that blobby, cauliflower-like, extraordinary thing inside your own head.

The Evolving Brain

Every human being shares common ancestors with bats, begonias, and bacteria that go back at least 3.5 billion years, to the very first microorganisms. Multicelled creatures emerged in the ancient seas 650 million years ago, and after 50 million more years, they'd grown complicated enough that they began to develop a nervous system to coordinate their sensory and motor systems. Mammals arose about 200 million years ago, and the first primates about 60 million years ago. By 2.5 million years ago, our hominid ancestor, *Homo habilis,* was intelligent enough to begin making stone tools, and our own species—*Homo sapiens*, the clever ape—emerged about 200,000 years ago.

Over the last 600 million years, solutions to survival problems faced by creatures ranging from jellyfish and clams to lizards, mice, monkeys, and early humans have gotten built into the evolving nervous system. The brain has roughly tripled in volume over the past several million years, while being carved by the intense pressures of natural selection. Our hominid and human predecessors lived in small hunting-and-gathering bands until organized farming began about 10,000 years ago. Their world was pristine and beautiful, and there was a simplicity, an easygoing pace, and a time for relationships that many long for today.

Nonetheless, the survival challenges they had to manage— such as the prospect of being attacked and eaten by predators— were very different from our own. Because they lived in small bands, it was uncommon for them to meet people they didn't know, and often dangerous when they did. While some bands interacted peacefully with each other, on average about one in eight men died in conflicts between bands, compared to one in a hundred men who died due to warfare in the twentieth century. There were also starvation, parasites, illness, injury, the hazards of childbirth, and no painkillers or police departments. This world was the womb of the human brain, which was pains-takingly adapted to its conditions. The results live on between your ears today, continuing to shape your experiences and guide your actions.

Bad Is Stronger Than Good

To pass on their genes, our reptilian, mammalian, primate, hom-inid, and human ancestors had to get things that were pleasur-able, such as the "carrots" of shelter, food, and sex. Meanwhile, they had to stay away from things that were painful, such as the "sticks" of predators, starvation, and aggression from others of their species. Carrots and sticks are both important, but there's a vital difference between them. From a survival standpoint, sticks have more urgency and impact than carrots. If you fail to get a carrot today, you'll have another chance to get one tomorrow, but if you fail to avoid a stick today—*whap!*—no more carrots forever. Rule #1 in the wild is: Eat lunch today—don't *be* lunch today. Over hundreds of millions of years, it was a matter of life and death to pay extra attention to sticks, react to them intensely, remember them well, and over time become even more sensitive to them.

Consequently, the brain evolved a built-in *negativity bias*. While this bias emerged in harsh settings very different from our own, it continues to operate inside us today as we drive in traffic, head into a meeting, settle a sibling squabble, try to diet, watch the news, juggle housework, pay bills, or go on a date. Your brain has a hair-trigger readiness to go negative to help you survive.

Looking Out for You

For starters, your brain is always on the lookout for potential dangers or losses, which is why news programs typically start their shows with the latest murder or disaster. As they say in journalism: If it bleeds, it leads. Over the course of evolution, animals that were nervous, driven, and clinging were more likely to pass on their genes, and these inclinations are now woven into our DNA. Even when you feel relaxed and happy and connected, your brain keeps scanning for potential dangers, disappointments, and interpersonal issues. Consequently, in the back of your mind, there's usually a subtle but noticeable sense of unease, dissatisfaction, and separation to motivate this vigilance.

Then when the least little thing goes wrong or could be trouble, the brain zooms in on it with a kind of tunnel vision that downplays everything else. If your boss gives you an excellent performance review that contains just one piece of critical feedback in a bucket of praise, you'll likely focus on that one negative comment. Negative stimuli are perceived more rapidly and easily than positive stimuli. We recognize angry faces more quickly than happy ones; in fact, the brain will react even without your conscious awareness when another person's face is angry.

The Power of Pain

Bad (painful, upsetting) experiences routinely overpower good (pleasurable, comforting) ones. The psychologist Daniel Kahnemann received a Nobel Prize in economics for showing that most of us will do more to avert a loss than to acquire an equivalent gain. Lasting intimate relationships usually need at least five positive interactions to balance every negative one. People really begin to thrive when positive moments outnumber negative ones by at least a three-to-one ratio, and ideally higher. Negative contaminates positive more than positive purifies negative; for example, a misdeed will harm a hero's reputation more than a good deed will improve a villain's.

The extra impact of the bad on your mind is based on its extra power in your brain, which responds more intensely to unpleasant things than to equally intense pleasant ones. In the middle of your head, the central circuit of overreactivity has three parts to it: the *amygdala,* the *hypothalamus,* and the *hippocampus.* The

almond-sized amygdala does respond to positive events and feelings, but in most people it is activated more by negative ones.

Think about a time that someone—perhaps your parent,
partner, or a coworker—got angry with you and you felt anxious about it. The other person's anger activated your amygdala
somewhat like a charging lion would have a million years ago.
To begin a fight-or-flight response, your amygdala sent alarm
signals to your hypothalamus and to *sympathetic nervous system* control centers in your brain stem. Your hypothalamus
sent out an urgent call for *adrenaline, cortisol, norepinephrine,*
and other stress hormones. Now your heart was beating faster,
your thoughts were speeding up, and you started feeling rattled
or upset. Your hippocampus formed an initial neural trace of
the experience—what happened, who said what, and how you
felt—and then guided its consolidation in cortical memory networks so you could learn from it later. Connected by the neural
equivalent of a four-lane superhighway, your activated amygdala
commanded your hippocampus to prioritize this stressful experience for storage, even marking new baby neurons to be, in
effect, forever fearful.

Vicious Circles

Over time, negative experiences make the amygdala even *more*
sensitive to the negative. This snowballing effect occurs because
the cortisol that the amygdala signals the hypothalamus to call
for enters the bloodstream and flows into your brain, where it
stimulates and strengthens the amygdala. Now the alarm bell of
your brain rings more easily and more loudly. Making matters
worse, even after the danger has passed or turns out to be a false

alarm, it takes many minutes to metabolize cortisol out of your body. For example, you may have had a close call while driving and still felt revved up and shaken twenty minutes later.

In the meantime, in a one-two punch, the cortisol in your brain overstimulates, weakens, and eventually kills cells in your hippocampus, gradually shrinking it. This is a problem because the hippocampus helps you put things in perspective while also calming down your amygdala and telling your hypothalamus to quit calling for stress hormones. So now it's harder to put the one thing going wrong in the context of the many things going right, plus harder to settle down a runaway amygdala and hypothalamus.

Consequently, feeling stressed, worried, irritated, or hurt today makes you more vulnerable to feeling stressed, etc., tomorrow, which makes you *really* vulnerable the day after that. Negativity leads to more negativity in a very vicious circle.

Paper Tiger Paranoia

One aspect of the negativity bias is so important that it deserves particular attention: the special power of fear. Our ancestors could make two kinds of mistakes: (1) thinking there was a tiger in the bushes when there wasn't one, and (2) thinking there was no tiger in the bushes when there actually was one. The cost of the first mistake was needless anxiety, while the cost of the second one was death. Consequently, we evolved to make the first mistake a thousand times to avoid making the second mistake even once.

People do still make the second mistake. Personally, I don't floss my teeth often enough and I drive too fast. A variation on the second mistake is to be overly optimistic about likely benefits compared to their costs; for example, many gamblers and rock star hopefuls inflate the chance of a payoff. But in general, the default setting of the brain is to *over*estimate threats, *under*estimate opportunities, and *under*estimate resources both for coping with threats and for fulfilling opportunities. Then we update these beliefs with information that confirms them, while ignoring or rejecting information that doesn't. There are even regions in the amygdala specifically designed to prevent the unlearning of fear, especially from childhood experiences. As a result, we end up preoccupied by threats that are actually smaller or more manageable than we'd feared, while overlooking opportunities that are actually greater than we'd hoped for. In effect, we've got a brain that's prone to "paper tiger paranoia."

These biologically based tendencies are intensified by multiple factors. Consider your temperament. Some people (like me) are constitutionally more anxious than others. Also, think about your personal history. Alarming or painful life experiences, especially traumatic ones, naturally make a person more fearful. If you grew up in a dangerous neighborhood, had angry or unpredictable parents, or were bullied in school, it's normal to still be watchful even if you now live in a safe place with nice people. Your current situations make a difference, too. Perhaps you live with someone who can fly off the handle without cause or you're being harassed at work. The economy plays a role as well. Understandably, people feel unsettled or worse when money is tight and daily life is racing and pressured. And throughout history, political groups have played on fears to gain or hold on to power.

What's your own experience of fear? It ranges from mild watchfulness, caution, apprehension, and unease to worries, anxiety, obsessing, panic, and terror. And what role does fear play in your life? When we're afraid, we dream smaller dreams, speak less freely, cling tighter to "us," and feel more fear and anger toward "them." Because others are just as vulnerable to the power of fear as we are, our actions when frightened feel threatening to them, so they overreact, making us feel more afraid than ever.

Velcro and Teflon

The negativity bias also affects the structure-building processes of your brain. Here's how this works. As we've seen, what flows through your mind changes your brain. The result is two kinds of learning, two kinds of memory: *explicit* and *implicit*. Explicit memory has all your personal recollections, from when you were a young child to whatever was going on ten minutes ago. These recollections tend to be positively biased the farther back in time you go. For example, I know logically that my feet must have been killing me in tight climbing shoes on a long route in Yosemite, but all I remember is how great it felt to stand on top with my friend. Explicit memory also includes what's called "declarative knowledge," which is a kind of encyclopedia of information about things such as what a bicycle is, the shape of Earth, and your Social Security number.

Implicit memory includes "procedural knowledge," which is how to do things, from riding that bicycle to navigating a delicate conversation with a friend. It also contains your assumptions and expectations, emotional residues of lived experience, models of relationships, values and inclinations, and the whole

inner atmosphere of your mind. It's like a vast storehouse holding most of your inner strengths as well as most of your feelings
of inadequacy, unfulfilled longings, defensiveness, and old pain.
What gets put into this storehouse is the foundation of how you
feel and function. Its contents usually have much more impact
on your life than the contents of your explicit memory.

Unfortunately, the formation of implicit memory is *negatively* biased. Uncomfortable experiences are immediately fast-
tracked into memory stores: once burned, twice shy. We usually
learn faster from pain than from pleasure. Strong dislikes are
acquired faster than strong likes. In relationships, trust is easy
to lose and hard to regain. Something bad about a person is
better remembered than something good, which is why negative ads dominate political campaigns. Whether between family
members or nations, long-remembered grievances fuel long-
running conflicts. Just a handful of painful experiences of futility can rapidly become a sense of helplessness—a major factor
in depression—and a person usually needs many times as many
counter-experiences of effectiveness in order to regain a sense of
confidence and capability. One way or another, negative mental
states can easily become negative neural traits.

On the other hand, unless it's intense or novel, most good
news has little or no lasting effect on implicit memory systems
in the brain. This happens for three reasons. First, we tend to
look past the good news because we're busy solving problems or
scanning for something to worry about. Ordinary good facts are
all around—birds are calling, people are smiling, hearts are still
beating—and we don't give them much attention. Second, when
we do recognize a good fact, it often fails to become a good
experience. We finish a task—good fact—and then shift to the
next one with little sense of accomplishment. Someone offers a

compliment, and it's brushed aside. We hear the children laughing, but it doesn't lift our hearts.

Third, even if you do notice a good fact and even if it does become a good experience, it probably does not get converted into neural structure, stored in implicit memory. Unless they're million-dollar moments, positive experiences use standard-issue memory systems, in which new information must be held in short-term buffers long enough for it to transfer to long-term storage. "Long enough" depends on the experience and the person, but loosely speaking it's at least a few seconds, and the longer the better. In effect, you have to *keep* resting your mind on a positive experience for it to shape your brain.

But how often do we stay with a positive experience for five, ten, or twenty seconds in a row? Or longer? I sure didn't until I began appreciating the importance of deliberately taking in the good and gradually filling the hole in my heart. Suppose something has happened and you feel peaceful, contented, or loved. Would you typically keep open to this feeling for (let's say) ten seconds, keeping it alive in your awareness, sinking into it as it sinks into you? Most people wouldn't. But if you're not doing this, much if not all of the value available in this experience will be lost. Your brain is like Velcro for negative experiences but Teflon for positive ones.

Wasted Efforts

Unless you consciously take in a good experience, it usually washes through your brain like water through a sieve, leaving little good behind. (In the meantime, your bad experiences are being caught in the sieve by negatively biased implicit memory.)

The experience felt good, but from the standpoint of building neural structure, it may as well not have happened. This is the central weakness in most formal programs of stress management, human resources training, character education for children, mindfulness or compassion training, coaching, psychotherapy, and drug and alcohol treatment. Informally, managers, educators, and parents encounter the same problem. With skill and effort, we create beneficial mental states. Each time this happens, it's good in the moment. But in most cases, we don't consistently and systematically take the extra seconds to *install* these experiences in the brain. I'm talking about myself here, too. As a therapist, it's been humbling and troubling to realize that a large fraction of the positive thoughts and feelings that I helped my clients to access have produced little enduring benefit for them.

The effects of the negativity bias are also frustrating and disheartening for the "learner," which I've been as well. You could be in a structured situation (e.g., leadership training, AA, parenting class) or informally just trying to feel less worried, blue, or stressed. You work hard to get something good going in your mind—some calming, happiness, or healing—and then a few hours later (or sooner, sadly), it's as if it never happened. It's like struggling to push a heavy stone uphill only to have it roll down again.

The negativity bias is not our fault. We didn't create it. Still, we *can* do something about it.

Leveling the Playing Field

The negativity bias doesn't mean you can't be happy. But if you're happy, you're happy in spite of it. It's a *bias*, ready to spring into action depending on events. When you feel good, it waits in the background, looking for a reason to make you feel bad. When you feel bad, it makes you feel worse.

This bias creates two kinds of problems. First, it *increases the negative.* It pulls your attention to what is or could be bad, makes you overreact to it, and stores the negative experience in implicit memory. It also creates vicious circles of negativity both inside your brain and with other people. In a variety of ways, this bias increases your stresses, worries, frustrations, irritations, hurts, sorrows, feelings of falling short, and conflicts with others.

Second, the negativity bias *decreases the positive.* It slides your attention past the good facts around you. It makes you under-react to the good facts you do notice. And it slips the good experiences you do have right through your brain, leaving little or no trace behind. This bias is a kind of bottleneck that makes it harder to get happiness into your brain.

The interest rate in a savings account determines how much you gain financially each day. Which would you rather have, a low rate or a high one? Similarly, the *conversion rate* of positive mental states to positive neural traits determines how much you gain psychologically each day. Here, too, which would you rather have, a low rate or a high one? Unfortunately, the negativity bias lowers this conversion rate, which flattens your gains in life: your happiness, contributions to others, and success.

In effect, the negativity bias is tilted toward immediate survival, but against quality of life, peaceful and fulfilling relationships, and lasting mental and physical health. This is the default setting of the Stone Age brain. If we don't take charge of it, it will continue to take charge of us.

Tilting toward the positive simply levels the playing field. Taking in the good corrects for the two tendencies of the negativity bias: This practice decreases negative feelings, thoughts, and actions while increasing positive ones.

And over time, taking in the good can help you experience that your core needs for safety, satisfaction, and connection are finally fully met. We'll explore how to do this in the next chapter.

TAKING IT IN

- Throughout history, people have wondered about the causes of suffering and happiness as they appeared in the *mind*. Now we are beginning to understand how our experiences are produced by the underlying structures and processes of the *brain*.

- The nervous system has been evolving for 600 million years, and solutions to survival problems faced by ancient reptiles, mammals, primates, and humans are active in your brain today.

- To survive and pass on their genes, our ancestors needed to be especially aware of dangers, losses, and conflicts. Consequently, the brain evolved a negativity bias that looks for bad news, reacts intensely to it, and quickly stores the experience in neural structure. We can still be happy, but this bias creates an ongoing vulnerability to stress, anxiety, disappointment, and hurt.

- A key aspect of the negativity bias is the special power of fear. We routinely overestimate threats and underestimate opportunities and resources. At the same time, negative experiences sensitize the brain to the negative, making it easier to have even more negative experiences in a vicious circle.

- Inner strengths such as happiness and resilience come mainly from positive experiences. But unless we pay mindful, sustained attention to them, most positive experiences flow through our brains like water through a sieve. They're momentarily pleasant but leave little lasting value in terms of changing neural structure. The brain is like Velcro for negative experiences but Teflon for positive ones.

- While the negativity bias is good for survival in harsh conditions, it's lousy for quality of life, fulfilling relationships, personal growth, and long-term health. It makes us overlearn from bad experiences and under-learn from good ones.

- The best way to compensate for the negativity bias is to regularly take in the good.

Chapter 3

Green Brain, Red Brain

Humans have long wondered about human nature, from ancient poets to ordinary people today looking out at the ocean or up to the stars, asking, *Who am I?* The answer matters for many reasons.

If at bottom we are fighters and flee-ers, greedy and addictive, and envious and mean-spirited, then we need to be kept in line by powerful authority figures, strict rules, and heavy guilt and shame. On the other hand, if underneath it all we are even-keeled, grateful, and warmhearted, then we can live more freely, more guided by our own conscience and caring.

Until recently, fact-based answers to fundamental questions about human nature were few and far between. But research in evolutionary neuropsychology and related fields is beginning to offer some clear answers that show how to find a *lasting* sense of security, fulfillment, and loving closeness. So let's explore your brain's three operating systems, the two settings of these systems, and one practice—taking in the good—that can bring you home to happiness. This material can get a little technical, but I think you'll find as I have that it is a really useful—and hopeful—way to understand yourself and others. And starting in the next chapter, we'll get into very practical ways to turn everyday good experiences into lasting happiness and other inner strengths.

Three Operating Systems

To simplify a long and elaborate process: Your brain developed in three stages that are loosely associated with the reptile, mammal, and primate/human phases of evolution. The three layers of your brain were built from the bottom up, like the three floors of a house. Your *brain stem* emerges from the top of your spinal cord. It manages fundamental survival functions such as breathing, and it energizes and guides behavior. The *subcortex* rests atop your brain stem and spreads across the middle of your head. It is the center of emotion, motivation, and bonding. The *cortex* is the outer shell of your brain, and it enables abstract reasoning, reflecting about the past and future, and key social abilities such as empathy, language, and cooperative planning.

Meanwhile, roughly in parallel with the building of the three floors of the brain, the autonomic nervous system was also evolving, along with the very important *vagus nerve.* The oldest branch of the vagus nerve supports the *parasympathetic* wing of your autonomic nervous system, which is calming and inhibiting, and can also promote withdrawal or freezing around threats. Complementing and often opposing the influence of the parasympathetic nervous system and the first branch of the vagus nerve, the *sympathetic* wing of your autonomic nervous system is energizing and exciting; it promotes both the sustained pursuit of opportunities and fighting and fleeing in response to threats. The most recent and uniquely mammalian branch of the vagus nerve supports the "social engagement system." Its tendrils extend down into the heart and other organs and up into the larynx to modulate your tone of voice and into the head to guide your facial expressions.

As the brain evolved, so did its capabilities to meet our three core needs—*safety*, *satisfaction*, and *connection*—through, respectively, three "operating systems" that *avoid* harms, *approach* rewards, and *attach* to others. (I've drawn on and adapted the influential work of Paul MacLean, Jaak Panksepp, Stephen Porges, Paul Gilbert, and E. Tory Higgins for this model.) This sounds complex, but daily life is full of simple examples. Imagine going out to see a friend for dinner. On your way to the restaurant, you avoid harms such as running a red light. Once you sit down at your table, you approach rewards like something good to eat. As you talk with your friend, you feel more connected, more attached to him or her.

To summarize, in general terms your avoiding harms system is linked to the brain stem, to the oldest branch of the vagus nerve, to the parasympathetic nervous system, and to the earliest stages of vertebrate evolution involving fish, amphibians, and reptiles. Your approaching rewards system is linked to the subcortex, to the sympathetic nervous system, and to the mammalian stage of evolution. And your attaching to others system is linked to the cortex, to the most recent branch of the vagus nerve, and to the primate and especially human stage of evolution. (To complicate things, the sympathetic nervous system can also be used to avoid harms through fighting and fleeing, and the mammalian stage of evolution certainly supports complex social behaviors.) It's a little silly, but it helps me to think of my own mind as containing a kind of lizard, mouse, and monkey related to the avoiding, approaching, and attaching systems. We meet our core needs for safety, satisfaction, and connection when we—metaphorically—pet the lizard, feed the mouse, and hug the monkey.

Of course, we can't take metaphors like these too seriously. Today, the three operating systems—avoiding, approaching, and attaching—use your brain as a whole to accomplish their aims; they're defined by the *functions* they serve, not by their anatomy. While these functions are rooted in ancient biological imperatives—swim away from a predator, eat a carrot, make a baby—they play out today in ways that would astonish a caveman, let alone a goldfish, gopher, or gorilla. For instance, the attaching to others system clicks into gear whether it's a high school girl putting on makeup before the prom, bonobos picking lice off each other, prairie voles experiencing elevated oxytocin levels in the presence of their mates, or a salmon swimming upstream to spawn. In effect, you experience life from inside a home that's taken hundreds of millions of years to build.

Each operating system has its own set of abilities, mental activities, and behaviors; for the details, see Table 1, "Features of the Avoiding, Approaching, and Attaching Systems." One system can use the other two to serve its purposes. For example, to avoid the harm of someone breaking into your home, you could approach a hardware store to get a bolt lock for your door and attach to a big dog. Two or three of these systems can be running at the same time. Shopping at a market, you could be joking with your preschooler who is riding in the cart (attaching) while getting groceries (approaching) and staying out of the aisle with the cookies (avoiding).

Table 1: Features of the Avoiding, Approaching, and Attaching Systems

Characteristic	Avoiding	Approaching	Attaching
Need	Safety	Satisfaction	Connection
Challenge	Threat	Loss	Rejection
Attends to	Risks	Opportunities	Relationships
Priorities	Preventing declines	Promoting improvements	Sexuality, intimacy, self-worth
Appreciates from others	Reassurance	Encouragement	Warmth
Capabilities	Freeze, flight, fight	Forage, sustained chase	Empathy, bonding, language
Behavioral inclination	Caution, inhibition, withdrawal	Eagerness, excitation, pursuit	Sociability, bonding, affection
Key neurotransmitter systems	Acetylcholine	Dopamine, opioids	Oxytocin, vasopressin
Branch of vagus nerve	First		Second
Key area of brain	Right hemisphere; less left prefrontal activation	Left hemisphere; more left prefrontal activation	"Social engagement system"

I've found it very useful to become more aware of when one of my core needs—safety, satisfaction, and connection—is being taken care of, what that system feels like when it's operating, and (as we'll explore in the next chapter) how to take in the key experiences that will especially help that particular system. The avoiding, approaching, and attaching systems manage how we meet challenges, and they organize and direct most of our experiences and actions. They pretty much run the show—and they do so in two very distinct and *very* far-reaching ways.

The Responsive Mode

Imagine a day in which you feel generally fine. After waking up, you spend a few minutes in bed lightly thinking ahead about some of the people you will see and the things you will do. You hit traffic on the way to work, but you don't fight it; you just listen to the radio and don't let the other drivers bother you. You may not be excited about your job, but today you're focusing on the sense of accomplishment you feel as you complete each task. On the way home, your partner calls and asks you to stop at the store; it's not your favorite thing to do after work, but you remind yourself it's just fifteen extra minutes. In the evening, you look forward to a TV show and you enjoy watching it.

Now let's look at the same day, but imagine approaching it in a different way. After waking up, you spend a few minutes in bed pessimistically anticipating the day ahead and thinking about how boring work will be. Today, the traffic really gets under your skin, and when a car cuts you off, you get angry and honk your horn. You're still rankled by the incident when you start work, and to make matters worse, you have an unbelievable number of rote tasks to get through. By the time you're driving home, you feel fried and don't want to do a single extra thing. Your partner calls to ask you to stop at the store. You feel put upon but don't say anything and go to the store. Then you spend much of the evening quietly seething that you do all the work around the house. Your favorite show is on, but it's hard to enjoy watching it, you feel so tired and irritated.

Over these two imaginary days, the same exact things happened. All that was different was how your brain dealt with them—the *setting* that it used.

Each of your brain's operating systems has essentially two settings: *responsive* and *reactive*. As long as you experience that the core need a system handles is basically being met, then that system defaults to its responsive setting. When you feel safe, your avoiding harms system enters its responsive mode, which brings feelings of relaxation, calm, and peace. When you feel satisfied, your approaching rewards system shifts into its responsive setting, with feelings such as gratitude, gladness, accomplishment, and contentment. And when you feel connected, your attaching to others system goes responsive, evoking feelings of belonging, intimacy, compassion, kindness, worth, and love. For simplicity, I think of this as the "green" setting of your brain.

In the responsive mode, you meet challenges without them becoming *stressors*. Events occur, even hard ones, but there's a kind of shock absorber in your brain that stops them from rattling you. You deal with threat, loss, or rejection without getting carried along by feelings of fear, frustration, or heartache. You're still engaged with life, and sometimes handling very difficult things, but on the basis of an underlying sense of security, fulfillment, and feeling cared about.

In other words, when your brain is not *disturbed* by threat, loss, or rejection, it settles into its resting state, its responsive mode. Neurochemical systems involving *oxytocin* and natural *opioids,* regions such as the *subgenual cingulate cortex,* and neural networks such as the parasympathetic nervous system (PNS) initiate and maintain this balanced, sustainable, *homeostatic* condition. In it, you'll often feel at ease, relaxed, and relatively calm, while moderate to high PNS activation slows your heart rate, lowers blood pressure, promotes digestion, and replenishes your body, brain, and mind. It's also possible to be active and energized in the responsive mode, with more sympathetic nervous system activation. Mammals, including us, become friendly, playful, curious, and creative when they feel safe, satisfied, and connected. When the lights on your brain's dashboard are green, you can still be strong and determined, asserting yourself, pursuing your goals with enthusiasm, standing up to injustice, living with passion, making love, creating art, cheering on your children, and howling happily at the moon on a good night with friends. Whether you're quiet or active, your emotions in this mode remain generally positive.

Table 2 summarizes the responsive mode of the avoiding, approaching, and attaching systems. In this mode, you're not pressured or rattled; nothing is out of whack. There's a sense of ease, comfort, ongoing all-rightness. Things may not be great, but they're okay and you're basically fine. You know what this feels like because it is your resting state, when there is no fundamental sense of deficit or disturbance. It is your natural home base. You don't have to scratch and claw your way to it. When whatever felt frightening, frustrating, or hurtful comes to an end, you'll soon come home to the lovely green meadow that has always been there, even if it was hidden for a while by the fogs and shadows of an unsettled mind. This is who you most essentially are, which is both inspiring and a relief to know.

Table 2: Responsive Mode of the Avoiding, Approaching, and Attaching Systems

Characteristic	Avoiding	Approaching	Attaching
Sense of self	Safe	Satisfied	Connected
View of world	Protection	Sufficiency	Inclusion
Stance	Confident	Fulfilled	Related
Copes through	Asserting	Aspiring	Caring
Related actions	Dignity, gravity, restraint	Generosity, creativity	Empathy, compassion, kindness, cooperation, affection
Central experience	Peace	Contentment	Love
Related feelings	Strong, calm, relaxed, tranquil, agency, efficacy	Grateful, glad, enthusiastic, accomplished, successful	Seen, liked, appreciated, worthy, cherished, special

It's Good to Be Home

Your brain is the master regulator of your body. In its responsive mode, it tells your body to conserve energy and to refuel and repair itself. Our ancestors evolved this setting of the brain to prevent, manage, end, and recover from depleting and damaging bursts of stressful activity. For example, the *endorphins*, other natural opioids, and *nitric oxide* that are released when your brain goes green kill bacteria, relieve pain, and reduce inflammation. Unlike pathogenic processes that cause bad health, the *salutogenic* responsive mode causes good health. Responsive type experiences prepare your mind and brain and body to meet future challenges in a responsive way. The responsive mode evolved to be pleasurable in order to motivate our ancestors to seek it. It feels good because it *is* good.

When your mind is in the green zone, your neural networks are no longer in a state of deficit or disturbance, and your hypothalamus becomes less active. As this central controller of thirst, hunger, lust, and other drives quiets down, so does your sense of lack, pressure, and demand. In your brain as a whole, there is less and less basis for aversion, grasping, and clinging: in a word, *craving*, broadly defined. As deficit- and disturbance-based motivations fall away, so do worry and irritability, disappointment and drivenness, hurt and shame. As you rest more and more fully in the responsive mode, the underlying neurobiological causes of stress, fear, frustration, and heartache—suffering, also broadly defined—are gradually extinguished.

Already feeling basically safe and strong, accomplished and grateful, and respected and liked, you're more able to be fair-minded, compassionate, and generous toward others. Your natural lovingness becomes unobstructed and can flow freely, nourished by the sense of your own core needs being met.

The green brain is contagious. When you come from a responsive place, it helps draw others there as well. When you're not irritated, pushy, or needy, you're less likely to provoke others; when you feel centered, it is harder for others to provoke you.

Positive circles grow. When a relationship "goes green," it can still have misunderstandings, bumps, and conflicts, but they're handled in a responsive way. People can also treat each other this way in families, groups, and organizations. Challenges are faced, competition and confrontations occur, but on a foundation of empathy and goodwill.

Your natural resting state, the responsive mode of your brain, is the foundation of psychological healing, everyday well-being and effectiveness, long-term health, fulfilling relationships, and the highest reaches of human potential. And every time you take in the good and experience that your core needs are being met, you strengthen the neural substrates of this mode. You could even be sensitizing your brain to positive experiences so that it will turn them increasingly quickly into neural structure.

Velcro for the Good

As our ancestors evolved, they had to respond to things that mattered, that were *salient*. Is it a stick? Avoid it. Is it a carrot? Approach it. Is it a friendly member of my species? Attach to it. Consequently, the brain evolved a *salience network* that reacts to good news, like the face of a friend, and to bad news, like the smell of smoke inside a building. This network tells you what's relevant, what you should care about and remember. Its messages guide the *executive control network*, centered in the prefrontal cortex behind and above your forehead, which shapes your actions, words, and thoughts.

If you've been stressed, your salience network becomes sensitized to bad news. Now you're on red alert. This negative sensitization might help you survive, but it also makes you feel bad and overreact. On the other hand, by taking in the good, you could sensitize your salience network to good news, in effect putting it on *green* alert.

Your brain can become sensitized to the good in a variety of ways. The upper and frontal parts of your *cingulate cortex* are like an internal bell that rings if you deviate from a goal or plan ("better get back on track"). Regularly looking for opportunities to take in the good could train this part of your brain to keep aiming you in the direction of positive experiences. Or take the insula, which is continually "listening" to your body as it tells the brain how it's doing. The central functions of your body are usually doing just fine, even if there are some aches or a wonky digestion. Repeatedly tuning into a mild but pleasant state of physical well-being, such as experiencing that there is plenty of air to breathe, could sensitize your insula to a viscerally important positive experience that is available with each breath.

And of course there is the amygdala, in many ways the hub of the salience network. Your amygdala reacts to both bad news and good news. Less amygdala reactivity to the bad would help you feel less anxious or angry, but it would not by itself make you more happy. For that, you need stronger reactions to the *positive*. You need what Wil Cunningham has called "a joyful amygdala."

In terms of amygdala activation, people seem to belong to one of three groups. Some react equally strongly to positive and negative stimuli. Others have a "grumpy amygdala" that reacts more to negative stimuli than to positive ones; risks and pains have more impact than opportunities and pleasures. A third group has stronger amygdala reactions to positive stimuli than to negative ones. These people—the ones with a joyful amygdala—are more focused on promoting the good than on preventing the bad. This is called an "approach orientation," which has numerous benefits for physical and mental health, relationships, and success. These people also have relatively high positive emotions compared to people in the other two groups. In fact, these happier individuals have more amygdala stimulation to the *nucleus accumbens,* a control center deep in the brain that initiates actions toward a person's goals. In effect, happiness encourages us to take practical steps toward our dreams.

Why would the brain have evolved the capacity to turn a grumpy amygdala into a joyful one? The amygdala quickly becomes sensitized to negative experiences through vicious circles involving the stress hormone cortisol. This helped our ancestors survive in tough conditions by highlighting the threats around them, making their brains like Velcro for the bad. But in good conditions, whether in the jungle millions of years ago or in the lives of most people today, it would be adaptive for survival to sensitize the amygdala to positive experiences, which would heighten the approach to opportunities and help make the brain like Velcro for the good.

Positive experiences, especially if they have a sense of freshness about them, increase the release of the neurotransmitter *dopamine.* While you are taking in the good, you typically prolong dopamine inputs to your amygdala. These sustained releases of dopamine make it react more intensely to good facts and experiences, with associated signals to your hippocampus saying essentially, "This is a keeper, remember this one." In sum, whether through your cingulate cortex, insula, amygdala, or other parts of the salience or executive control networks, repeatedly taking in positive experiences will likely make your brain "stickier" for them, which will increase your positive experiences, making your brain even stickier in a positive circle.

The Reactive Mode

Then there is the other setting of your brain, the one that evolved to keep our ancestors alive when they were disturbed by threat, loss, or rejection. Multiple neural systems continually scan for any sense that something's wrong, any sense that one of your three core needs—for safety, satisfaction, and connection—is not being met. While the responsive mode is our resting state, the negativity bias makes us very vulnerable to being knocked out of that state and into the reactive mode. Perhaps you feel apprehensive or exasperated, pulled in different directions, or left out or criticized. This disturbs the healthy equilibrium of the responsive mode and triggers the reactive mode, the "red" setting of your brain, which evolved to help our ancestors to escape the eager jaws of predators, scrabble for the last bits of food, and protect babies at any cost.

In the red zone, the amygdala sends an alarm both to your hypothalamus to release stress hormones and to your sympathetic nervous system for the *hyper*-arousal of fleeing or fighting. (If there's a history of trauma, the amygdala could instead trigger extreme parasympathetic activation to initiate the *hypo*-arousal of freezing, numbing, or dissociation.) The neural circuits our ancestors used for raw survival light up today when we're worried about money, feeling pressured about a project at work, or hurt by a frown across a dinner table.

The reactive mode assumes that there are urgent demands, so it's not concerned with your long-term needs. In this disturbed, *allostatic* state—which ranges from subtle to intense—bodily resources are depleted while building projects such as strengthening the immune system are put on hold, adrenaline and cortisol course through the blood, and fear, frustration, and heartache color the mind. At the same time, the negativity bias is heightening the storage of the negative experience in your implicit memory. In a broad sense, the reactive mode is the neural foundation of craving (by which I mean coming from a sense of deficit or disturbance), and the suffering and harm it causes you and others. See Table 3 for a summary of the features of this setting of your brain.

Stuck on Red

The natural, biologically based rhythm is for animals, including us, to spend most of their time in the responsive mode. In the background, the negativity bias is operating, creating an inclination toward occasional reactive bursts. These bursts are supposed to end quickly . . . one way or another. The reactive mode is a departure from the responsive baseline, and we're designed by evolution to return to this baseline as soon as possible. Just entering the red zone triggers neurochemical processes (involving natural opioids, nitric oxide, and other chemicals) designed to bring you home to green, followed by a nice long recovery there. Even though reactive experiences feel bad, as long as they follow the evolutionary blueprint—infrequent, brief, and usually moderate—they will likely have few lasting consequences.

Unfortunately, much of modern life violates this ancient design. While most people are no longer exposed to the intense pressures of predation, starvation, and lethal conflict, we do commonly face ongoing mild to moderate stressors—such as doing multiple things at once, processing dense incoming streams of information and stimulation, racing from here to there, working long hours, and rapidly shifting gears—with little time for

Table 3: Reactive Mode of the Avoiding, Approaching, and Attaching Systems

Characteristic	Avoiding	Approaching	Attaching
Sense of self	Unsafe	Dissatisfied	Disconnected
View of world	Danger	Scarcity	Exclusion
Stance	Aversive	Coveting	Separated
Copes through	Resisting	Grasping	Clinging
Related actions	Appease, freeze, flee, fight	Drivenness, addiction	Reproach, quarreling, prejudice
Central experience	Fear	Frustration	Heartache
Related feelings	Angry, immobilized, defeated, weak, overwhelmed, helpless	Disappointed, failed, sad, grieving	Hurt, dismissed, abandoned, mistreated, provoked, aggrieved, envious, jealous, rejected, lonely, ashamed, inadequate, unworthy

responsive recovery between them. In the wild, regular exercise helped clear stress-based cortisol out of the body, but our sedentary lifestyle allows cortisol to keep circulating, which increases reactivity in a vicious circle. Modern economies require consumerism, so you're continually encouraged to chase more rewards. Meanwhile, the news is full of pains and perils you can't do anything about. All this puts the brain on high alert. Its ancient reptile, mammal, primate, and Stone Age circuits keep flashing red: *Something's wrong, watch out!* Due to the negativity bias, these experiences are swiftly encoded in neural structure. And because of our unique human ability to sustain states of mind unrelated to our immediate environment, internalized psychological factors—such as a sense of inadequacy about getting everything done in time—can keep you feeling stressed long after a challenge has passed.

As a result, while the reactive mode is designed to be a short-lived departure from the home base of healthy equilibrium, for many people it's become the new normal, a kind of chronic inner homelessness. This may not feel awful—you may "just" carry around a background sense of being pressed, hassled, tense, prickly, drained, inadequate, uneasy, or glum—but it's bad for your well-being, health, and relationships.

Costs of the Reactive Mode

Going red feels bad emotionally, shifts perspectives negatively, and impairs learning. It sucks up resources that could have been used for pleasure and ease, and for personal healing and growth. It makes us hunker down, muzzle self-expression, and dream smaller dreams. It promotes problematic self-soothing or "self-medicating" through overeating, drugs and alcohol, video games, or pornography. Meanwhile, your body's stress reactions halt long-term building and repair. The red zone feels bad because it *is* bad. Its unpleasantness is a primal signal that you should leave it as fast as you can and avoid it if possible.

We shouldn't underestimate the growing impact of reactive experiences. Over time, they are risk factors for depression and other mental issues. Many psychological disorders involve reactive extremes in one of the brain's three operating systems. For example, generalized anxiety, agoraphobia, post-traumatic stress disorder (PTSD), obsessive-compulsive disorder (OCD), dissociative disorder, social anxiety, and panic are related to the avoiding system. Substance abuse or dependence, and other addictive processes, are related to the approaching system. Insecure attachment, narcissism, borderline personality disorder, antisocial behavior, and the consequences of child abuse and neglect are related to the attaching system.

In your body, the gradually accumulating burden of reactive experiences is called *allostatic load,* which increases inflammation, weakens your immune system, and wears on your cardiovascular system. In your brain, allostatic load causes neurons to atrophy in the prefrontal cortex, the center of top-down executive control; in the hippocampus, the center of learning and memory; and in other regions. It impairs *myelination,* the insulating of neural fibers to speed along their signals, which can weaken the connectivity between different regions of your brain, so they don't work together as well as they should. For example, it could become harder for you to stay in touch with the big picture if someone else is provoking you. Chronic stress also reduces the *neurotrophin,* BDNF, which we need to protect neurons and promote learning, particularly in the prefrontal cortex.

In relationships, "seeing red" has powerful negative effects.

I've been very hurt by people who've put me down or let me down, and I know I've hurt others in similar ways. Just think about how it felt when you were wronged or mistreated in a significant relationship. Simply regarding others as "them," even when there is no conflict, reduces our capacity for empathy and increases our tendency to dehumanize and devalue those people. Compared to other animals, humans are particularly prone to retaliation. Reactivity feeds conflict, which feeds reactivity, in an escalating cycle of grievance, grudge, and payback.

Let's step back and consider the wider implications. The brain is the most influential organ in the body. The primary source of the brain's contribution to our overreactions, unhappiness, psychopathology, lifestyle-based illnesses, and relationship problems is its red, reactive setting.

The Choice

These two ways in which the brain operates, responsive and reactive, green and red, are the foundation of human nature. We have no choice about the vital needs the brain serves—avoiding harms, approaching rewards, and attaching to others—nor about its capacity to be in either mode, green or red. Our only choice is which mode we're in. (See Table 4 for a comparison of the two modes.)

Living under the shadow of danger and pain, hunger and loss, and social aggression and humiliation, primates and early humans evolved a brain that is prone to crave and suffer in order to survive. When conditions were harsh, most individuals died young, and bands feared and fought each other, the short-term benefits of the reactive mode outweighed its long-term costs. But these days, when conditions are better, people want a long and healthy life, and billions of us need to live cooperatively together, the costs of the reactive mode greatly outweigh its benefits. In effect, one of the brain's major design features for passing on genes is now a design flaw, a "bug," in the twenty-first century. What can you do about it?

Table 4: Summary of Responsive and Reactive Modes

Characteristic	Responsive	Reactive
Sense of self	Safe, satisfied, connected	Unsafe, dissatisfied, disconnected
View of world	Protection, sufficiency, inclusion	Danger, scarcity, exclusion
Stance	Confident, fulfilled, related	Aversive, coveting, separated
Copes through	Asserting, aspiring, caring	Resisting, grasping, clinging
Metabolism	Replenishment	Depletion
Bodily systems	Building up	Wearing down
Effect on health	Salutogenic	Pathogenic
Equilibrium	Stable, homeostatic	Disturbed, allostatic
Central experience	Peace, contentment, love	Fear, frustration, heartache

You can use your mind to change your brain for the better. In particular, you can *engage life from the responsive mode as much as possible, contain and calm reactive states when they occur, and return to your responsive home base as soon as you can.* This is the better path, the alternative to stress, unhappiness, conflicts with others, and many health problems. And as you follow this path, it will become easier to stay on it, since your brain will become increasingly biased toward it.

Developing a Responsivity Bias

We saw in chapter 2 that the negativity bias has five basic features. It makes you (1) get reactive when conditions are challenging; (2) feel uneasy, dissatisfied, and disconnected even when conditions are fine; (3) over-learn from bad experiences; (4) become quickly sensitized toward reactivity; and (5) return slowly to the responsive mode even when the coast is clear. But we are not stuck with being this way.

Over time, taking in the good could actually turn your brain's negativity bias into a *responsivity bias*—with five very different features—that will help you stay centered, strong, healthy, and happy. First, whether you go responsive or reactive when you're challenged depends on what's been woven into your brain. Repeatedly internalizing positive experiences builds up inner strengths so you can meet life's challenges without fear, frustration, or heartache. Second, taking in the good shows you again and again that you are basically all right right now, that there are always grounds for gratitude and gladness, and that you are cared about and worthy.

Third, your increasingly positive experiences and growing inner strengths will prevent negative experiences from slipping into your mind and sinking into your brain. As your mental garden fills with flowers, there's less room for weeds to grow. Fourth, as we saw earlier in this chapter, you'll be sensitizing your brain to the positive, making it like Velcro for good. Fifth, if you've already become stressed, upset, or unhappy, starting to take in the good as soon as you can do so authentically begins the recovery process from reactive states. Further, as taking in the good builds up your inner strengths, your body will become increasingly resilient and your mind will become increasingly centered in a fundamental peace, contentment, and love, so you'll recover more quickly from negative experiences in general.

Taking in the good brings you home. Home to a comfortable intimacy with your own experience, to a confident openness to life, to a sense of competence, even mastery, with your own mind. Reactive material may still come up for you—it does for me—but you'll be increasingly able to hold it in a responsive framework. When my mother passed away, I felt sad and lost, but these feelings were like storm clouds in a big sky of acceptance, gratitude, and love for my family. Even if one of your brain's operating systems is blinking red, the other two can remain green. For instance, you might feel worried about an unexpected bill (avoiding) while also being glad about having a steady job (approaching) and feeling supported by your mate (attaching).

Even in hard times, you can still take simple actions within your reach that have been designed by Mother Nature to dial down the red, dial up the green, and bring you back to your resting state—actions such as exhaling slowly, remembering a time you felt strong, savoring a physical pleasure, thinking about someone who cares about you, and feeling loving yourself. These are not miracle cures. But with time and effort and practice, it is perfectly natural for you to spend most minutes of most days resting in the responsive mode of your brain.

Peace, contentment, and love are important *aims* for most people. These are the rewards, the fruits, of a good life. Additionally, because of experience-dependent neuroplasticity, these experiences are a powerful *method*, a wonderful path, for transforming your brain. Every time you take in the sense of feeling safe, satisfied, or connected, you stimulate responsive circuits in your brain. When you stimulate a neural circuit, you strengthen it. To borrow a Tibetan saying, taking in the good is "taking the fruit as the path." Happiness is skillful means.

TAKING IT IN

- The brain was built in three stages—brain stem, subcortex, and cortex—that are loosely related to reptilian, mammalian, and primate evolution. In a parallel process, the two branches of the vagus nerve also developed.

- As the brain evolved, so did its capability to meet our three core needs—*safety*, *satisfaction*, and *connection*—through, respectively, three "operating systems" that *avoid* harms, *approach* rewards, and *attach* to others.

- The avoiding, approaching, and attaching systems in your brain have essentially two settings. When you experience that your core needs are met in any system, it returns to its resting state, its "green," *responsive* mode. In this homeostatic setting, the home base of the brain, your body refuels and repairs itself. Meanwhile, your mind rests in a basic sense of peace, contentment, and love, in terms of the avoiding, approaching, and attaching systems. You still engage life with all of its challenges, but with an underlying sense of security, fulfillment, and caring.

- When your brain goes green, you are not *disturbed* by threat, loss, or rejection, and thus there is no real basis for aversion, grasping, or clinging—for our *craving*. In the responsive mode, there is little or no fuel for stress, anxiety, irritation, drivenness, dissatisfaction, sadness, hurt, envy, or conflicts—for our *suffering*.

- On the other hand, when you experience that a core need is not met, due to the negativity bias, your brain quickly shifts into its "red," fight/flight/freeze *reactive* mode. In this *allostatic* setting, bodily resources are drained while building projects are put on hold. In the red zone, your mind is colored by fear, frustration, and heartache, in terms of the avoiding, approaching, and attaching systems.

- Our reptilian, mammalian, primate, and human ancestors typically spent long periods in the responsive mode punctuated by brief bursts of reactive stress followed by another long stretch of responsive recovery. Modern life violates this ancient template with its pervasive mild to moderate stressors. Consequently, the reactive mode has become the new normal for many people, a kind of chronic inner homelessness that has harmful effects on mental and physical health, and on relationships.

- Taking in the good draws you out of reactive episodes and strengthens the responsive capacities of your brain. As you weave an underlying sense of strength and well-being into yourself, your happiness becomes increasingly unconditional, less and less based on external conditions. Remarkably, the experiences of peace, contentment, and love that are important *aims* for a good life are also powerful *methods* for achieving it.

PART TWO

How

Chapter 4

HEAL Yourself

A friend of mine suddenly lost her relationship after more than a decade of happiness with her partner. He was the love of her life. After he left, she felt empty and despairing. She talked with her friends, exercised, meditated, and saw a therapist, all of which helped. But her grief still felt intense, and sometimes overwhelming.

Then she decided to add taking in the good to the other things she was doing to feel better, and something began to shift. "When I went for a run," she told me later, "I felt good. When I stayed with how this felt, it was like the good feelings were soaking into my mind from the body up." The same thing happened when she took a hot bath and let the relaxation sink in, or took the extra seconds to enjoy the satisfaction she felt when she finished a project at work. "My sadness and hopelessness began to pass away." After a few weeks, she said that taking in good feelings a few times each day had played a real role in easing her sense of loss. "I honestly feel it helped me learn to be happy again."

Her story is pretty dramatic, but it's true. My friend didn't try to paper over her hurt and sadness with positive thinking. She let her grief be, and slowly, over many months, it let go. Along the way, when she could, she let in positive experiences of vitality, relaxation, satisfaction, and eventually joy.

When you tilt toward the good, you're not denying or resisting the bad. You're simply acknowledging, enjoying, and using the good. You're aware of the whole truth, *all* the tiles of the mosaic of life, not only the negative ones. You recognize the good in yourself, in others, in the world, and in the future we can make together. And when you choose to, you take it in.

The Four Steps of Taking In the Good

Technically, taking in the good is *the deliberate internalization of positive experiences in implicit memory.* It involves four simple steps:

1. **Have a positive experience.**
2. **Enrich it.**
3. **Absorb it.**
4. **Link positive and negative material.**

Step 1 *activates* a positive mental state, and steps 2, 3, and 4 *install* it in your brain. The first letter of each step produces the acronym **HEAL.** The first three steps focus entirely on positive experiences. The fourth step is optional, but powerful: It uses positive thoughts and feelings to soothe, reduce, and potentially replace negative ones.

A Quick Walk Up the Steps

I'll summarize the steps here, and then chapters 5 to 10 will cover them in depth. (If you'd like to get an experiential sense of this practice, see the box "A Taste of Taking in the Good," page 62.) When you're actually taking in the good, the three or four steps tend to blend together, but when you're first learning this practice, it helps to be clear about what is specifically happening within each one.

STEP 1. **Have a positive experience** Notice a positive experience that's already present in the foreground or background of your awareness, such as a physical pleasure, a sense of determination, or feeling close to someone. Or create a positive experience for yourself. For example, you could think about things for which you're grateful, bring to mind a friend, or recognize a task you've completed. As much as you can, help ideas like these become emotionally rewarding *experiences*; otherwise, it's merely positive *thinking*.

STEP 2. **Enrich it** Stay with the positive experience for five to ten seconds or longer. Open to the feelings in it and try to sense it in your body; let it fill your mind. Enjoy it. Gently encourage the experience to be more intense. Find something fresh or novel about it. Recognize how it's personally relevant, how it could nourish or help you, or make a difference in your life. Get those neurons really firing together, so they'll really wire together.

STEP 3. **Absorb it** Intend and sense that the experience is sinking into you as you sink into it. Let it really land in your mind. Perhaps visualize it sifting down into you like golden dust, or feel it easing you like a soothing balm. Or place it like a jewel in the treasure chest of your heart. Know that the experience is becoming part of you, a resource inside that you can take with you wherever you go.

A TASTE OF TAKING IN THE GOOD

Would you like to get a sense of how it feels to take in the good? I'll suggest some prompts here that you can use for the first three steps; we'll explore the fourth one in chapter 8. Take my prompt and go through the first three steps on your own.

- Notice something pleasant that's already present in your experience. Perhaps a relaxed sense of breathing, comfort, or curiosity.
- Find something good in your immediate situation. Perhaps something sturdy, well made, protective, useful, or beautiful, such as a cozy chair, a tree out the window, or a picture on the wall.
- Think of something you are glad about, in your life these days or in your past. It could be as simple as having a roof over your head.
- Bring to mind someone who makes you feel cared about. It need not be a perfect relationship, but the caring—the warmth for you, the wishing you well—is genuine.
- Bring to mind someone you like.
- Think of some things that help you feel strong . . . peaceful . . . grateful . . . happy . . . loved . . . loving.

STEP 4. **Link positive and negative material** (optional) While having a vivid and stable sense of a positive experience in the foreground of awareness, also be aware of something negative in the background. For example, when you feel included and liked these days, you could sense this experience making contact with feelings of loneliness from your past. If the negative material hijacks your attention, drop it and focus only on the positive; when you feel recentered in the positive, you can let the negative also be present in awareness if you like. Whenever you want, let go of all negative material and rest only in the positive. Then, to continue uprooting the negative material, a few times over the next hour be aware of only neutral or positive material while also bringing to mind neutral things (e.g., people, situations, ideas) that have become associated with the negative material.

Getting Good at Taking In the Good

You already know how to take in the good even if you haven't done it consciously. We've all had the experience of savoring a delicious meal or enjoying a good time with friends. But as with any other skill, you can probably get better at it. So I'm going to offer some suggestions here. As you try them, become more aware of how it feels to take in the good, like marking a path in the woods so you know how to come back the same way again.

Appreciating the Little Things

Most opportunities for a good experience arrive with little fanfare. You finished an e-mail, the telephone works, you have a friend. And most good experiences are relatively mild; on the zero to ten intensity scale, they're ones and twos. No matter. These moments still count in their own right. Plus they can add up over time to change your brain for the better.

Finding Good Times for Good Experiences

Typically you'll take in the good during the flow of life. As I write this, our elderly brown and silver cat is curled up on my desk, giving me a cozy feeling of family that is good to take in. As you move through your day, look for chances to let good experiences sink into you.

You can also take in the good at specific times. For example, on first waking, you could call to mind an experience that's important to you, such as good wishes toward others. Meals are a traditional opportunity to feel thankful. Just before bed, your mind is very receptive, so no matter what went wrong that day, find something that went right, open to it, and let good feelings come and ease you into sleep.

Doing It Your Way

People take in the good in different ways, and that's fine. Consider gratitude. One person might approach this conceptually. I'm blown away by the fact that anything exists at all, that this universe is here with us in it. Talk about gifts! Another person might relate to gratitude concretely, such as by appreciating a friend. Your family background could also play a role. In some homes, sharing pleasures together is warm and connecting, while in others, positive experiences are more private.

Enjoying It

Sometimes it might be hard to let yourself have a good experience. So consider "the friend test." If your friend could have a positive experience, would you wish that for him or her? Would you want your friend to be able to enjoy the experience and to take it in? Well, it is equally valid to wish to have positive experiences yourself. You're not looking at the world through rose-tinted glasses, but rather correcting your brain's tendency to look at it through smog-tinted ones. And by taking in the good, you become more able to deal with the bad. This doesn't mean putting on a happy face if you feel stressed or let down. But when you have the opportunity, why not let yourself feel good, and grow more strengths inside?

Of course, every experience, no matter how positive, is impermanent. When you take in the good, stay in the present, enjoying what is flowing through your awareness without trying to grab it as it goes by, opening to it so that it sinks into you.

Being for Yourself

To take in the good, you have to want to help yourself. Being for yourself, not against others but on your own side, is the foundation of all practices of health, well-being, and effectiveness. Without this stance, you wouldn't be motivated to act on your own behalf. Unfortunately, for reasons such as being criticized a lot as a child, many people are a much better friend to others than they are to themselves. The more that others didn't stick up for you in the past, the more important it is for you to stick up for yourself today. (To take in and thus strengthen this sense of being on your own side, try the guided practice in the following box.

BEING FOR YOURSELF

This practice uses the first three steps of taking in the good. Adapt my suggestions as you like.

1. **HAVE** Notice any quality of being for yourself already present in the foreground or background of awareness. Perhaps you can sense or feel a determination to take care of your own needs, or good wishes for yourself. Or, create this feeling. Bring to mind a time when you were strong on your own behalf, when you self-advocated or were kind to yourself. If it's hard to get on your own side, start by remembering the experience of being for some-one else. Feel what this is like, and then see if you can bring the same attitude to yourself. Perhaps get an image or memory of yourself as a young, vulnerable child and see if you can feel supportive toward that young person.

2. **ENRICH** Open to this feeling. Let it fill your body and mind and become more intense. Stay with it, help it last, make a sanctuary for it in your mind. Notice different aspects of the experience. Imagine how you would sit or stand or speak if you were on your own side, and then let your pos-ture or facial expression shift in this direction. Be aware of how being on your own side would matter for you at home or work.

3. **ABSORB** Sense and intend that this feeling of being on your own side is sinking into you as you sink into it. Let this good experience become a part of you. Give yourself over to it. Let being kind toward yourself, wishing yourself well, be increasingly how you treat yourself.

Making It a Habit

The brain is a physical system that, like a muscle, gets stronger the more you exercise it. So make taking in the good a regular part of your life. This will be deliberate at first, but it will become increasingly automatic. Hardly thinking about it, you'll be weaving good experiences into your brain. You can routinely take in the good with even the simplest experiences, as this man wrote me: *I love to take in the good whenever I eat an orange. I have at least two a day, so I get an opportunity to experience this moment often. As I break through the skin, I gently close my eyes and breathe in the sweet scent. I hold that pleasure in my mind and think about how I am the first person ever to see inside this orange and taste its fruit. Although this experience takes less than a minute, it has an enormously positive effect on my mood and energy level. I look forward to it throughout the day.*

Taking In What You Need

You can use the HEAL steps for any positive experience. But as you've probably seen in your own life, some experiences feel more nourishing than other ones do. How can you focus on the experiences that will help you the most? This is where taking in the good gets very personal—and very wonderful, for you can take in the experiences that are *specifically* aimed at your own wants and needs.

Perhaps you'd like to feel less worried, self-critical, or insecure. Perhaps you're dealing with a tough situation at home or work, or you'd like to feel motivated to exercise more or drink less. Perhaps you'd simply like to feel happier, more at ease in life, and more loved. What, if you had more of it inside you, would make a big difference for you?

A good way to answer this question is in terms of your brain's three operating systems. If you feel worried, tense, pushed on, or helpless, that triggers the avoiding harms system, so you'd be particularly helped by "resource experiences" related to this system, such as protection, safety, relaxation, strength, and agency. Sadness, disappointment, frustration, drivenness, pressure, or boredom engage the approaching rewards system and are best addressed by related resource experiences of gratitude, pleasure, accomplishment, and satisfaction. Feeling left out, hurt, inadequate, envious, lonely, resentful, or provoked involves the attaching to others system, so resource experiences of belonging, self-compassion, being appreciated, friendship, kindness, and assertiveness would especially help here.

In other words, a problem requires a solution that's matched to it. If you have scurvy, you need vitamin C. For years I tried to fulfill my need for love—a need that everyone has—by piling up accomplishments, but this never worked because I was trying to fix an attaching to others type of problem with an approaching rewards type of solution. In effect, I took a lot of iron pills for scurvy, which didn't help. Only by taking in attaching type experiences—feeling seen, included, respected, liked, and cherished—have I been able to gradually take care of this need of mine.

So what's your own vitamin C? It could be related to a current situation, a long-standing difficulty with another person, or an old wound from your childhood. When you know what you want to take in and grow inside yourself, you can look for opportunities in daily life to experience it and install it in your brain by using the HEAL steps. You're being on your own side, a good friend to yourself, giving yourself the psychological nutrient you need. Once it's installed, this inner strength will be easier to activate the next time you need it, and then you can reinstall it, deepening its neural trace in a positive circle. And of course you can use this approach for more than one "vitamin," for more than one resource experience.

Here's an example of taking in experiences that are specifically targeted at a person's needs, in this case in the avoiding harms system: *I was having panic attacks, and so each day I went out on my back porch and focused on my garden. I would look at the plants I love and watch the insects buzz around, the birds hop between plants, and the sunshine filter through the leaves. For a few minutes, I would take in the feelings of safety I had in my garden. Sometimes I imagined this confidence and peace making a golden protective bubble around me. Then I would pick up a small object from the garden and put it in my pocket. When I started to feel uncomfortable anxiety, I held the object, remembering how I felt in my garden, and bringing those feelings of strength and peace into my mind.*

Even if you can't get every bit of the experience you want, at least you can get parts of it. You've got to start somewhere, so take the step that's in front of you. When I first went to college, I was very shy. One night my roommate asked if I wanted to come along with him and a group of young women. This made me very nervous. But it was a step toward the relationship experiences I knew I needed. So I made myself go with him and stayed quiet, but it turned out all right. They were nice to me and I felt included. Over the next few days, I ran mental replays of what had happened, taking in these good feelings again and again. This helped me be a little more open the next time I got asked along, which brought me even richer experiences of being wanted, appreciated, and liked. One good thing led to another. I really broke out of my shell in college, which put me on a life path I couldn't have dreamed of as a dorky kid in high school. Looking back nearly forty years later, I see that a key step on that path was saying yes to my roommate that night.

It's Good to Take In the Good

It takes a little effort to take in the good, especially in the beginning. Plus you might have some internal blocks to doing it, such as the belief that it's selfish to feel good (to get through blocks like this one, see chapter 9). Motivation is the key to sticking with anything, thus it helps to know *why* taking in the good is good for you and others. So I'd like to summarize the benefits of this practice, including some I've already mentioned.

By taking just a few extra seconds to stay with a positive experience—even the comfort in a single breath—you'll help turn a passing mental state into lasting neural structure. Over time, you can fill up your inner storehouse with the strengths you need, such as feeling at ease rather than irritable, loved rather than mistreated, and resourced rather than running on empty. These strengths will foster well-being and effectiveness, heal psychological issues such as anxiety, and support creativity, self-actualization, and spiritual practice.

Inherently, taking in the good is a way to be active rather than passive—a hammer rather than a nail—at a time when many people feel pushed and prodded by events and their reactions to them. It's also a way to treat yourself like you matter, which is especially important if others haven't. This practice brings you into the present moment and reduces rumination, that repetitive rehashing of things in your mind that fosters mental and physical health problems. It teaches you to have more control over your attention, so you can keep it on what's good for you and others and pull it away from what's bad. All the while, you'll be sensitizing your brain to positive experiences, making it like Velcro for the good—a far-reaching benefit.

Growing your inner strengths through taking in the good is like deepening the keel of a sailboat so that it's less jostled by the worldly winds, it recovers more quickly from big storms, and you can now safely head out into deeper waters in pursuit of your dreams. You'll be turning moments of *hedonic* well-being into a more fundamental ongoing sense of fulfillment and meaning: what's called *eudaimonic* well-being. In a positive circle, feeling better helps you act better, which helps the world treat you better, which helps you feel better.

Taking in the good is not about chasing after pleasure or chasing away pain. It's about bringing the chase to an end. When you get good experiences into your brain—when you build up the sense of being already peaceful, contented, and loved—your well-being becomes increasingly *unconditional*, less dependent on external conditions such as a partner being nice or a good day at work. As your positive mental states become positive neural traits, you'll gradually rest in a happiness that emerges naturally inside you.

Everyday Jewels

If you take in a lot of good, you might do it five or ten times a day, ten to thirty seconds at a time—five minutes at most. It won't take over your life. You won't become self-absorbed or overly positive. You'll still recognize challenges, you'll still feel bad sometimes. You won't ignore health problems, financial trouble, mistreatment from others, or emotional pain. You won't forget that here and around the world, terrible things happen every day to millions of people—and might happen to any one of us.

But just as good facts do not cancel bad ones, bad facts do not cancel good ones. Good facts are all around you, even in a challenging life—things large and small that support your happiness and welfare and the happiness and welfare of others. Chocolate is delicious, beautiful sights and sounds are all around, you do get many things done each day, and you do make a difference to others. You can enjoy the results of the hard work of countless people who've made our world today. Turn on a tap and there's water, flip a switch and there's light. You have the good fortune of a human body, brain, and mind, painstakingly crafted through 3.5 billion years of evolution. More vastly, you've been gifted by the universe altogether. Every atom heavier than helium—the oxygen in air and water, the calcium in teeth and bones, the iron in blood—was born inside a star. You're literally made out of stardust.

There are people who wish you well, who like you, who see the good in you. Almost certainly, you are loved. Your kind heart and good intentions are real, they exist. You've created much good in the past and you continue to do so in the present. Like me, you're not a perfect person—no one is—but you are a good one.

Good facts abide and abound no matter how obscured. In this moment—and in most others—you are all right right now. Each moment of experience is saturated with an almost overwhelming fullness. You are continuously connected with all things. If you have a sense of something transcendental such as God, Spirit, or whatever is meaningful to you, then this, too, is a marvelous goodness.

Besides the good here in the present, there were good facts in your past and there will be good ones in your future. Just think of some of the pleasurable, fulfilling, or meaningful times you've had, or some of your accomplishments, or people who've seen the light in you and loved you. Think of the future, the good that could happen, the love you could give and get.

All this good means that each day is like a winding path strewn with pearls and diamonds, emeralds and rubies, each one an opportunity for a positive experience. Unfortunately, most people hurry by without noticing them. And even when they do see a jewel, they rarely *feel* anything about it. Jewel after jewel left behind, lost forever.

But it doesn't have to be this way. With a little intention and skill, you can take some seconds here and there each day to weave a handful of these jewels into the fabric of your brain, your being, and your life. Little moments of ease, pleasure, calm, determination, joy, insight, and caring becoming neural structure.

It's just a few jewels each day. But day after day, gradually adding up, they become the good that lasts. It's the law of little things: lots of little bad things take people to a hard and painful place, and lots of little good things take them to a better one. I'm often struck by how big a change a few moments can make, inside my own mind or inside someone else's. I find this really hopeful, since it's the little things that we have the most influence over. You can't do anything about the past, but you do have the power to take in the good during the next few moments. As a proverb puts it: *If you take care of the minutes, the years will take care of themselves.*

TAKING IT IN

- Taking in the good is the deliberate internalization of positive experiences in implicit memory. It involves four simple steps (the fourth one is optional). (1) **H**ave a positive experience. (2) **E**nrich it. (3) **A**bsorb it. (4) **L**ink positive and negative material. The first letter of each step forms the acronym HEAL. Step 1 *activates* a positive experience, and steps 2 to 4 *install* it in your brain.

- It's natural to take in the good. We all know its essence: have a positive experience and then really enjoy it. But as with any other skill, you can get better at it through both learning and practice.

- Most positive experiences are relatively brief and mild. But taking in half a dozen of them a day, half a minute or less at a time, will add up to something big for you.

- You can take in good experiences both in the flow of daily life and during special times such as at a meal or just before bed.

- Taking in the good involves being a good friend to yourself. If this is hard for you, as it is for many people, you can deliberately create and take in experiences of being on your own side.

- Some experiences are particularly valuable to take in. When your brain's avoiding harms system is threatened, you need key experiences that are directly related to it, such as a sense of protection or strength. The same is true for the approaching and attaching systems. You can use the HEAL steps to look for and take in the experiences that would really help you these days.

- Drawing on the hidden power of seemingly ordinary experiences, this deceptively simple practice builds resilience, heals distress and dysfunction, improves relationships, promotes physical health, and grows a durable happiness.

<u>Chapter 5</u>

Take Notice

This chapter is about *noticing* positive experiences that are already present, and chapter 6 will explore how to *create* new ones; these two chapters cover how to *activate* positive experiences: the first step—Have—of taking in the good. Then chapters 7 and 8 will show you how to *install* them in your brain, using the second, third, and fourth steps of taking in the good: Enrich, Absorb, and Link. Chapter 9 will apply the skills you've learned in the previous chapters to specific situations, such as a relationship, and to particular issues or needs, such as replacing anxiety with confidence, sadness with gladness, and self-criticism with self-compassion. Chapter 10 will offer guided practices for twenty-one key experiences and inner strengths. (In the guided practices in this book, there is some repetition of suggestions, which you can skim over if you like.)

The fourth step of taking in the good can be powerful, but it needs to be used skillfully since it involves negative psychological material such as anger, grief, or shame. Until we explore the fourth step in depth in chapter 8, the guided practices will contain only the first three steps.

Since taking in the good is experiential, not conceptual, let's start with a direct experience of it.

Noticing a Pleasant Sensation

You can take half a minute or more with this practice, with your eyes open or closed. It's fine to do it along with other activities, but in the beginning you'll probably get a better sense of it if you first stop whatever else you're doing.

1. **Have** Find a pleasant sensation that's already present in the foreground or background of your awareness. Perhaps a relaxed feeling of breathing, a comfortable warmth or coolness, or a bodily sense of vitality or aliveness. This sensation could be subtle or mild, yet it still feels good. There may be other sensations, or thoughts or feelings, that are uncomfortable, and that's all right. Just let go of these for now and bring your attention to the pleasant sensation. When you find a pleasant sensation, move into the next step.

2. **Enrich** Stay with the pleasant sensation. Explore it a little. What's it like? Help it last. Keep your attention on it for ten, twenty, or more seconds in a row. Come back to it if your attention wanders. Open to this sensation in your mind and body. Without stress or strain, see if it can become even fuller, even more intense. Enjoy it. Let the pleasure of this sensation help keep it going. See if you can embody it through small actions, such as shifting your body to breathe more fully or smiling softly.

3. **Absorb** Both during the second step and right after it, intend and sense that the pleasant sensation is sinking into you as you sink into it.

When you're done with this practice, see how you feel. Get a sense of what it's like to take in the good.

If you weren't able to notice any pleasant sensations, either you were overwhelmed with agonizing pain (I hope not!) or you just need to try it a few more times. It's natural to have difficulties with the first step of taking in the good, and easy to underestimate it. When working with your mind, it helps to have a gentle yet persistent spirit of exploration. Keep looking. If you can't find something positive right now, maybe it will arise a moment later.

The Music of Experience

Listening to a song, you can hear different parts of it, such as the vocals, guitar, piano, and drums. Similarly, your experience has different parts to it, including thoughts, sense perceptions, emotions, desires, and actions. At dinner earlier tonight, before writing this, our son and daughter were laughing together affectionately. The "song" of my experience included thinking how much they cared about each other, seeing their happy faces, feeling contented as a father, wanting them to always love each other, and leaning in toward them to bask in their warmth.

Often you'll take in an experience as a whole. When I hike in the hills near my home, the beautiful views, the sense of vitality, and the pleasure in being outdoors all blend together. But there is also value in learning to tune into the separate parts of your experience. Becoming more aware of all aspects of your experience gives you a greater sense of integration, of inner wholeness. Plus, it enables you to turn up the volume, as it were, on different parts when you need them. You could focus on a *thought* that other people's happiness is primarily up to them not you, a *sensation* of easing in your body, an *emotion* of calm, a *desire* to be less perfectionistic, or an *action* of unplugging from e-mails. Staying with one part of your experience brings you its benefits in the moment plus helps it sink into your brain, which makes it easier to call up again in the future.

So let's take a tour of the major parts of your experience and the rewards they could offer you. See if you can find something in each of these parts that would be good to bring more to mind. For instance, you could focus on the feeling of gratitude if you've been disappointed, or the sensation of relaxation if you're stressed.

Thoughts

Your thoughts include factual knowledge, ideas, beliefs, expectations, viewpoints, insights, images, and memories. Some thoughts are verbal (mental self-talk) while others consist of imagery or a blend of words and pictures.

Many studies demonstrate the benefits of cognitive therapy focused on changing thoughts for the better. For instance, in my mid-twenties, I realized that I had been a nerd, not a wimp, while growing up. This was a very important thought for me! A woman client once walked into my office, exhaled slowly, and said she'd been thinking, "It's not my fault that my husband's an alcoholic." This thought helped her stop blaming herself for his drinking and helped her confront him more directly. It's good to take in thoughts that are true and useful rather than untrue and harmful. These good thoughts include seeing yourself, others, the past, and the future more accurately; understanding how your actions lead to different results; and putting things in perspective.

While thoughts are of course important, in general, we especially enjoy or suffer what we sense and feel and want and do. Therefore, the practices in this book emphasize these more embodied parts of your experience.

Sense Perceptions

This is the realm of sight, sound, taste, smell, touch, and *interoception* (the internal sensations of your body, such as gurgling in your stomach). Sense perceptions are the pathway to experiences of pleasure, relaxation, vitality, and strength.

Each sense is a potential doorway to *pleasure*, such as seeing a pretty dress, hearing good music, biting into a juicy peach, smelling freshly baked bread, scratching an itch, or, frankly, finally getting to a restroom. Besides being enjoyable in its own right, pleasure typically reduces your sense of stress and initiates the process of recovering from it. Pleasure is an underrated resource for physical and mental health. When you find it, let yourself receive it fully, as this man wrote me: *Near my apartment in North Carolina, the huge expanse of the ancient mountains across the skyline makes me feel there is room for every part of me. When I take in this view, I feel myself "unzip" from my head to my toes and open up in a way that feels wonderful. I fill myself up with the majestic view, which makes me feel good every time I think of it later.*

Relaxation involves the "rest and digest" parasympathetic

wing of the nervous system, the natural counterbalance to the "fight or flight" sympathetic wing. Much like pleasure, relaxation dials down stress. It also strengthens the immune system, increases resilience, and lowers anxiety. It's almost impossible to be very upset about something if you feel deeply relaxed.

Vitality can feel intense, such as when you experience excitement at your sports team winning a game or passion in dancing or lovemaking. But much of the time vitality is milder, such as when you simply feel alive. Whether it's powerful or subtle, taking in a quality of vitality is especially helpful if you feel rundown, melancholy, or overtaxed at home or work.

Some experiences of *strength* have a "ka-pow!" quality to them, but dogged endurance, such as simply getting through a tough childhood, relationship, or job is more common. One night I watched a man trudging home from a late shift and sensed from his movement and the expression on his face the stamina it took for him to just keep on going.

Emotions

Emotions consist of feelings and moods. Feelings are specific, often fairly brief, and caused by an inner or outer stimulus. A friend smiling at you makes you happy; a minute later, his or her snippy comment makes you irritated. Moods are more diffuse, enduring, and independent of stimuli. Sadness is a feeling, while depression is a mood.

Feelings grow moods. For example, repeatedly taking in feelings of gladness and gratitude will tend to develop a mood of contentment. In turn, moods grow feelings. A basic sense of contentment with life fosters feelings of thankfulness and joy.

Consequently, taking in positive feelings can lift your mood, which will bring you more positive feelings, which can lift your mood further.

One of the sweetest emotions, of course, is love, as this woman told me about: *Every night before I turn out the lights, I check on my young, sleeping son and say quietly: "May you be happy, healthy, safe, and at peace." The love I feel from doing this sinks into me. One night, after I returned to my room and pulled up the covers, the joy in my heart continued to expand, and I decided to extend it toward my husband. I thought about how much I loved him and the feelings of joy kept flowing into me. I had a huge smile on my face, in the dark, and I went to sleep a very happy person!*

Desires

Our desires include hopes, wishes, longings, wants, and needs. They also include motivations and inclinations, values, morals, aspirations, purposes, and goals, as well as aversion, drivenness, clinging, craving, and any addiction. Your desires can be aimed at the outer world—wishing that someone would not blow off your needs, let's say—or at the inner one, such as intending to stay strong when you speak up against this treatment. Positive desires lead to happiness and benefit, such as intending to get a glass of water when you're thirsty; while negative ones lead to suffering and harm, such as intending to get a cigarette when you're stressed.

Therefore, when you are experiencing a positive desire, notice it and take it in. Be aware of factors in your mind that support good desires, such as determination or conviction, and take these in as well. When you do *not* act on a bad desire, notice the good results, and take in the relief, satisfaction, and sense of worth that you've earned.

Actions

I'm using "actions" broadly to include both what we do outwardly—behaviors, facial expressions, posture, the words we speak or write—and the internal inclinations and skills that produce our observable actions, such as a tendency to reach out to others who are hurting and the capacity to listen empathically. You can help yourself act more effectively by really registering the actions you want to support, either while actually engaging in them or simply imagining doing them. For example, suppose you'd like to be more assertive with pushy people, which could involve leaning forward rather than back, lifting up your chest, making confident gestures, or speaking firmly. Then, when you do or imagine any of these actions, stay with your experience of this for ten or more seconds, helping it sink in.

One woman used these methods to help herself change how she got her kids ready for school: *My seven- and nine-year-old daughters love to sleep in, so getting them up has never been easy, and we'd usually have a rushed, hectic, cranky morning. Eventually I decided to learn a different way. I started going in early to each of their rooms. I lean over next to their sleeping little bodies to give them a good, long sniff as I kiss them on the cheek. They still smell like babies, and I know this will not last forever. These motherly feelings sink into me, which makes me comfortable with this way of waking my girls. I take in the goodness of their baby smell and hold it in my heart for a few moments, while they're still sleeping. It makes me so happy! Then I playfully, gently rub their hair and back and wake them, and the sweetness I feel doing this becomes a part of me. This almost always results in a happy, pleasant wake-up, with smiles and hugs. And I get to savor the moments that will be gone much too soon.*

The Stage of Awareness

When earlier in this chapter you did the practice of noticing a pleasant sensation, you used the simplest way to have a positive experience: to *notice* something good that's already present in your mind. Awareness is like the stage in a theater. At any moment, something is in the foreground of awareness, under the spotlight of attention, such as these words that you're reading. Simultaneously, in the background of awareness, off to the side of the stage, you're experiencing other things, too, such as sensations, sounds, and feelings. This gives you two places to look for good experiences that you're already having.

See if you can find something pleasurable or useful in the *foreground* of your awareness, under the spotlight right now. Perhaps a sense of interest, well-being, or determination. Maybe you just ate and feel pleasantly full. It doesn't have to be big or intense; it's still positive.

Similarly, as you go through your day, there will be many moments when there's something positive in the front of your mind, such as the good smell of coffee, warm feelings for a friend, or a sense of relief as the day finally winds down. Each time you notice and take in one of these good experiences is a break in the daily race, a kind of pit stop for respite and refueling, as this person found one morning: *It was dark when I awoke, and I listened to the magical sound of light rain on the skylights, warmly snuggled under my comforter. I felt safe and loved, and soaked in this feeling. After getting up, the dogs and I headed to the dog park, which we had to ourselves in the early morning. It was quiet—no birds chirping, very few cars going by, a sense of peace and solitude in a busy city. I felt so grateful. I closed my eyes, breathed deeply, and gave myself to it.*

Next, see if you can find something positive in the *background* of your awareness. It's like eating a meal: Even though most of your attention is on the food, you're also conscious of other sounds and the room as a whole. In the same way, as you read now, there could be a pleasant background sense of relaxation in your body. Or an attitude of curiosity or hopefulness floating in the back of your mind.

Once you find something positive in the background of your awareness, focus on it to bring it to the foreground. Learn what it's like to shift things from the back to the front of your mind. Since there is usually *something* pleasant or beneficial somewhere in your awareness, getting more skillful with this shifting creates many opportunities to have the core of your experience at any moment—what's in the foreground—be positive. Further, since neural encoding increases for what's under the spotlight of attention, moving an aspect of your experience to the front of your awareness heightens its transfer into brain structure. (For a sense of shifting a part of your experience from the background to the foreground, try the practice in the box "Bringing a Feeling to the Front of Awareness," page 86.)

To stay with something good in the foreground, you need to remain undistracted by things in the background. Simply let them be, without resisting or chasing after them. You can bring attention to them later if it feels right.

BRINGING A FEELING TO
THE FRONT OF AWARENESS

This practice involves noticing something good in the background of awareness and moving it to the foreground. You'll be applying this process to one part of your experience: *feelings*.

1. **HAVE** While you are reading here, various feelings are naturally operating in the back of your mind related to this book or to other things. They could be mild or subtle, and they might include negative feelings, but probably at least one or more of these feelings is positive, such as calm, confidence, basic well-being, or warm feelings toward others. Take a moment to be quiet with yourself and listen to what's murmuring in the back of your mind. Find a feeling you like and focus on it.

2. **ENRICH** Once a positive feeling is in the foreground of your awareness, stay with it, let it get more intense if possible, and feel it in your body.

3. **ABSORB** Meanwhile, get a sense that the feeling is sinking into you as you sink into it. Open to this feeling and receive it.

How do you feel after doing this practice? Take a moment to replay this process to deepen your sense of moving things from the back to the front of your mind.

Liking and Wanting

Once you start having a good experience, a natural tendency is to want to keep hold of it. But if you do this, you're no longer flowing with the experience and are instead standing apart from it trying to freeze and possess it. Then there is no more good experience. It's like listening to music. If you hear a great riff and try to replay it in your mind while the song continues, the enjoyment goes out of the music. Therefore, the art is to *like* the good experience without *wanting* it.

Liking involves enjoying, appreciating, and relishing. By *wanting*, I mean drivenness, insistence, compulsion, pressure, grasping after, getting attached to, craving, and clinging. In your subcortex and brain stem, connected but separate circuits handle liking and wanting. This means you can like something without wanting it, such as enjoying the taste of ice cream while still turning down a second serving after a big meal. People can also want something without liking it, such as the ones I've seen mechanically pulling the slot machine handle over and over in a casino, hardly seeming to care if it pays off.

Liking what's pleasant is natural, and there's no harm in it. The trouble comes when we want things that aren't good for us or for others, such as wanting to drink too much or to win arguments at any cost. Trouble also comes when what we want is good but how we try to get it is bad. For example, I want to get to work on time (good), but I often drive too fast to get there (bad). And honestly, I think there is trouble in the sheer experience of wanting itself. Notice what it feels like to want, to have a strong sense of desire, to be driven toward a goal. The Norse root of the word *want* means "lack." Wanting is different from

inspiration, aspiration, commitment, intention, ambition, or passion. Can you aim high and work hard without getting caught
up in drivenness? Based on a deficit or disturbance, wanting activates the reactive mode of your brain and feels contracted and
stressful. Consider this saying: *Liking without wanting is heaven,
while wanting without liking is hell.*

The practical take-away here is to enjoy your experiences as
they flow through you without getting attached to them, and to
pursue good ends with good means without becoming driven
about it. When you notice something good in your experience,
gently encourage it to last without trying to hold on to it. Your
brain tends to keep looking for something new to want. By repeatedly taking in experiences that you like without tipping into wanting them, you could gradually undo the habit of wanting itself.

Low-Hanging Fruit

It's quite remarkable to recognize that your awareness in any
moment usually contains some positive elements. Unless you're
overwhelmed by something terrible, in your stream of consciousness right now are aspects of the peace, contentment, and love
you've always wished for.

With just a little use of attention, good experiences are available to you throughout the day. They're like low-hanging fruit
that you only have to notice. As soon as you notice them, yum!
They're delicious. Most of the good experiences you are already
having are like small sweet cherries—a relaxing breath, a good
intention, a pleasant sight or sound, or a shared joke with a
friend. Whenever you like, you can nibble on these experiences
simply by noticing them and letting them nourish you.

Even awareness itself, a kind of space that holds all the parts of your experience, has positive aspects that you can always notice. A TV screen is not changed by either the beautiful or the ugly images it shows. Similarly, awareness is never stained or damaged by what passes through it. This gives awareness an inherent quality of reliability and tranquility. Even if you are depressed or in great pain, you can find refuge and relief in the awareness that contains these, and any other difficult contents of mind.

TAKING IT IN

- There are two ways to do step 1 (Have) of taking in the good: notice a positive experience that is already present or create one.

- You can notice a positive experience in either the foreground or background of your awareness. Try to be more aware of the experiences hovering in the background, which will give you more good things to take in.

- Be aware of the different parts of your experience, including thoughts, sense perceptions, emotions, desires, and actions. Each of these could be good to take in.

- Thoughts include inner speech as well as images, expectations, perspectives, plans, and memories. Useful sensory experiences include pleasure, relaxation, vitality, and strength. Emotions consist of changeable feelings and enduring moods; repeatedly taking in certain feelings could shift a related mood. Desires include your hopes, intentions, morals, and wants. Actions include your behaviors as well as your inclinations and skills.

- Your brain has separate systems for liking and wanting. Consequently, it is possible to like something without wanting it. If you let yourself have positive experiences without trying to hold on to them, you'll enjoy them more and won't get carried away by the drivenness and pressure of wanting them.

- Noticing good experiences gives you many opportunities to take in the good each day. Even noticing your own awareness is an opportunity for a good experience, since awareness is inherently peaceful and never tainted or harmed by what passes through it.

Chapter 6

Creating Positive Experiences

In the previous chapter, we explored how to notice a good experience that was already present. The other way to have a good experience is to *create* one, and we'll look at how to do that in this chapter. Creating a positive experience can be as simple as looking around to find a pleasant sight or thinking of something that makes you happy. Often you'll do this just because it feels good. At other times, you'll call up the experience of an inner strength to respond to a challenge: Perhaps a plane ride is alarmingly shaky, so you take some deep breaths to calm down; or someone cuts you off in traffic, and you remind yourself not to take it personally.

Whether you're doing it simply to feel good or to meet a challenge, being able to self-activate useful states of mind—to get the song playing that *you* want on your inner radio station—is fundamental to psychological healing, everyday well-being and effectiveness, personal growth, and spiritual practice. Nonetheless, it's hard at first for many people to call up positive experiences at will—particularly ones that would be helpful in certain situations or for certain needs. For example, if you're feeling stressed, it can take practice to create a sense of relaxation in your body. If you've been hurt, it can take a while to remember a friend and feel seen and appreciated. The states of mind that would be most useful for a person are often the hardest to self-generate. But with practice, you will get better at this. And as you repeatedly internalize the experiences you create, they will begin to emerge naturally for you as inner strengths when life goes bump.

FROM IDEA TO EMBODIED EXPERIENCE

Try these ways to help *thoughts* about a good fact become good *feelings*, *sensations*, *desires*, and *actions* related to it:

- Be aware of your body as well as the good fact.
- Soften and open your mind and body, with a sense of receiving the fact.
- Think about aspects of the good fact that naturally encourage positive emotions, sensations, desires, and actions.
- Be kind toward yourself—like an inner voice saying, "Go ahead, this is real, it's true, it's all right to feel good about it."
- Imagine that this good fact is in the life of a friend. What experience would you wish for him or her? Could you wish this same experience for yourself?

Try this with various experiences. For example, let seeing strong walls become a feeling of protection. Let knowing that a hard day is behind you bring relief. Let remembering some of your accomplishments support a sense of worth. Let observing that you are included in a group nurture a feeling of belonging.

Let's explore a variety of ways to create a good experience, with some examples for each one. Many of these methods are based on finding good facts. You're not making anything up. You're seeing what's *true*, what's objective reality. Recognizing good facts does not deny bad facts. You're simply focusing on facts that could legitimately prompt a good experience.

Often we see a good fact but don't have any feelings about it. This seemingly small step—from idea to embodied experience—is critically important, for without it, there's not much to install in your brain. In terms of building neural structure, what matters is not the event or circumstance or condition itself but your *experience* of it. Knowing without feeling is like a menu without a meal. For ways to turn a good fact into a good experience see the box "From Idea to Embodied Experience," page 92.

Current Setting

At almost any time, wherever you are, you can find a good fact in your immediate situation. Look around right now. Can you see anything that is appealing or beautiful and get a good feeling from it? Can you hear anything that could give you a sense of comfort or reassurance? Are you touching something—such as a chair, clothing, or pages of a book—that you're glad to have in your life? Are there people nearby whom you like or appreciate?

Include things that are small or that you normally pass over. For instance, typing these words, I began paying attention to my keyboard (recognizing a good fact) and then started appreciating what a clever and useful invention it is (having a good experience). On the 0 to 10 intensity scale, my gratitude for keyboards is a 1, but it's still a positive experience. I've used keyboards for forty years, but never had any particular feeling about them until now. Under my nose all along was an opportunity that I'd missed. There's a bonus in recognizing a previously overlooked good fact. Once you do see it, there's a multiplier effect in which you'll keep recognizing that good fact in the future.

Here's one woman's story of finding good facts in an unlikely setting: *I live in Detroit, where 40 percent of the land has been abandoned, which means that it's like living in nature amidst urban ruins. The other day when I was out in the "urban prairie," I was literally stopped in my tracks by a tree full of raucous birds. I looked up, taking in the sounds and the sights, letting them fill every part of me. I became aware of the hum of a distant freeway, which created a symphony played by birds and cars. Taking in moments like these has helped me see the world in a new way. Sometimes, late afternoon sunlight on the red brick of an abandoned building can be almost too beautiful for words.*

Recent Events

In the last day or so, it's likely that many things have happened that you could rightfully feel good about. Consider things that were physically pleasurable, such as splashing water on your face in the morning or snuggling into your pillow at night. How about things you got done, even as simple as a load of laundry or returning some e-mails? Finding positive meaning in ordinary events is a good way to create a positive experience. Probably in the last twenty-four hours, you had a meal, someone felt good about you, and you saw or heard something you liked. Before going to sleep, you could take in good feelings about at least one thing from the day. One person told me about doing this for a whole year: *On New Year's Day, I started a Good Year box. Each day I put a note inside about something good that happened. I will read them all on New Year's Eve. Now when a little something good happens in my day, I feel it instead of busily glossing over it.*

Also think about the many, *many* things that could have gone badly but didn't, such as the accident that didn't occur on the way to work, the dish that didn't break, and the flu that didn't send you to bed. We don't recognize this sort of good fact for two reasons. First, there's no stimulus to attract attention. It's hard to notice something that *didn't* happen. Second, the absence of a daily flood of bad events is, happily, the norm in most lives. Your brain filters out things that don't change, both the refrigerator's hum and the routine absence of disasters. While this process, called *habituation*, is an efficient use of neural resources, it makes us miss opportunities for good experiences. Try to recognize at least one thing a day that could have been a real mess but wasn't, and then take a moment to feel good about it.

Ongoing Conditions

In contrast to transient events, many good things are relatively stable and reliable—and these facts are all opportunities for good experiences. Right now, many places you love are still here and doing fine. For example, when I'm getting drilled at the dentist, I'll imagine Tuolumne Meadows in Yosemite Park, and see in my mind the granite domes and hear the soft wind in the pine trees. Good people are in your life and others wish you well. Look around your home, from closet to kitchen, and notice things that keep on existing, even naming them to yourself, such as: *This sink will be here for me tomorrow . . . these clothes will be here . . . these walls will still be painted, this table and lamp will keep on being useful.*

Looking in widening circles, consider the imperfect but still positive aspects of your society—hopefully including the rule of law, democracy, and civil rights—especially when compared to the alternatives, both in history and still widespread today. Think about culture and our easy access to music, ideas, art, entertainment, and wisdom teachings. Science and technology have advanced, offering things like refrigeration, air travel, flush toilets, aspirin, and the Internet. Wider still, you can count on nature's gifts, from scampering dogs to clouds in the sky or the sound of the sea. Here's a beautiful example: *There's a hillside near my house that's covered with flowers most of the year. When I'm at work in an office building, I know the hill is still beautiful: the colors, the brilliant purples, oranges, blues, and pinks. In my mind I can see the squirrels running over the mossy rocks. It's like my little sanctuary at work, to know that the flowers are there while I sit in meetings.*

Sure, conditions can change—fall turns to winter, children leave home, loved ones pass away—and positive conditions can have downsides (a big job may mean long hours of work). Still, the good conditions that *do* exist can be recognized, each one a valid basis for a sense of comfort, security, gratitude, relief, awe, or ease.

Your Personal Qualities

There are undoubtedly many good qualities in your character, personality, and capabilities, such as fairness, a sense of humor, and various talents and skills. Seeing these facts and feeling good about them will lift your mood and help heal feelings of inadequacy or shame. Feeling good about yourself doesn't make you conceited; as your sense of worth grows, there's actually less need to impress others.

Neither halo nor heroics are needed to have positive qualities; we all have some! But feeling that you are a fundamentally decent and capable person can be challenging if self-criticism makes you feel inadequate or self-doubting. Standing up for the truth to *yourself* and to others that you are a basically good person—not a perfect person, but a good one—can feel taboo.

Consider a friend's positive qualities—perhaps honesty, likable quirks, and a warm heart. Would denying these qualities be a fair way to treat this friend? How would your friend benefit, instead, if you appreciated his or her positive qualities? Now turn it around: Can you see your own good qualities? It's a matter of justice: You are telling the truth about yourself, much as you would tell the truth about a friend. Why would it be good to see good in your friend, but bad to see it in yourself? The Golden Rule is a two-way street: We should also treat *ourselves* as we would treat others.

Observe virtues and strengths in yourself such as endurance, patience, determination, empathy, compassion, and integrity. Also notice abilities, even seemingly simple ones like cooking a meal, working a spreadsheet, or being a good friend. These are facts, not fiction. If negative thoughts tug at you—*But*

I'm not always *this way, plus this good thing is erased by the bad things about me*—that's normal. Just be aware of these negative thoughts and then bring your attention back to the facts of your virtues, strengths, and abilities. Reflect on what different friends or family members appreciate, like, or love about you. Or imagine that you are observing the life of someone just like you: What does he or she give to others? What is honorable and admirable about this person? Or imagine the fairest and most loving being in the universe whispering in your ear, telling you about your own goodness.

Really try to admit the *truth* of your good qualities. Pick one and get a clear sense of it. Maybe you are a helpful friend, or a good cook, or a decent person. Whatever it is, know that it is real. Let this recognition of one of your good qualities become a sense of gladness, confidence, and worth. Open to these positive feelings sinking into you. Consider how it helps you and others when you feel good about yourself in this way. Then repeat this process with other good things about you. Take in the sense that you are a fundamentally good person.

This woman took in the good she felt about the quality of her work: *There's an awkward stage in medical residency when haunting doubts about your professional competency hover like dark clouds. To cope, I really took it in when things did go well, such as the gratitude from a schizophrenic patient others had given up on, who told me he cherished our therapy sessions together as he slowly began to regain his life. The more I let in real examples of being competent, the less I heard the negative tape playing in my head and the happier and more engaged I felt.*

The Past

A wonderful source of good experiences is the treasure chest of the past. If I'm challenged by a situation, sometimes I'll remember pulling through an overhang when rock climbing (fact) while getting a sense in my body of that determination and power (feeling). Or maybe there's been a setback in my work, so I'll bring to mind some past successes. If someone is critical, after trying to sort through what happened and what I can learn, I might muse about a good time with a friend, and feel cared about and valued.

Sometimes your past experiences will blend together. Over many years, I've been to hundreds of beaches, and now there is a distilled sense of vastness and exhilaration when I think about times I've been at the seashore. Or you might have a vague recollection of a period in your life that you could draw upon. For instance, knowing that you got through a financial crisis could evoke a positive sense of endurance and being an honorable person. In fact, you don't need any clear memories at all. You could use photos from places you don't recall or stories from when you were little to imagine good feelings you must have had. I know for a fact that I was really wanted and loved as a baby, the firstborn in my family after my mother had a couple of miscarriages, and I've imagined what it must have felt like to be so cuddled with love by my mom and dad.

When you reflect on the past, there may be a bittersweet sense of the passing of good things, and that's all right. Try not to let your attention get caught up in regret or loss. You honor what was once sweet when you taste it again today.

The Future

The future is another kind of treasure chest that's full of potential good experiences, whether it's looking forward to getting out of a tight pair of shoes after work or daydreaming about a vacation next summer. This mental time travel draws on midline networks in the cortex that were an important evolutionary development, enabling our ancestors to plan more effectively.

Take a moment to imagine something good that will happen later today, and then let this become a pleasant feeling for you. Imagine a good experience you might have in the future if you were to speak or act differently in a difficult relationship. Or imagine the benefits down the road from making a change in your life that you've been considering, such as getting a different job or meditating regularly.

Sharing Good with Others

Studies show that talking about good things with others intensifies the experience. Humans are the most social animals on the planet, so we have highly developed neural networks for empathy, the ability to tune into others. When two or more people have a shared positive experience, the good feelings in these empathy networks bounce back and forth in a chain reaction. As John Milton wrote in *Paradise Lost*: "Good, the more communicated, more abundant grows."

You can reminisce about the past with someone: perhaps a fun time or a challenge you got through together. You can also celebrate the present, such as murmuring "this is nice" to your mate when watching your kids in a play, sharing a happy glance as you enjoy a sunset, or smiling in pleasure at each other as you dive into a scrumptious dessert. And you can happily plan for a nice future, from what to do this Saturday night to where to live after you retire.

Finding the Good in the Bad

In 2011, a routine mole check revealed a malignant melanoma on my right ear. My brother-in-law had recently died from skin cancer. While the top of my mind was solving problems like where to go for treatment, a deeper layer felt like a little animal curled up and shaking. I was on pins and needles for ten days before the cancer was removed and tests showed that it hadn't spread. Nonetheless, I'm at heightened risk for a recurrence. I could interpret all this in a glum, negative way: "Sunscreen is such a hassle. Will it even help? I hate having cancer hanging over my head." But I don't. Instead, mostly I feel glad that this happened. It's made me more compassionate for people with an illness and given me more appreciation for life since I'm still here to enjoy it.

Your *perspective* on the facts—the context in which you place them and the meaning you give them—really shapes your experience of them. In particular, finding positive meaning in negative events, which is called *reframing*, is helpful for coping and recovery. This is not to suggest that a tough experience is any less painful, or that it is all right for people to mistreat you. My point is that even a horrible event or situation may have some opportunities in it for a positive experience.

Consider past hardships. Did these make you stronger in any way? What lessons did you learn from them? What about losses:

Have these helped you appreciate what you still have? Consider a current challenge and ask yourself, "Has this made me realize I need to change my course in some way?" Reflect on what you have learned about taking care of yourself from people who mistreated you. Or suppose you are in the middle of a major transition: What might you gain in this new chapter of your life?

One woman found something peaceful in the passing of her father: *My dad was a U.S. Marine in World War Two, who drew his last breath on a sunny Memorial Day. We heard the loud noise of fighter jets flying overhead at the exact moment he died. The bedroom was quiet after the flyby. I was filled with sorrow and didn't know if I could take losing my father, but at the same time, I was awed by the love, peace, and calm that filled the room after he passed. I bathed myself in it. It felt as if time stood still. It was a very intense moment. That experience gave me a sense memory that carried me through the whole experience of losing my beloved father—and it carries me to this day still. Anytime that I now feel lost or stressed, I remember those moments of intense calm and bathe in them again.*

Caring About Others

Thinking about a friend, speaking kindly, or being generous are warmhearted opportunities for a positive experience. Loving thoughts, words, and deeds usually feel good. In fact, one study found that reward centers in the brain activated more when people chose to give money to charity rather than to keep it for themselves.

Caring includes both inner experiences and outer behaviors. Internally, you could recall someone you like. Externally, you could smile at a stranger, touch someone in sympathy, tuck a child into bed, or stop interrupting your wife (I've been working on this one myself). For extra benefits, you can be happy while anticipating an act of caring, happy while doing it, and happy while remembering it. And your caring toward others just might evoke more caring from them toward you.

Here is one man's example of taking in a loving experience: *Holding my baby grandson in my arms as I swayed and sang gently, his eyes closed, his breathing became regular, and he went to sleep. I savored the sense of holding something precious for several minutes and allowed the sense of this moment to dwell within, abiding here. Astonishing.*

Seeing Good in the Lives of Others

One kind of caring about others is so important that I want to single it out here. Our ancestors lived in small bands in which individuals needed to cooperate to keep their children and one another alive in tough conditions. The evolving capacity to take pleasure in the joys and successes of others likely helped deepen the bonds of caring that promoted survival and the passing on of genes. Being happy that others are happy is an innate and powerful inclination of the human heart. And it gives you endless opportunities to feel good since there is always someone somewhere who is happy about something.

Think about a good fact in the life of someone you care about. Then see if you can feel pleased and glad for this person. This is sometimes called *altruistic joy*, happiness at the good fortune of others. If it is hard to have much sense of this, try it with a child you know or can imagine: perhaps a little kid opening a present, or licking an ice cream cone, or playing with a puppy. If other feelings come up, such as sadness about your own difficulties, that's common. Be aware of such feelings but then gently bring your attention back to what you want to encourage in your mind: happiness at the welfare of others.

Try this with various people in your life. Then with people you don't know, such as strangers on the street, or in the news, or imagined far away. Personally, I love this practice. Besides being kind to others, it gradually opens your heart. Plus, it's a great way to undo feelings of envy, jealousy, or ill will. When you do this practice, thoughts about what's bad in your life are replaced by warm feelings about what's good in the lives of others.

Imagining Good Facts

The midline cortical networks that enable our uniquely human abilities to think about the future and the past are the neural foundation of that wonderful inner movie theater, the imagination. If you're like me, it's way too easy to use that theater for bad purposes like replaying again and again a hurtful interaction. Instead, use it for good purposes, such as imagining good facts that could be true—and even ones that couldn't be.

Things That Could Be True

I haven't surfed, but I really like videos of people riding huge waves. When I think about doing this myself, it makes me feel excited and happy. This imagined fact will likely never come to pass, but at least it's possible, and thus a potential source of a positive experience.

You can use this method in a variety of ways. You could imagine a loved one's voice talking you through a challenging situation. If you have talents that haven't been fully used, consider what it might be like if they were. If you wished you felt stronger, imagine having a black belt in karate. If you'd like to feel more peaceful, imagine sitting quietly in nature. In each case, be realistic about what you might feel; don't overdo it, which would undermine the power of this practice.

Things That Couldn't Be True

You can also use your inner theater to imagine good facts that could never be true for you. Deep down in the emotional memory centers of your brain, imagined experiences build neural structures through mechanisms similar to those that actual, lived experiences use. You're not using this method to delude yourself about what's been missing, or to slip into a rosy fantasy world that distracts you from improving this one. You still know what's true. You just suffer it less.

For example, I've known people who never received any kind of loving parenting. Feeling loved in this way is important for healthy psychological development, and the lack of it leaves a wound in the heart. For these people, it was a powerful experience to imagine a loving parent and then take in feelings of being cuddled, soothed, and cherished. This didn't mean they forgot what had actually happened in their childhood. But they were resourceful on their own behalf, finding ways to give themselves at least *some* sense of a vital experience, feeling cherished by a loving parent. Though it wasn't a miracle cure, this practice made a big difference to them.

Producing Good Facts

Most days hold opportunities for creating good facts, and each of these new facts is a chance for a good experience. You could compliment someone, put a flower in a vase, turn on music, rearrange some furniture, take a different route to work, eat protein at breakfast, invite the cat up into your lap, or put on a fresh pillowcase. The point is not to pile new demands on yourself, but simply to be open to the chance to create a fact that could foster a good experience.

One way to create a good fact is to make something that makes you happy. A friend made a little box that she keeps in her handbag, with seashells from a trip to Italy, a picture of her dog, and a cross; when she wants a boost, she opens it and looks inside. Another friend got a photo of herself as a child and put it next to her driver's license, so that when she shows her ID, she sees this lovable girl.

Restraint is another way to create good facts. Turn off a nerve-jangling TV program. Don't criticize. Refuse to worry more than three times about something you can't change; three strikes and the worry is out. If you're caught up in something bad and disengage from it, that alone creates something good; take a moment to register this and enjoy it before shifting to the next thing you're doing.

Each morning, you could pick one good fact that you're going to bring into being that day. And when you create this fact, really enjoy the experience that follows.

Directly Evoking a Positive Experience

As you build up the neural traces of positive experiences, it becomes easier to activate positive states of mind at will, without having to think about any good facts to evoke them. See if you can call up a good feeling directly. Start with an experience that's easy to access. Perhaps a sense of strength, calm, love, or gladness. In the beginning this works best if your mind isn't disturbed by worries or stress. But with practice, you'll learn to light up the neural circuits of positive states even when you're rattled or upset, like reaching through clutter to get the tool you need.

Seeing Life as Opportunity

In the previous chapter and in this one, we've explored many different ways to do step 1 of taking in the good: to Have—to activate—a positive experience. These are:

Notice a positive experience that's *already* present

1. in the *foreground* of awareness
2. in the *background* of awareness

Create a positive experience by

3. finding good facts in your *current setting*
4. finding good facts in *recent events*
5. finding good facts in *ongoing conditions*

6. finding good facts in your *personal qualities*
7. finding good facts in the *past*
8. anticipating good facts in the *future*
9. *sharing* the good with others
10. finding the *good in the bad*
11. *caring* about others
12. *seeing good* in the lives of others
13. *imagining* good facts
14. *producing* good facts
15. *directly evoking* a positive experience
16. seeing life as *opportunity*

Good facts are all around, even if life is difficult. The sun rose today, others are happy, and food smells good. Good facts persist inside you: Your body keeps going, your mind is full of abilities, and you are a fundamentally good person. Even bad facts often contain opportunities for good experiences. And there are many ways to have a good experience without reference to facts at all.

Sometimes it is impossible to notice or create a good experience. The mind could be shattered by agonizing pain or a terrible loss, or smothered by an overwhelming depression, or flooded with panic. Then all you can do is ride out the storm—being with it, letting it be—hopefully with some underlying compassion for yourself.

But most of the time, it *is* possible to notice or create a good experience, whether it's looking around for something you like seeing, recognizing your good intentions, or thinking of someone you love. Or it could be as simple as shifting in your chair to a more comfortable position. Recognizing that each day offers many ways to generate a good experience feels good in its own right. Imagine discovering that you could give good experiences to a dear friend, or to someone who was hurting. It would probably make you happy to know that you could do this. Well, you have the same power to give good experiences to yourself. This is the sixteenth way to have a positive experience: seeing life as opportunity.

Even in the middle of hardship and pain, it is usually within your power to ignite a good thought, sense perception, emotion, desire, or action. It's also usually in your power to add fuel to the good experience to keep it going, and we'll explore how to do this in the next chapter.

TAKING IT IN

- Being able to self-activate positive experiences—to call up inner strengths at will—is fundamental to coping, well-being, and everyday effectiveness. With practice, these experiences and strengths will increasingly activate on their own.

- In order to turn the idea of a good fact into a more embodied experience, tune in to your body, soften and open, and think about aspects of the fact that naturally generate positive emotions, sensations, desires, or actions.

- Good facts can be found in your current setting as well as in recent events, ongoing conditions, your personal qualities, the past, and the lives of others. You can also create good facts. Any good fact is the potential basis for a good experience.

- Additional ways to create positive experiences include imagining the future, sharing good experiences with others, finding the good in the bad, being caring, imagining good facts (both ones that could be true and ones that couldn't be), and directly evoking a positive experience.

- Sometimes you just can't have a positive experience. But most of the time, it is possible to notice or create one. This fact is another source of good experiences: seeing life as opportunity.

Chapter 7

Brain Building

Using the methods in the previous two chapters, let's say you're feeling relaxed, grateful, or loving. You've got a good thing going: step 1 of taking in the good. Now what?

You help that good experience sink into your brain. This is where steps 2 and 3 come in. In step 2, you *enrich* the experience by staying with it and growing it inside your mind. In step 3, you *absorb* it, intending and sensing that the experience is becoming a part of you. These two steps *install* experiences into your brain, turning good mental states into good neural traits.

Enriching an Experience

Five major factors heighten learning, the conversion of fleeting mental events into lasting neural structure. The greater the *duration, intensity, multimodality, novelty,* and *personal relevance,* the greater the retention in memory. Each of these is a way to increase neural firing so you get more wiring during an episode of taking in the good. Repeated episodes of taking in the good will further strengthen these neural traces.

The upper reaches of the mind/brain system can produce lofty flights of fancy, subtle mathematical insights, richly textured feelings, and exquisite images and melodies, but down in the basement, as it were, building new structure is a mechanical process. The more tools you have and the more often you use them and the more seconds that tick by while you're using them, the more neural structure you'll grow. More is better. Plus, it's nice to have five different options for enriching an experience; if one isn't applicable or isn't working for you right now, you can try other ones.

Duration

So often a good experience seems to fly on past. Instead, help it last, staying with it at least five to ten seconds in a row; the longer, the better. You can use the methods that activated the good experience to reactivate it again and again to keep it going. One man sent me a vivid example of how he does this: *I bring up a memory of eating chocolate cake and ice cream. Not only the flavors, but also the textures and temperatures. I recognize how much pleasure I'm experiencing, and imagine my brain having smiley faces floating around in it as I enjoy the flavors. I remember to stretch out as long as I can the pleasure obtained by eating chocolate cake and ice cream. When thoughts distract me, I take another mental bite. I try to stay with this experience for thirty seconds, a minute, several minutes, longer. Later on, if something bothers me, I say to myself, "Time for cake and ice cream!"*

Let yourself have your good experience. Be devoted to it, renouncing all else for as long as you like. Give your mind over to it; in a good sense, let it have you. Make room for it, preserve a kind of sanctuary for it in your mind.

STAYING AWARE OF A POSITIVE EXPERIENCE

- Deliberately *apply* your attention to the experience and then *sustain* it. It's a little like ice skating. Planting your foot is like applying your attention and then gliding along is like staying in touch with the experience. From time to time, you can reapply your attention to it and sustain your contact with it.

- Keep a bit of attention on your own attention so you can bring it back if it wanders. Gentle instructions to yourself can help, like a soft voice in the back of your mind saying "stay with this."

- To reduce distractions from tension and stress, take one or more long exhalations, which will activate the calming and relaxing parasympathetic wing of your nervous system.

- Softly name the experience to yourself, such as: "calming . . . relaxing . . . safe."

- If you're distractible, try to take in particularly stimulating experiences. These include physical pleasures, energizing emotions such as delight, awe, joy, affection, and eagerness, and embodied attitudes like fierce determination.

If your attention wanders, that's normal. When you notice this, try to return the spotlight of attention back to the positive experience without criticizing yourself. Negative experiences, such as uncomfortable feelings or sensations, may come up for you alongside positive ones. Recognize these, let them be, and stay with the positive experience. Remember that you can think about other things later. Also, try the suggestions in the box "Staying Aware of a Positive Experience," page 113.

Intensity

As the intensity of an experience increases, so do levels of the neurotransmitter norepinephrine, which promotes the formation of new synapses; the more that an experience fosters new synapses, the more that it gets woven into your brain. And as an experience becomes more pleasurable—particularly if it was more rewarding than your brain initially expected because you deliberately intensified it and opened to it through taking in the good—dopamine levels rise as well, which also promotes new synapses. In essence, as the pleasurable intensity of an experience grows, so does its conversion into lasting neural structure. Consequently, encouraging positive experiences to get more intense and feel as good as possible is a great way to get lasting benefit from them.

To do this, encourage the positive experience to become richer, fuller, and bigger in your body and mind. Sink into the experience and let it become as intense as possible. Be aware of things that are rewarding about it, such as how good something feels on your skin or how touched you are when someone is kind to you. You could inhale a little faster or get a sense of pumping up energy inside yourself. Perhaps close your eyes or look down at something unchanging so you can really focus on this delicious experience. An experience may be subtle—such as serenity, belonging, or fulfillment—yet it can still pervade your mind. Savor it, relish it. Enjoy it!

Multimodality

Multimodality means that you're aware of as many aspects of the experience as possible. Suppose you are thinking about a friend's good qualities. You could also tune into related sensations, emotions, desires, and actions. Or if you're feeling grateful, get an image of a stream of good things coming into your life, sense your body easing, notice the wish to share some of what you've been given with others, and imagine speaking your thanks out loud.

In particular, try to sense good experiences in your whole body. Let your attention move down into your body like water moving down into the earth. Bring awareness to your breathing, which will help you stay in touch with your body. See if you can even get a sense of breathing as the whole body, with feelings like happiness or love or peace woven into the breathing.

It's so obvious that it's easy to forget that we engage life as a very physical *body*. Subcortical control centers are continually monitoring the state of your body and sending calls for action and related emotion signals up into your cortex. These subcortical signals shape the views and values held in the cortex, with results that reverberate back down to the subcortex and brain stem. Through this loop, action shapes thinking and thinking shapes action, which is the basis of what's called *embodied cognition*. For example, studies show that leaning toward a reward increases the brain's response to it, and that your facial expressions, posture, and even whether you open or close your hands all influence your experience and behavior.

Consequently, you can enrich an experience by embodying it through various kinds of action, even subtle ones. Early in my marriage, when my wife was telling me about a problem and, ah, it was starting to look like it was me, I would pull back physically ("get me out of here"). But gradually I found that leaning toward her helped keep my mind in the conversation and my heart open to her. Similarly, you could use a soft half smile to lift your mood, sit up a little straighter to become more alert, or widen your stance to feel a little stronger. In general, the more actively and bodily we engage positive experiences, the greater their impacts.

A creative way to engage an experience with multiple senses is to be artistic with it. Even simple things can be powerful, as you can see in this example from a middle school counselor (for more on taking in the good with children, see chapter 9): *I facilitate advisory groups for students who are academically disengaged, and I've introduced a gratitude exercise in which we practice taking in the good. I pass out strips of different colored paper, glue sticks, and markers; everyone gets three strips. I ask the students to close their eyes and to take a few minutes to think about what they're grateful for in their lives. Then I tell them to pick three of these things and write each one on a paper strip. I let them know that what they choose can be grand or as simple as melted cheese, hot water, or seedless watermelon (three of my favorites). Next, each student constructs a paper chain out of his or her strips of paper. Each time a link is added, we pause to reflect on the goodness of the added experience. I remind the students to let the experience sink in and become a part of them. What I notice most of all when doing this exercise are the peace and quiet that fill our space and the gentle smiles on all the faces.*

Novelty

Your brain is a novelty detector, always looking for something unexpected and then storing it rapidly in memory. So try to find what's fresh in your positive experiences, especially if they are commonplace ones, such as eating a slice of bread, arriving home from work, or looking into the eyes of someone you love. Let these moments be new ones. Look for unexpected rewards in your experiences—such as a sense of "I didn't expect this subtle flavor of curry in my soup" or "I didn't know it would feel this good to hug you"—which will tend to lift dopamine levels and thus promote the registration of the experience in your brain.

Bring your attention to different aspects of an experience. Try this with something you know well, such as breathing. Take a few breaths and explore some of their many sensations in the belly, chest, diaphragm (between belly and chest), and throat. Notice cool air coming in and warm air going out. Notice sensations around the upper lip, in your back, in the small movements of shoulders, neck, head, and hips. Each time your attention moves to another aspect of an experience, it's a new stimulus to your brain.

Notice things as they are changing, which also brings a sense of novelty. When talking with a friend, be aware of expressions flickering over his or her face, and the ebb and flow of feelings inside you about what your friend is saying. Or while sitting calmly with a sense of basic well-being, observe how sights, sounds, tastes, touches, smells, and thoughts continually arise in awareness and then pass away.

As you saw in chapter 2, the hippocampus is very important for memory and thus for taking in the good, but its neurons are also vulnerable to being weakened or killed by the stress hormone cortisol. Fortunately, the hippocampus is the primary site in the brain where new neurons are born (called *neurogenesis*). The survival of these baby neurons is increased by the novelty of your experiences. Since no experience is exactly like any other, focusing on and taking in different aspects of your experience will promote a sense of freshness and novelty and thus may support neurogenesis and help repair your hippocampus.

Personal Relevance

Imagine walking through a mall or looking at a website. Your brain is continually scanning to find things that could matter to you. *Relevant to my needs, interests, or concerns?* Zero in on it. *Not relevant?* Move on. And when your brain does find something that's relevant to you, it files that experience in storage.

Consequently, you can use this natural process of relevance-seeking to build up the neural traces of your positive experiences. Be aware of how an experience that you're taking in could help you, why it's valuable. For example, relaxation and calm could ease stress and worry; some shared humor with your partner could help you feel more connected when your busy schedules make it hard to be close.

You're placing the experience in the context of your life. You could even say to yourself, during an experience, "This applies to me because _____." Built into the sense of its relevance to you is kindness to yourself, a feeling that "this is what I need, this feels good, this is right for me." You're not delivering supplies to your ego, but rather giving yourself an experience that *matters* just as you'd offer it to a friend who could use it.

Absorbing an Experience

One time while on vacation, my wife and I watched a sunset that was extraordinary even by Hawaiian standards. I told myself, "Remember this one," and now as I write twenty years later I can still see the vivid glowing purples and pinks across the sky.

By itself, enriching an experience—the second step of taking in the good—will heighten its installation in your brain since you're intensifying and prolonging neural activity, which naturally tends to build neural structure. And just as you do when taking a mental snapshot of a beautiful sunset, you can increase this installation further by intending and sensing that the experience is sinking in, becoming part of you, in the third step of taking in the good, Absorb.

In effect, taking in the good is like making a fire. Step 1 lights it, step 2 adds fuel to keep it going, and step 3 fills you with its warmth. You can start the third step after clearly ending the second step, but much of the time, the sense of absorbing a positive experience mingles with and overlaps the sense of enriching it. It's like being warmed by a fire even as you add sticks to it.

In doing the third step, some people visualize the positive experience sifting down into them like gentle rain or soft golden dust, or being placed like a jewel in the treasure chest of their heart. One person gave me a striking visual metaphor for absorbing an experience: *If you take a clear glass of water and add a drop of oil, the oil stays at the surface. If you take another glass of water and add a drop of food coloring, the drop gradually makes its way through the water and tints it that color. This is how I visually explain taking in the good to others. The oil represents a fleeting experience that makes no difference, while the coloring represents a tangible change, one that takes its time to sink in.*

Others sense that the positive experience is warming them like a cup of hot cocoa, or easing hurt places inside like a soothing balm. Or they simply know that they're receiving, registering, and retaining the experience; that it is settling down into their brain, becoming a part of them, a resource inside they can take with them wherever they go. Find what works for you, and trust that the good experience will make its way into your brain. As you are sinking into it, it is sinking into you.

Here's an example of how one woman repeatedly absorbed a positive experience: *Recently, one of my cats got sick. I took Sammy, who is eleven years old, to the vet, thinking she would get some medicine and be good as new in no time. Instead, I learned that her little chest was filled with fluid, which made it hard for her to breathe. She had an incurable illness. After talking it over with my vet and my partner, I decided it was best to put Sammy down. Animals are incredibly precious, but the unthinkable decision had to be made. The euthanasia was seared into my brain and heart. I cried for days. After some time passed and I became a little more centered, I started trying to take in the good. I held memories of the precious good times I had with Sammy and savored each one for well over thirty seconds. I sensed those positive feelings sinking in deep, like a salve, and healing those last terrible moments with her. In a way, it felt like Sammy herself was becoming a part of me. A comfort was coming into me from remembering her sitting on my lap or chasing a toy.*

Whatever methods you use to absorb an experience, try to have the willingness, even the courage, to be changed, to grow, to become a little different as a result. For example, as you take in an experience of gratitude, see if you can feel yourself actually becoming a little more thankful and appreciative. As you take in a feeling of strength, see if you can let yourself truly become a little stronger. The mind (and brain) takes its shape from what it rests upon, and you're letting it mold itself around the positive experience that you are taking in.

Peace, Contentment, and Love

Let's pull the pieces together with an extended practice of taking in the good applied to the foundational experiences of peace, contentment, and love, which will bring you home to the responsive mode of your brain. When you first do this practice, it can help to take a little time with each part of it so that you develop a clear sense of it. Then, increasingly, you will be able to go directly to an integrated sense of peace, contentment, and love. I often use this practice myself, including when I first wake up. (For a very brief version of it, see "One Minute for Good" on page 176.)

Here we go:

Come into a sense of being present with whatever is moving through your awareness: thoughts, sense perceptions, emotions, desires, and actions. Let these be; let them come and go.

Recognize some of the ways you are protected right now, including the walls around you and good people nearby. Recognize some of your resources, such as capabilities, decent credit, or a driver's license. Bring to mind a sense of strength, of determination. Notice that your body is basically all right right now, that your heart is beating, that breathing is happening just fine, that you are okay even if not perfect.

Be aware of any needless sense of being threatened, and see if you can let it go. Try to disengage from worrying or planning; you can do these later. You are not struggling or contending with anything or anyone. Any annoyance, exasperation, irritability, or anger is falling away. Be aware of any unnecessary guarding, bracing, or anxiety—and see if you can let it go. Open to feeling as safe as you reasonably can. You are getting calmer and more relaxed. Perhaps you feel a sense of tranquility, like a still mountain lake. There is no basis for aversion; you're not resisting anything either inside yourself or out in the world. You're allowing, uncovering, a sense of peace.

Stay with peace, enjoy it, enrich and absorb the sense of it. Sink into peace as it sinks into you. Stay with this as long as you like.

Now let the sense of peace move into the background of your mind, and bring into the foreground something that helps you feel thankful, appreciative, grateful. Think about something else that brings you pleasure, gladness, delight, or joy. Remember a time when you got something done. Be aware of things you've achieved, goals you've met. Recall times of satisfaction and fulfillment. Call to mind more things that bring you feelings of fullness and well-being. Let go of disappointments, frustrations, dissatisfactions. Be kind to yourself about losses while accepting the reality of them. See if you can find a sense of enough-ness in this moment, even abundance, with no wish for this moment to be anything other than what it is. Feel a growing contentment. There is no basis for grasping; you're not chasing after anything inside the mind or out in the world. You're allowing, uncovering, a sense of contentment.

Stay with contentment, enjoy it, enrich and absorb the sense of it. *Sink into contentment as it sinks into you. Stay with this as long as you like.*

Now let the sense of contentment move into the background of your mind, and bring into the foreground things that help you feel loved and loving. Open to and find a sense of emotional connection with another being—perhaps a person, a pet, or a group of people. Think of someone who is warm or friendly toward you, and help this become a feeling of being cared about. Recall a time you felt included, seen and understood, appreciated or respected, even liked and loved. Let feeling cared about fill you, softening your face and throat and eyes, easing and warming your heart. Let rejections fall away, and resentments, and past sorrows in relationships. Know what it's like to feel loved. Recognize some of the ways you are a good person, that you care about others. Be aware of some of your contributions to others, some of your abilities. Let feelings of worth sink in. Again, let it land inside that you truly are a good person.

Bring to mind someone you like, someone who matters to you, someone you love. Find compassion—the wish that living beings not suffer—for someone, perhaps a friend in difficulty, a child in pain, or impoverished people far away or close to home. Find kindness, the wish that beings be happy. Bring to mind someone, somewhere, who is happy. Be glad about the good fortune of others. Let any envy or jealousy fall away; you needn't be disturbed by them. Feel more and more connected, to other people, to all life, even to the whole planet and beyond. There is no basis for clinging to anyone; you are already related to others, already loved and loving. Love flowing in and love flowing out. You're allowing, uncovering, a sense of love.

Stay with love, enjoy it, enrich and absorb the sense of it.

Sink into love as it sinks into you. Stay with this as long as you like.

Now get a sense of peace, contentment, and love all present together in your mind. Supporting one another. A sense of wholeness, your natural state. There is an integrated sense of balance and well-being as you rest in the responsive mode of your brain. There may be challenges to face or pain in your body or concerns in your mind, but these do not disturb the core of you. There is no need for craving, for drivenness of any kind. You are experiencing that your core needs for safety, satisfaction, and connection are basically being met in this moment.

Being home.

TAKING IT IN

- The second and third steps of HEAL are to Enrich and Absorb a positive experience in order to install it in your brain.

- Five major factors enrich an experience and heighten its conversion into neural structure: duration, intensity, multimodality, novelty, and personal relevance.

- You can absorb the experience by visualizing it sinking into you, by sensing it coming into your body, and by letting yourself be changed by it.

- Routinely giving yourself a basic sense of peace, contentment, and love is a wonderful way to come home to the responsive mode and deepen its neural traces.

Chapter 8

Flowers Pulling Weeds

The first three steps of taking in the good involve only the positive. You might be using these steps to address a challenge or to ease something that's still bothering you, but while doing the steps you're focusing entirely on positive experiences. For example, I had some embarrassing times as a nerdy kid getting picked last for sports teams. So, when I was older, I took in many good experiences of playing football and rock climbing with friends. In the moment of doing this, there was no sense in my mind of the old embarrassments, even though part of what motivated me to look for and take in these experiences was knowing I had this lingering issue from childhood.

In contrast, in the fourth step of taking in the good—Link— you hold *both* positive and negative material in your awareness at the same time. You keep the positive material more prominent and intense, and sense it connecting with and gradually soothing, perhaps even replacing, the negative material. In this step, the flowers of positive experiences crowd out and gradually replace the weeds of negative thoughts, feelings, and desires.

Let me explain first why this method works and then give you some suggestions for how to use it effectively.

Negative Material Has Costs

Unpleasant experiences are a natural part of life. And some of them have benefits. Sorrow can tenderize your heart, hardship can make you stronger, and anger can energize you to deal with mistreatment. Further, if you resist unpleasant experiences, this blocks their flow through your mind and body, and they stick around. If you go negative on the negative, you just have more negative.

But when unpleasant experiences become negative material stored in your brain, that's not good. Negative material has negative consequences. It darkens your mood, increases anxiety and irritability, and gives you a background sense of falling short, of inadequacy. This material contains painful beliefs like "no one would want me." The desires and inclinations in it take you to bad places. It can numb you and muzzle you. Or it can make you overreact to others, which can create vicious circles of negativity between you and them. Negative material impacts your body, wears down long-term mental and physical health, and can potentially shorten your life span.

Overall, negative material in your brain is like a strong current continually tugging you toward the reactive mode. Understanding the neural machinery of how this material is activated and then stored suggests ways to actually *change* it, even to the point of clearing it out entirely.

How Negative Material Works in Your Brain

Sometimes we experience negative thoughts, sensations, emotions, desires, or actions related to *explicit* recollections. If I'm reminded of the time we were driving with our kids and our car nearly slid off a snowy cliff near Yosemite, I get a sickening feeling of dread and helplessness. But negative material usually emerges from *implicit* memory stores. Suppose you bought a pair of jeans that were tighter than usual, which reactivated a whole sludgy package of self-criticism about your weight. Or perhaps you were out for a walk, began thinking about money, and it was like taking the lid off of a bucket of anxiety.

Whether the negative material comes from explicit or implicit memory, it's not usually activated the way you'd open a document on your computer. Unless it's a "flashbulb memory" of trauma with every painful detail imprinted on your mind, it is not retrieved as a whole but *reconstructed* from underlying seeds. The brain does this so quickly that it seems like a particular folder of crud is pulled from a filing cabinet somewhere inside your head, but actually there is an active process in which vast numbers of synapses—millions if not billions of them— take several tenths of a second to sync up together into a kind of confederation or *coalition* that represents the conscious experience of this negative material.

Then when the negative material—such as an anxious preoccupation, an image from a battlefield, a muzzling of self-expression around authority figures, an edgy reactivity with a mate, or a growing feeling as a single person of being unwantable—is no longer active in awareness, it becomes gradually *reconsolidated* in memory structures. Little molecular machines need at least several minutes and probably several hours to rewire the negative material back into your brain. The fact that this is an active process which takes time gives you two methods for soothing, healing, and potentially replacing negative material.

Two Methods for Changing Negative Material

If something other than negative material is also present in awareness, it is represented by its own coalition of synapses. The two coalitions start linking together, since neurons that fire together wire together. Therefore, you can deliberately be aware of both positive and negative material, so that—especially if what's positive is vividly present in the foreground of awareness—the positive will connect with the negative. In effect, strongly positive thoughts and feelings will begin weaving their way into the negative material. When the negative material leaves awareness to be reconsolidated in neural structure, it will tend to take some of these positive links with it. When the negative material is next reactivated, it will also tend to bring along some of these positive associations, these positive thoughts and feelings.

Overwrite the Negative

Let's say you had a minor argument with a friend or your mate. It was awkward and uncomfortable, but you know rationally that you two will be all right. Still, you can't stop worrying about it. So what you could do is to be aware, at the same time, of both your anxiety and a feeling of being cared about by someone (who could be the other person). Keep making the positive feelings stronger than the negative ones while being aware of both of them at once. After a dozen or more seconds, let the anxiety go and stay with the feeling of being cared about for another dozen seconds or so. If the worry about the relationship returns, it could be a little (or a lot) milder as a result of this brief practice. And as with any mental practice, the more you do it, the greater its impact on your brain. This is the first method for using positive material to reduce negative material.

Still, as beneficial as this infusion of positive into negative is, research indicates that it can sometimes merely "overwrite" the negative material without actually erasing it, like a pretty picture painted on top of a grim older one. When negative material is overwritten, it might return with a vengeance if the right trigger is present. Or it could be easier to reacquire down the road.

Erase the Negative

To deal with these potential weaknesses of overwriting negative material with positive material, new research is pointing to a second method for reducing negative material: certain psychological protocols literally erase negative associations in neural structure, rather than just overwriting them. Here's how it works. Negative material is often associated with a neutral "trigger." Suppose that in your childhood you had a male sports coach who was loud, critical, and scary. In this case, male authority—a neutral trigger, since male authority is not inherently negative—became connected in your brain to experiences of fear and humiliation (negative material). If so, these days you might still feel uncomfortable around a male authority figure at work even though you know intellectually that he's not going to treat you like your coach did when you were young. How can you break the chain that ties the neutral trigger to the negative material?

In your brain, there's a "window of reconsolidation," which lasts at least an hour, that you can use to do this. For at least an hour after the negative material has been activated and then left awareness, repeatedly bringing to mind the neutral trigger while feeling only neutral or positive (for roughly a dozen seconds or longer) will disrupt the reconsolidation of the negative associations to the neutral trigger in neural structure, even reducing amygdala activation related to the neutral trigger.

Working with the example here of a male authority figure, you could use both methods for reducing negative material. First, hold in mind a strong sense of self-worth along with a memory in the background of awareness of being embarrassed by the coach when you were young; in doing this, you're consciously linking positive and negative material. Second, after letting go of the painful memory, for a few times over the next hour or so, be aware of only neutral or positive things—such as a feeling of worth—while also bringing to mind the idea of male authority or a memory or an image of a male authority figure that you know (the neutral trigger) for a dozen seconds or longer.

You could use this method in your everyday activities as well. Just before a meeting with a man who is an authority figure, you could link in awareness both the strong sense of worth and the painful memory of the sports coach. Then, during the meeting with the man, re-access the sense of worth several times with no reference to the old memory of your coach. You could also try this approach in a lower-key way, such as by simply watching the male authority figure across a room while repeatedly renewing your sense of worth.

Powerful Possibilities

In sum, during their reconstruction and reconsolidation phases, the neural patterns underlying negative material *can be changed* by linking them to positive material in two ways. First, you can infuse positive influences into negative material. This will frame it in a larger, more realistic, and more hopeful perspective, plus soothe and ease its feelings, sensations, and desires. Second, you can disrupt the reconsolidation of associations between negative material and neutral triggers in neural structure, gradually erasing them.

These are powerful tools for reducing and clearing negative material. Here's one of my favorite examples of using them: *I was dog-sitting my daughter's two Cardigan Welsh corgis. I know them well, and we like each other. I decided to lie down quietly on the floor to see what they would do. Within seconds, they came over, put their front paws on my chest, licked my face and lips, very gently bit at my nose and ears, snuffled at my neck, ran around me, and then started all over. Needless to say, I was laughing and giggling. It was such a lovely experience of unconditional love. Then it occurred to me that I could use this experience to heal a very painful memory from when I was about three or four years old. My grandmother was nasty and cruel and had locked me outside the house and told me that the cows in the field next door were going to come eat me and other such crazy stories that terrified me. I repeatedly held in mind the lovely experience of the corgis jumping all over me and licking my face with unconditional love, while also remembering that painful time with my grandmother. It worked! Now, I cannot think of my grandmother without immediately thinking of the corgis. The old memory fades away, replaced by joy and love.*

This is the fourth step of taking in the good: by linking positive and negative, you're injecting "medicine" for what ails your mind directly into the neural networks where pain and distress and dysfunction are rooted.

This linking may seem exotic or risky, but actually it's natural. I bet you do this yourself already sometimes, holding positive and negative together in your mind. You may remember a friend's support when you're worried about your kids, talk yourself down when you get upset about something, go for a walk in nature if you are feeling blue, pray about an illness or loss, or hold chronic pain in a large and peaceful space of awareness.

Linking positive and negative can be done informally in everyday life as well as formally in various psychotherapies. For example, psychoanalysis connects a new interpretation to a person's neurotic symptoms and Rogerian therapy holds a client's pain in the therapist's unconditional positive regard. In particular, coherence therapy, developed by Bruce Ecker and colleagues, systematically links positive and negative material.

Taking the Fourth Step

So let's get into the details of the fourth step of taking in the good. You begin as usual with the first three steps—Have, Enrich, and Absorb—and then, when you feel solid in the positive experience, you Link it with some negative material. You can hold both positive and negative material in awareness as long as you like. When you are done, let go of the negative and allow yourself to marinate entirely in the positive for another few seconds at least.

If a neutral situation, action, relationship, or desire (i.e., the trigger) has become associated with negative material in your mind, several times over the next hour, with no sense of the negative being present, try to be aware of neutral or positive things along with the neutral trigger for a dozen seconds or longer. Sometimes there is no clear neutral trigger, or at least you can't think of one. If so, no worries, just skip this part of the fourth step. The holding in awareness of both positive and negative material that you've done will still have benefits for you.

Holding Two Things in Mind

It can feel a little odd at first to be aware of two things at once, but you already have many experiences of this, from listening while taking notes to keeping a preschooler happy in the back-seat while driving to school. With a little practice, you will get even better at it.

Keep the negative material in the background of awareness, so that it is dim, small, and mild. Meanwhile, hold the positive material in the foreground, so that it is bright, big, and intense. If the negative gets too strong, drop it like a hot potato. Be on your own side. You are *for* the positive. You want it to win! If it's useful, imagine allies with you, supporting you, strengthening you, cheering you on.

If the negative is especially intense or compelling, you can simply be aware of the *idea* of it, nothing more, while immersing yourself in the positive. Or you could have a more detailed sense of the negative material but still keep it far off in the wings of the stage of awareness, with the positive material under the spotlight. Most challenging but probably most powerful, you could sense the positive making direct contact with the negative. For example, you could imagine the positive material sifting down into the negative like a warm, gentle, and persistent rain; like a golden balm that touches and soothes places inside that feel raw, hurt, or bruised; or like water filling up old hollows.

Making Connections

You could also imagine that the positive material is connecting with younger layers in your psyche, as this person did: *My mother abandoned our family on my third birthday. Regularly, I take in the good while walking on a nearby trail along a lagoon. Every day I see things there that nourish me, such as the graceful flight of a large flock of birds or the tender new leaves on a bush. When I notice such things, I stop for maybe thirty seconds to drink them in. I breathe deeply and imagine the goodness of the experience sinking into me—I find the image of filling a treasure chest in my heart effective. I began pairing this beautiful experience with the thought of my mother's leaving. At first, it was bewildering to think of her. But after doing this practice for a few months, I can now think of my mother without it feeling painful.*

You could even get the sense that the child inside you—since there are younger layers inside everyone's psyche—is finally getting some things that he or she always needed. Perhaps visualize a nurturing adult part of you holding and comforting young parts of you in your lap, as this woman did: *Recently a deep childhood hurt appeared out of the rabbit hole of memory. In the past it would have swept me away. But this time I asked myself: What does this very scared and alone small child need? The answer was for someone to hold her with love and bear witness to her sadness. So I just stayed with the sense of a caring, gentle, caressing presence who listened to this little girl and didn't try to talk her out of her feelings. Many, many years later, that small child was finally heard, felt, and held. This hurt has reappeared several times since, but it keeps getting softer.*

As a bonus, if it's real for you, explore a sense of receiving the positive material *into* the negative. Like a sense of being soothed. Or a sense of young parts of you receiving and taking in at least a little of what they've longed for. This involves a kind of dual perspective in which one part of you experiences offering a positive experience while another part of you experiences receiving it.

Three Requirements

Overall, the fourth step has three requirements. First, you have to be able to hold two things in mind at once. Second, you can't allow yourself to get hijacked by the negative material. Consequently, I recommend that you don't use this method yourself for the black hole at the center of trauma (though a trained therapist might use the fourth step with his or her clients). Third, you need to keep the positive material more prominent. Otherwise, it could get infused with negativity.

This may all seem complicated at first, but after you try the fourth step of HEAL a few times, it will feel straightforward and even simple.

Antidote Experiences

The fourth step of taking in the good is a very useful way to match key resource experiences—which we explored in chapter 4—with your own issues and needs. For instance, you could link feeling all right right now with anxiety, ease with irritability, gladness and gratitude with sadness, connection with separation, feeling loved with feeling hurt, worthiness with inadequacy, and motivation with feeling stuck. In effect, you would be using a particular positive experience as a kind of "antidote" for certain negative material. For other examples, see Table 5 opposite, "Matching Some Antidote Experiences to Negative Material"; it organizes positive and negative experiences in terms of your three core needs, for safety, satisfaction, and connection. (Of course, the "antidotes" listed are not the only way to address the negative materials.)

This woman used her memories of positive experiences with a loved one to ease the pain of his death: *I lost my close friend eight months ago. He was an exceptional person who loved me deeply. I feel the grief, and then focus on one of the wonderful moments we shared. I relive the memory as vividly as I can and allow the happy feelings of those times to soak in. Then the sadness becomes softer, and I bear it with a love that feels like what we used to share.*

Perhaps something has been bothering you lately, or you're dealing with chronic anxiety or guilt, or you're trying to heal an old pain such as a shocking loss when you were a child. Try to name the issue to yourself, and then ask: What experiences would help with this issue? Once you have some kind of answer—and it doesn't need to be a perfect one—you can look for opportunities to have these antidote experiences in daily life and use them in the fourth step of the HEAL process. Additionally, see chapter 10 for guided practices you can use to call up and take in these key experiences on your own.

Repeatedly linking antidote experiences to negative material has been deeply helpful to me. It's been the main way I've gradually filled the hole in my heart.

Table 5: Matching Some Antidote Experiences to Negative Material

Avoiding Harms

Negative Material	Positive Experience
Weakness	Strength
Helplessness, feeling at effect	Efficacy, feeling at cause
Alarm	Protection, safety, calm
Anxiety, fear, worry	Reassurance, relaxation, seeing strengths, noticing you're all right right now
Feeling contaminated	Cleansing, sensing ways the body and mind *are* healthy
Sensitivity, quick activation of the fight-or-flight sympathetic nervous system	Soothing of the senses, activation of the calming, rest-and-digest parasympathetic nervous system
Immobilization, freezing	Physical activity, venting

Approaching Rewards

Negative Material	Positive Experience
Disappointment, sadness, loss	Gratitude, gladness, beauty, pleasure, gain
Frustration	Accomplishment, seeing goals attained
Failure	Success

(continued)

Negative Material	Positive Experience
Drivenness	Satisfaction, fulfillment
Boredom, apathy	Feeling the rich fullness of this moment

Attaching to Others

Negative Material	Positive Experience
Abandoned, neglected	Feeling loved
Ignored, misunderstood	Feeling seen, receiving empathy
Left out, excluded	Belonging, feeling wanted
Inadequacy, shame, worthlessness	Feeling recognized, appreciated, prized
Loneliness	Friendship, being kind to others, being caring toward oneself
False front, "imposter syndrome"	Feeling accepted, accepting oneself, sincerity
Resentment, anger at someone	Assertiveness, support from others, self-compassion

Starting with the Negative

Most of the time when you do the fourth step, you will begin with positive material, in the sequence I've described so far. But you can also use negative material as your starting point.

Let's say that something negative has gotten reactivated inside you. In terms of the three fundamental ways to engage the mind, you start with the first one: *being with* what's there. You step back from the negative material to observe it. After a while, it will feel right to shift into the second one: *decreasing the negative.* You might relax a little, cry, or try to let go of some harmful thoughts. At some point, you'll be ready for the third way to engage the mind: *increasing the positive.* Then you use the HEAL steps, with a particular focus on the key experiences that will provide an "antidote" to the negative material that began this process.

I use this sequence often, usually for mildly negative experiences. Let's say I'm getting frustrated with writing an e-mail. I'll start by being with my reactions, trying to sort out what's bugging me so much. Maybe it's that I feel pressed to get a lot done in a short amount of time. Next I'll begin letting go of that sense of stress by exhaling slowly and looking out the window. As my inner stress needle climbs down from orange to yellow and even yellow-green, I'll shift into letting in some good feelings, such as a sense of accomplishment from the stuff I have gotten done today and an overall feeling that things will be okay even if I don't finish this e-mail right now. Then, using the fourth step of taking in the good, I'll help these good feelings connect with the frazzled parts of my mind, sinking into them, reassuring them, making them less alarmed. So the next time my e-mail in-box starts overflowing, I won't feel so pressured about it.

When they're stressed, worried, frustrated, or hurt about something, people frequently use the first two ways to engage the mind—letting be and letting go—but skip the third one: letting in. Unfortunately, in terms of the garden of the mind, then they miss a chance to grow flowers—inner strengths—in the space left by the weeds they pulled. Plus, as any gardener knows, if you don't replace weeds with flowers, the weeds come back. So when the bad feelings pass, or at least some of them, remember to take in some good ones.

Linking Positive Material and Negative Situations

A variation on the fourth step is to deliberately encourage a strongly positive experience in settings or with people that are difficult for you. Over time, the positive material you've repeatedly taken in will start activating automatically as an inner strength in these previously challenging situations. I'll use an example here of relaxing and calming your body in increasingly tense situations.

Start with the easiest situations and work your way upward, on a 1 to 10 scale of difficulty. Perhaps you're waiting in a lunch line at a deli to order your sandwich and you feel a little nervous about getting back to work on time; suppose this is a 1 on the challenge scale. So you use your relaxation methods while in line (e.g., exhaling slowly, remembering happy times) and gradually feel more at ease. Next, pick a slightly harder challenge, a 2 or 3 or 4. Perhaps you've got an important meeting today and you're agonizing more than you need to about what would be the right blouse or tie to wear. Keep calming your body until you feel more settled down. Then raise the bar further. A 6 might be speaking up to disagree with a coworker, while an 8 could be disagreeing with your boss (obviously, don't do things that wouldn't be good for you). Keep relaxing your body even in these situations. You don't have to be perfect; if it's a 6, let alone an 8 or a 10, it's natural to still be somewhat nervous or revved up. When you're ready, you can approach that 10 of telling a significant person how you really feel about something that's very vulnerable and important to you.

You can also use this method with ongoing, difficult conditions. This woman learned to link positive feelings with chronic pain: *I suffer from severe back pain, which is aggravated by the fear I have about it. To counter this, I started focusing on when my back was* not *in pain. When I'd go to work and afterward my back felt okay, I'd spend minutes acknowledging this and feeling good about it. I imagined a kind of warmth—sometimes a warm light, like sunlight, or sometimes a warm, sparkling, gooey liquid, a bit like melted chocolate—that would seep into every cell in my body, especially my back. It really felt like this warm goodness was soothing my back, like putting oil on a squeaky door joint. Each time I did this I was making a kind of mental video of my back being and feeling all right. Eventually I had hundreds of these good videos, in which I had actually been comfortable and moving easily. Increasingly, these became my expectation instead of a dreaded agony that I was always bracing against. It was as if being more flexible in my mind allowed me to be more flexible in my body.*

Practicing the Fourth Step

The practice that follows focuses on key experiences in the approaching rewards system. We will start with a positive experience that is an antidote to the negative feelings people can have when they don't reach a goal, such as frustration, disappointment, failure, or inadequacy. Antidote experiences that can soothe and replace this negative material include feelings of success, arriving, satisfaction, and being praised or valued.

To do this practice, you need to know both what the negative material is that you are trying to ease and heal, and what its positive antidote is. This clarity alone will be helpful to you because then you'll know better what positive experiences to look for or create for yourself. I suggest you pick negative material that is mild to moderate in its intensity. See if an inherently neutral situation, action, or desire (the neutral trigger) has become connected with the negative material in your mind; for example, making a to do list, setting goals, or telling others about your hopes and dreams—which are neutral if not positive—may have become connected to experiences of disappointment or failure. If you can't identify a neutral trigger, that's all right; you can still do the fourth step. If you get sucked into the negative material, drop it and stay with only positive material. Once you are stable in the positive, if you want, bring the negative back into awareness.

1. **Have** Bring to mind one or more times when you attained a goal. Perhaps it is a major achievement, or a series of tasks done, or a kind of speeded up movie of your life that quickly notes numerous milestones reached. It could be things learned or finished or otherwise succeeded at, both large and small.

Let knowing these facts become an experience of accomplishing, contributing, and adding value. Let knowing them become an experience of being adequate, being more than adequate, being a success.

2. **Enrich** Open to this experience, and stay with it. Let it become more intense. Sink into it. Help it become big in your

mind. Explore different aspects of it, finding things that are new or fresh in it. Consider how this experience of being successful is relevant to you.

3. **Absorb** Intend and sense that this experience is sinking into you. Let feeling successful sink into you as you sink into it. As you feel increasingly accomplished and successful, let any drivenness fall away, along with any inner sense of grasping after or straining toward rewards of any kind.

4. **Link** When you're ready, try the fourth step. In the background of your awareness, bring to mind some knowing of the negative material. You could just have an idea of it in passing, or a quick survey of it, or a sense of how it feels in your body, or a noting of a negative memory. Meanwhile, keep the positive material prominent in awareness in addition to this negative material. Hold both at the same time, perhaps like two things on stage at once, the positive material in the front, under the spotlight, with the negative material dim and back in the wings.

You could also get a sense of the positive connecting with the negative, going into it somehow, infusing it, sinking into it like a warm golden salve soothing hurt places inside. Or like golden dust sifting down into difficult places, or light moving into shadows. Perhaps imagine beautiful jewels or anything else you like gradually filling your own hole in the heart.

You may have a sense of younger parts or layers of yourself being given what they've longed for. There could be an image or feeling of something nurturing and kind holding a young version of yourself and giving something to it.

If you get too drawn into the negative, turn up the positive, making it more prominent in awareness, big in the front of your mind. If the negative remains too powerful, drop it. Recenter yourself in the positive. After a while, if you want, bring the negative material up into the background of awareness, to be infused again with the more powerful positive material.

If it's real for you, see if you can get a sense of *receiving* the positive material—a sense of it sinking into vulnerable, young, bruised, hungry, needy, or longing places inside you.

Then let go of the negative material altogether, and stay with the positive. If this feels difficult or unnatural, try telling yourself that it is okay to be with the positive, that you're allowed to do this, that it will be good for you and others. And be on your own side, using determination to focus on just the positive experience.

A few times over the next hour, for a dozen or more seconds at a time, be aware of only neutral or positive things, perhaps including a sense of accomplishment or success, while also bringing to mind neutral triggers (e.g., people, situations, ideas) of a sense of failure.

You need some courage to try the fourth step. So be especially kind to yourself, recognizing the moxie it takes to open to the negative. Over time, let it sink in that the actual *experience* of much if not most negative material is fairly brief and not overwhelming. This fact is itself good news.

TAKING IT IN

- Unpleasant experiences are part of life, and sometimes have value. But due to the negativity bias, it's easy for unpleasant experiences to get stored in your brain as negative material, which has negative consequences for you and often others.

- When negative material is activated, typically from implicit memory stores, it is not retrieved *as a unit* from storage but rather is reconstructed in a dynamic process. Once it comes into consciousness, it starts associating with whatever else is present in awareness. Then, when it's no longer activated, it gets reconsolidated back into memory, also in a dynamic process.

- The dynamic nature of memory reconstruction and reconsolidation gives you two good methods for changing negative material. First, when you are aware of prominently positive material alongside the negative, what's positive can soothe, compensate for, and sometimes eventually overwrite the negative. Second, during the "window of reconsolidation," if you bring to mind a neutral trigger associated with the negative material while feeling only neutral or positive, this can disrupt the reconsolidation process and gradually erase the association between the neutral trigger and the negative material.

- To do the fourth step of HEAL—Linking positive and negative material—you need to be able to hold both positive and negative in awareness while keeping the positive more prominent and not getting hijacked by the negative.

- Once you have identified key positive experiences for yourself, you can use the fourth step for old pain or other issues. Look for opportunities to have these good experiences, and once they're activated, help them connect with the negative material as an "antidote."

- You can also use the fourth step in situations that start with a negative experience. First, be with the difficult experience, witnessing it with self-compassion. Second, when it feels right, try to let it go. Third, call up an appropriate positive experience and link it with the original negative material.

- Connect positive experiences to negative situations, either ones you are in or ones you imagine. Over time, this could help you be more comfortable and capable in these situations.

Chapter 9

Good Uses

Now that we have explored the four HEAL steps of taking in the good, let's consider how you can use this practice in different situations and with different issues.

Letting Good Lessons Land

Everyday life holds many opportunities to learn something important and shift a bit as a result. Recently my wife has been telling me I sometimes make her wait, whether it's to leave together in the car or to start a TV program we want to see. After getting through my personal "Erk, go away!" at being caught and criticized, I know that I don't really want to keep her waiting. So I've been encouraging a feeling of consideration for her inside myself about this issue, giving myself over to this feeling so it will carry me along to the living room the next time we're going to watch some show.

More formally, you could be doing a structured activity such as human resources training, prayer, meditation, journaling, yoga, a mindfulness workshop, or psychotherapy. While you're doing this activity, when something really touches you and seems important, take the time to take it in. When the activity ends, use a few moments to let whatever was especially nourishing settle into you and stick to your mental ribs.

You can apply the steps of taking in the good to learning any new skill, from using a stick shift to staying cool when a teenager gets hot. The stronger the sensations and emotions related to the skill, and the more you replay the sense of it in your mind, the greater its memory trace will generally be, and the faster you will learn it.

Wanting What's Good for You

One key to a good life is learning to want the things that are good for you that, honestly, you *don't* particularly want. For example, I don't want to slog uphill on my treadmill for half an hour, but it's good for me. At work, a person may not naturally want to speak in public, but it could further his or her career to do so. Maybe you sort of want to do something—such as practice the piano daily—but you don't stick with it.

Sure, you could grit your teeth and exercise willpower, but this takes deliberate effort that's draining and hard to sustain. Plus, some people naturally have a genetic variation that produces less effective dopamine receptors, so they need a greater sense of reward to avoid running out of motivational gas. On the other hand, if you take in rewarding experiences related to the wants you'd like to encourage, this will make your brain lean in that direction, like the proverbial donkey trying to get the carrot. Using the piano as an example, when you think about playing it, call up a sense of enjoyment and other good feelings about it. While playing, keep refocusing attention on what's pleasant or fun and help these experiences sink in. Right after playing, take in feelings of satisfaction, congratulation, aesthetic pleasure, worth, and happiness. And if you can, be aware of wanting to play the piano while at the same time being aware of the rewards of playing it; this way, the wanting and the rewards will start associating together.

These methods are also helpful if you're being caught by a problematic desire such as drugs, alcohol, overeating, or gambling and are trying to take a higher road. The powerful rewards of the low road make it hard to appreciate the often milder but more wholesome rewards of the high road; for example, if you give a young child lots of candy, apples stop tasting sweet. So along with other resources (e.g., being honest about your issue with a close friend, therapy, AA), use taking in the good to intensify the rewards and thus the attraction of the high road. Suppose you are trying to drink moderately or not at all. When out to dinner with friends, notice how you feel just fine with only one glass of wine. See how good it feels to have an unclouded mind. Feel a sense of worth in staying true to your purpose; notice any positive reactions from others and let yourself feel respected. When you wake in the morning, feel glad about stopping at one drink. I've heard it said that wisdom is choosing a greater happiness over a lesser one. Over time, repeatedly internalizing rich experiences of the rewards of the greater happiness will gradually help tilt your brain toward it, and away from the lesser one.

If you want, you can remind yourself to take in the good with a simple checklist like the one that follows, "Hardwiring Your Happiness." Fill in the column headings with whatever

experiences you want to take in, such as those that would help
you want what's good for you or any others that are important
for you. Examples include strength, relaxation, enthusiasm, feeling cared about, and love. I left the column headings blank so
you can make copies of the table and then adapt it to your own
needs. Feel free to share or use this table with others (e.g., par-
ticipants in a training at work, children).

Hardwiring Your Happiness

- Fill in the column headings with the experiences you'd like
  to take in. You could make a copy of this table with blank
  column headings, print a few, and then add headings as
  you like.
- In the columns below, mark each day that you did the
  practice. (You can add marks if you did it more than once.)

Monday					
Tuesday					
Wednesday					
Thursday					
Friday					
Saturday					
Sunday					

A Slice of the Pie

In life, we get preoccupied with conditions, situations, and events—*circumstances* such as having money, getting to work on time, or being praised—but really, the point of these circumstances is what they help us *experience*. This fact gives us very useful options when we do not have the circumstances we want.

Let's say you want to have a romantic partner—a circumstance—but don't have one. I'm not trying to minimize the importance of this kind of relationship or the pain of not having one. But there could be other ways to have at least *some* of the experiences you'd get from a romantic relationship, such as fun, affection, security, physical pleasure, and friendship. If a romantic partner would make you feel loved, how else could you have some of this experience? The experience of being loved by a friend, parent, or child has many aspects of the experience of romantic love. It's not everything you want, but it's not nothing. It's a chance to feel loved in some ways. If you can't have the whole pie, at least eat a slice of it.

Unfortunately, many people turn away from opportunities to have elements of the experience they long for because it isn't everything they want. They fear that eating a slice will somehow stop them from ever getting the whole pie. But this just isn't true. Why would taking in respect from someone at work or warmth from friends or love from a parent block a person from getting a romantic partner? In fact, taking in the slices that *are* available often moves people forward toward eventually getting the whole pie.

People also think that eating a slice will mean letting others off the hook who should have given them the whole pie in the past but didn't—and maybe gave them no pie at all. Yes, those parents, teachers, siblings, classmates, lovers, or life partners really should have delivered the whole pie. I don't mean my pie metaphor to trivialize the loss, pain, even abuse, that may have happened. If it was bad, it really was bad. If anything, in my experience, most people downplay the bad things that have happened in their lives—especially when they were young—and how much it hurt. But turning down slices of the pie that *are* available reminds me of the saying in Alcoholics Anonymous that resentment is like taking poison and waiting for others to die. What's more important: feeling aggrieved and reproachful about the past, or feeling loved in the present? Plus you can certainly be clear about how others hurt you while also giving yourself at least some of the experiences that would feed your heart.

Filling the Hole in Your Heart

I weeded a lot of dandelions as a kid and learned that if you didn't get the tip of the root, the weed grew back. In the same way, it really helps for your key, "antidote" experiences to sink down into and get at the youngest, deepest layers of your issues. Some fortunate people had a very benign childhood, but in my experience many more people had a rocky one. In terms of the avoiding harms system, perhaps you felt unsafe as a child, unprotected, with fears or phobias; perhaps you were picked on or even assaulted. In the approaching rewards system, you could have suffered a loss or not had the resources you needed to succeed in school. In terms of the attaching to others system, you might have been put down a lot by an older brother or sister, felt like an outsider, been betrayed and humiliated by your first boyfriend or girlfriend, or been ostracized because of your appearance, ethnicity, or social class.

Many people are embarrassed about "still carrying the past." They ask, *Why haven't I gotten over this by now, what's wrong with me?* But the brain is designed to be continually remodeled by experiences in ways that last. If we can be changed for the better by life, we must also be changeable for the worse; in fact, the brain's negativity bias makes us especially changeable by negative experiences. Your brain is also designed to hyper-learn during childhood, so issues from that time—such as abuse, neglect, humiliation, bullying, discrimination, harsh scolding, poverty or financial hardship, burdensome secrets, creepy experiences, exclusion, family tension, injuries, disabilities, and illnesses—cast a long shadow. Even relatively moderate things add up, like feeling a little awkward socially. Your temperament affects how events land on you, so what may have been unpleasant but tolerable for someone else could have been very hurtful to you. Naturally, we're impacted by the bad things that happened when we were young and by the good things that didn't. Your personal history matters, it has consequences. It can leave you with a hole in your heart.

You can't change the past, but you *can* use key experiences today to fill that hole. Consider a significant issue from your childhood. In which of the three systems—avoiding, approaching, and attaching—does it mainly belong? Next take a look at the table "Matching Some Antidote Experiences to Negative Material" on page 137 for a key experience that would help with this issue. It could also be useful to ask yourself these questions: *What would have made all the difference when I was young? Deep down, what do I most long for?* The answers will suggest one or more key antidote experiences. Then, try to repeatedly have and take in these experiences.

You are not trying to deny the past or resist painful feelings in the present. You are simply *resourcing* yourself to deal with what you can and to bear what you can't. Over time, you can gradually give yourself some and perhaps even most of what you should have been given when you were young. This is what I did for myself, in the story that began this book, as I took in experiences of being included and valued to fill my own hole in the heart.

Lifting a Blue Mood

People in my family as well as many of my clients have been burdened by depression, which is painfully common. Many psychological approaches (e.g., psychotherapy, books) for dysthymic disorder (chronic blues) and for mild to moderate depression include the encouragement of a sense of agency rather than entrapment and helplessness, enjoyable and rewarding activities, good times with friends, self-compassion, and replacing catastrophizing or critical thoughts with realistic and supportive ones. Therefore, using the HEAL steps to heighten the impact of these interventions can be helpful—and more generally, can bring more good into your life and into your brain.

In general, taking in the good should not be used with severe depression, in which it's very hard if not impossible to create a positive experience. Trying to do this yourself or asking others to do so, such as a client if you are a therapist, would only be frustrating or worse. The potential exception involves experiences of simple physical pleasure, such as eating something sweet or warming up when chilled. Even if someone is severely depressed, there will still likely be some basic capacity for at least brief experiences of pleasure. Applied to physical pleasure, the methods for enriching and absorbing experiences in chapter 7 might help a severely depressed person gradually recover more capacity for enjoyment.

Recovering from Trauma

Whether it was a car accident, mugging, rape, injury, or childhood abuse, any trauma involves an incapacity to stop a terrible thing from happening; of course, this incapacity is not the fault of the person experiencing the trauma. Consequently, one aspect of treating and recovering from trauma is to nurture greater capacities, greater strengths, inside that person. In this general way, while working with a therapist or on your own, taking in the good may be useful. For example, a central aspect of trauma is entrapment, immobilization, and helplessness: The person cannot escape the awfulness. So it might help to take in experiences of agency (page 195 in chapter 10), of being able if only inside the mind to make something happen. Another common feature of trauma is being intimidated from communicating fully and firmly, so taking in experiences of assertiveness (page 215 in chapter 10) could be useful. But be careful: Simply knowing that a positive experience is an intended resource for dealing with the trauma can remind a person of the trauma and then reactivate it. First of all, do no harm.

Trauma is like a black hole that can suck you in if you are not careful, and getting sucked in—reexperiencing the trauma—

can be a re-traumatization. Since the fourth step of taking in the good brings negative material into awareness, I recommend not using this step on your own with the central experiences of the trauma itself, though it could be beneficial to use it with a skilled therapist (many therapies for trauma link positive and negative material). But you might be able to use the fourth step by yourself with issues around the edges, as it were, of the trauma. For example, a person could take in self-compassion (page 211 in chapter 10) linked to the pain of being let down by failed protectors, such as caregivers who did not pick up on the signs of child abuse and stop it.

For more about treating and recovering from trauma, see the work of Judith Herman, Peter Levine, Pat Ogden, and Bessel van der Kolk.

Feeding Relationships

Whether at home or at work or in other settings, a relationship is like a tapestry. The busyness and inevitable aggravations of daily life continually tear at its threads. If both people don't keep registering good experiences in the relationship, its fabric will fray and may eventually tear apart. I don't mean ignoring real problems, but rather *also* paying attention to the good qualities in the other person, to what there is to like, and to the being behind his or her eyes. The seemingly little things are often the most touching, as this woman writes: *Each morning I take a moment to feel grateful for my husband. I remember things I appreciate about him, like how he decorates a salad with little pepper rings and carrot curls. He isn't a cook, but he so wants to do something to please me. I smile and take in the feeling of a husband who loves me. When my mind goes to the annoyances—like how he doesn't put his dirty clothes in the hamper but has to put them on the floor next to it—I soon come back to how it feels when he does want to please. This little practice of appreciating my husband has truly changed my life and my marriage.*

Appreciating the good aspects of a relationship will feed your heart, help you feel good, and put hassles and irritations in perspective. Plus the other person will probably treat you better, since he or she will feel more seen and appreciated.

If you do need to mend a relationship, it's especially important to take in positive experiences that happen in it. Otherwise, staying fixated on the bad parts of a relationship and overlooking or minimizing the good ones feels bad for you, plus it is disheartening to the other person and doesn't encourage continued efforts in a positive direction. And if you like, you could ask the other person to be more aware of positive experiences with *you* and more open to letting them in.

Helping Others

Sometimes it might be useful to help others to take in the good, especially if you are a health care professional, manager, human resources trainer, yoga instructor, fitness trainer, mindfulness teacher, executive coach, or psychotherapist. At www.Rick Hanson.net, you can get many freely offered resources for doing this (see the section on pages 159–62 for using the HEAL steps with children, as a parent or teacher).

You can use taking in the good with others in one or more of the four ways it's possible to offer a method to anyone. First, you could do it implicitly without drawing attention to it, such as by bringing someone's attention back to a well-earned acknowledgment if he or she deflects it. Second, you could describe it but leave it up to the other person whether he or she uses it. Third, you could explicitly take the other person through the steps of taking in the good (leaving off the last step if appropriate). Fourth, you could encourage the person to do it on his or her own, and follow up to see what happened.

I've known many people who responded very well to taking in the good, both in general and for a particular issue. Suppose you're a manager who wants to encourage more creativity in an employee. What strengths inside would promote creativity? One might be feeling valued by others rather than anxious about making mistakes. So you could ask the person to look for times when he or she is in fact appreciated, and then to take in this experience. Or suppose you're a therapist working with someone raised by emotionally distant parents. What feeling inside would make a big difference for this person? Let's say that it's feeling special. You could suggest that the person look for times these days or in the past when someone cherished, prized, or wanted him or her, and then take in these experiences.

Taking in the good can improve the results of formal programs such as mindfulness training and psychotherapy as well as informal efforts to help others become healthier and happier. The "return on investment" in positive mental states grows much higher as more of these passing experiences become turned into enduring neural structures.

HEALing Children

I've used taking in the good with young people in therapy and also spoken with parents and teachers who have used it with their own children or students. As with an adult, there are four ways to offer the HEAL steps to a child, while naturally adapting them to the child's age and situation.

First, you can guide a child through the steps of taking in the good without drawing explicit attention to them. You either encourage a positive experience in the first place or if one is already happening, you try to keep it going, sometimes with encouragement to let it sink in. Suppose you're helping a toddler or preschooler build up a stronger sense inside of being soothed, so that he or she feels better and fusses less. When the child does feel soothed, you can take ten or more seconds to murmur things like "Yes, you're feeling better . . . it's nice to feel good . . . Susie feels better . . . you're feeling good inside." Or, suppose your sixth grader has been thinking he or she is unpopular. Hearing that your child enjoyed sitting with some other kids at lunch, you could draw him or her out about what felt good about it, not playing therapist or getting into your anxieties about your child's social issues but being simply an interested listener. As appropriate, offer words for the experiences or mirror back to your child what he or she is saying to help keep attention with the good feelings, and not rush on from them to something else. If it feels right, you might mention that feeling liked could go down into any places inside that have felt bad (drawing your child into the fourth step of HEAL). You can also use this approach with character qualities you're encouraging. Suppose you're trying to help an older child become less possessive about toys with a younger sibling; when a younger brother or sister returns a toy and it's unbroken, you could help the relief sink in as well as your appreciation of your older child's generosity.

Second, you could name the four steps but leave it up to the child whether he or she uses them. I find this approach especially helpful with teenagers or other children who place a premium on being independent. Since taking in the good is quick and usually feels good, children like it. It's straightforward to teach; give examples, and share your own experience with it. You could talk with the child about possible times that he or she could take in the good, such as when another child is nice or when the child succeeds at a task. With children roughly six and older, I find it helpful to say a few words about the brain being like Velcro for the bad but Teflon for the good; the child immediately gets that this is true, and doesn't want that bad stuff getting stuck to his or her brain. As appropriate, I'll say that the brain is controlling the child and pushing him or her around—which no child likes—but that the child can take charge of it if he or she wants to.

Third, you could draw children through the steps in an explicit way. Much as we teach children to read, we can teach inner skills of emotional intelligence, including taking in the good. If we value inner skills—which have great benefit over the life span—then we can ask children to learn them much as we can ask them to learn the multiplication table. For example, putting a child to bed, you could take a minute or more to review the day or think about good things in order for the child to have a good experience. Perhaps your son or daughter learned something new or played well in soccer, or perhaps your child knows that a grandmother loves him or her. Once the positive experience is activated, you could suggest that your child enrich it by letting it become big and strong, and absorb it like putting a jewel in the treasure chest of the heart. You might also suggest that your child link this good experience with any sadness or hurt inside, so that the good feelings gradually replace any bad ones, like flowers pushing out weeds. In a classroom, you could use a minute at the beginning of the day to go through the first three steps of taking in the good in order to encourage children to find some excitement about learning new things and then to take this in, or use another minute at the end of the day to feel and take in a sense of accomplishment.

Fourth, you could ask children to use the HEAL steps on their own, perhaps in certain situations, such as when other kids are nice or when a task is done successfully. Then follow up as appropriate. After a recess in school or at the end of the day at home, you could ask a child if he or she has taken in the good. If the child has, you could ask how it felt; if the child hasn't, you could explore why not. Of course, kids don't like being interrogated any more than adults do, and a little gentle inquiry goes a long way.

Overall, an easygoing and matter-of-fact approach works best. Children often do the HEAL steps faster than adults, so five or ten seconds at a time could be plenty. Young people feel things keenly but often don't have words for their experiences, so asking a child to describe them could put the child on the spot and turn him or her off to taking in the good. It's fine to gently offer words yourself for what the child may be feeling. If you have an idea about the key experiences that a child needs— such as feeling successful at something, anything, to overcome a sense of failure and inadequacy in school—then you can look for natural opportunities for the child to take in these experiences. Take a look at Table 5 in the previous chapter for potential "antidote experiences" that might help your child the most.

While all young people gain from taking in the good, for some it is particularly helpful. Children who are anxious or rigid tend to overlook the good news of life plus need to build up inner strengths such as feeling safe and determined. Children who are spirited or considered to have attention deficit/hyperactivity disorder (ADHD) (e.g., highly distractible, impulsive, or stimulation-seeking) tend to move on so quickly that even good experiences don't have time to sink in, plus they need to build up more self-control. Additionally, many of these spirited or ADHD children have a genetic variation that produces less effective dopamine receptors, so they need more repeated experiences of rewards to stay focused on tasks. Kids who are grappling with problems or challenges such as a learning disability or a death in the family benefit from taking in key experiences aimed at their needs, such as feeling loved by others even though a beloved grandparent has passed away. Most teenagers are interested in themselves and (unfortunately) have many negative experiences, so I've found that they can be pretty motivated to take in the good, especially related to key experiences of feeling attractive and liked.

Ask yourself what experiences might have made a difference for you as a child. Let this knowledge plus your intuition guide you in helping the children in your life to have and take in the experiences that will make a difference for them.

Handling Blocks

When you try to take in the good, sometimes you bump into a block, such as distracting thoughts. Blocks are common. They're not bad or wrong—but they do get in the way. What works is to explore them with self-acceptance, and see what you can learn about yourself. One valuable aspect of taking in the good is that it often reveals other issues, such as an underlying reluctance to let yourself feel good. Then you can address these issues with the suggestions below. With practice and time, blocks usually fade away.

Blocks to Any Inner Practice

- **Distractibility**—Focus on the stimulating aspects of positive experiences, which will keep your attention engaged with them.

- **Just not in touch with your body or your feelings**—Explore and get used to simple pleasant sensations, such as the taste of pancakes with syrup, the feeling of warm water on your hands, or the ease in exhaling.

- **Uncomfortable tuning into your own experience**—Put yourself in a safe setting, and remind yourself that you don't have to be externally vigilant. Look around for objects or people that give you comfort and a sense of protection. Bring to mind what it feels like to be with someone who cares about you. Remember that you can shift your attention away from your experience at any time you want. Be aware of something pleasant in your experience, such as a pretty sight or enjoyable sound, and notice again and

again that continuing to be aware of it is all right for you,
that nothing bad is happening to you.

- **Overanalyzing, pulling out of the experience**—Bring attention back into your body and emotions. For example,
follow one breath from beginning to end, or gently name
what you're feeling to yourself (e.g., revved up . . . exasperated . . . calming . . . feeling better).

Blocks Specific to Taking In the Good

- **It's hard to receive, including a good experience**—Inhale
and sense that it's okay to let something in. Pick a simple
positive emotion such as relief or gladness, open to it and
let it come into your mind, and recognize that you're still
fine.

- **Concern that you'll lose your edge in business or life if
you no longer feel "hungry"**—Realize that building up inner resources such as confidence and happiness can only
aid your success. On a foundation of well-being, you can
still be very determined and ambitious. Additionally, taking in the good trains your mind to see the *whole* picture,
which could help you spot more opportunities.

- **Fear that you'll lower your guard if you feel better, and
that's when people get whacked**—Remind yourself that
you can still be watchful while also feeling good. Focus
on building up inner strengths such as determination, resilience, confidence, and feeling cared about so you can
become less worried about lowering your guard.

- **Belief that seeking to feel good is selfish, vain, or sinful,
or that it's disloyal or unfair to those who suffer, or that
you don't deserve it**—It's moral to seek the welfare of *all*

beings, and "all beings" includes the one wearing your name tag. You matter, too. Increasing your happiness will not increase the suffering of others, nor will increasing your suffering make them happier. In fact, developing your inner strengths, including peace, contentment, and love, will provide you with more to offer others. Taking in praise or a sense of accomplishment won't make you conceited; as people feel fuller inside, they're less likely to get puffed up or arrogant.

- **Fear that if you let yourself feel good, you'll want more but be disappointed**—Recognize that if you feel good today, there's a good chance you will also feel good tomorrow, and thus not get disappointed. Even if you do become disappointed, know that this will be unpleasant but not overwhelming. Put the risks of disappointment in perspective: What's greater, the cost of occasional disappointment or the benefit of feeling good and building up strengths inside?

- **As a woman, you've been socialized to make others happy, not yourself**—Your needs and wants have the same standing as theirs. And if you want to care for others, you have to nurture yourself.

- **As a man, you've been socialized to be stoic and not care about your experience**—You need to refuel or you'll run out of gas. Also, building up your inner "muscles" makes you stronger, not weaker.

- **Positive experiences activate negative ones**—This is counterintuitive, but it's actually common. For example, feeling cared about could stir up feelings of not being loved by the right person. If something like this happens for you, know that whatever is negative does not change the truth of what is positive. Then refocus on the positive experience, particularly its enjoyable aspects (which will help keep your attention in it).

- **There are payoffs in not feeling good**—Sometimes, let's face it, there can be a certain gratification in being outraged, aggrieved, hurt, resentful, righteously indignant, or even blue. But, at the end of the day, what's better for you: these payoffs . . . or actually feeling good?
- **You've been punished for being energized or happy**—Really recognize that you spend time with different people today than those in your childhood. Notice the people who are fine with you feeling good. Wouldn't you have liked it if someone had stood up for you when you were young and lively and joyful? Well, you can be that person for yourself today.
- **Belief that there is nothing good inside you**—The good that others see in you is not a delusion of theirs. It is *real*, as real as your hands. Hold on to the knowing of the reality of your helpful actions, good intentions, and caring feelings. If people put you down or shamed you in the past, recognizing the realness of your goodness is a way to be fair and kind toward yourself today. (For more, see the section on recognizing the good in yourself in chapter 6, and the practice "Feeling Like a Good Person" on page 213.)
- **Belief that there's no point in feeling good since some things are still bad**—Know that the bad things that exist do not remove the good ones; the hole does not get rid of the donut. Plus, one way to deal with the bad is to grow the good. I love this proverb: Better to light a single candle than to curse the darkness.

Dealing with Challenges
in a Responsive Way

Life has many challenges, from aggravating relatives to serious illnesses. One way to think about these is in terms of your core needs for safety, satisfaction, and connection. To handle a problem in a responsive rather than a reactive way, try to call upon the inner strengths and related experiences that can best take care of the core need that is being challenged.

Suppose that you are dealing with a person who is being aggressive or threatening toward you, even in subtle ways; this would be someone who is activating the avoiding harms system in your brain, someone around whom you don't feel completely safe. A reactive approach to this person would involve feelings of anxiety (from unease to stark fear), anger (from exasperation to outrage), or numbing; and involve actions such as fighting (e.g., quarreling), fleeing (e.g., withdrawal), or freezing (e.g., getting immobilized). As understandable and common as "going red" is, it also has costs for you and others.

Alternately, imagine a responsive approach to this person. You could start by getting on your own side, having compassion for yourself, and buying yourself time to understand what's going on and to form a plan to handle it. Then you could draw on inner strengths and related experiences in the avoiding harms system. Remind yourself of protections and resources in your life, and call up previous experiences of feeling strong and determined. Double-check your assumptions and thinking, and make sure you are not under- or overestimating the threat; put the threat, whatever it is, in perspective. Exhale and do other relaxing things to feel less tense, and to feel cooler, calmer, and more collected. Build up your resources, such as the support of other people; try to have a sense of allies who are with you. When you do take action, be appropriately cautious but not cowed or intimidated. Be considered, serious, and sustained rather than impulsive, self-deprecating, or quick to give up. Imagine the likely results of "going green." While this approach is no guarantee of a good outcome, it's usually your best-odds strategy for one.

You can take a similar approach with conditions that challenge your needs for satisfaction or connection. Take a look at the table "Matching Some Antidote Experiences to Negative Material," in the previous chapter (page 137), and see what key experiences and inner strengths could help you stay responsive with any difficult conditions in your life these days. As you activate and draw on these experiences and strengths, you will have an opportunity to take them in again and again, installing them in your brain ever more deeply.

Besides drawing on the key experiences that are matched to difficult conditions in the thick of the moment, you can also *imagine* yourself coping in a responsive way in the future. This is called *mental rehearsal*, which has been shown to improve performance on various tasks. Try the practice below, adapting it as you like. It includes inner strengths for all three of your core needs, and you can focus on the ones that will be most useful for a particular challenge; the next chapter offers guided practices that explore many of these inner strengths in detail. Here we go:

Settle into yourself, taking a few breaths, getting centered. Pick a challenge and observe it as if from a bird's-eye view. Consider some of the reactions it has stirred up in you, and how you would like to approach it in the future.

To begin with, call up a sense of being on your own side, of caring for yourself, of having compassion for whatever is hard or painful for you. Find a sense of strength and determination. Let it sink in that you are basically all right right now.

Regarding the challenge, be aware of ways you are protected and supported. Exhale slowly and relax some. Imagine dealing with the challenge while staying in control of yourself, being reasonably calm even if you need to be firm, not getting tangled up with others, not going to war with anyone or anything. Exhaling and relaxing some more. Seeing if you can find some sense of peace related to the challenge.

Call up a sense of gratitude and gladness for the larger whole of your life. Be aware of the many things still going fine in spite of the challenge. Feel fed by the fullness of this moment. Focus on what is within your power to influence regarding this challenge. Begin to make plans for what is possible for you to do. Notice some of the many other ways in your life you can feel accomplished and successful. Imagine how you could approach this challenge from a place of feeling already contented and fulfilled.

Imagine being grounded in a sense of being cared about by others as you engage this challenge. Feel encouraged by them, receive compassion and sympathy and support from them. Try to get a sense of love from them flowing to you, into you, filling your heart. Also imagine caring and friendliness and love flowing out from you. See if you can feel lifted and carried by warmheartedness, so that you are dealing with difficulties from a place of compassion for yourself and others. Wish yourself and others well even as you strongly stand up for yourself. Imagine how you could deal with the challenge if you had a strong internal sense of being loved and loving.

Imagine feeling an overall sense of peace, contentment, and love as you deal with this challenge. Hold any negative experiences in a large untroubled space of awareness. Imagine some of the good results of staying fundamentally peaceful, contented, and loving with regard to this challenge. Let the knowing and appreciating of these good results motivate you to bring a responsive approach to this challenge in the days ahead.

TAKING IT IN

- In formal and informal settings when you get a good lesson, use the HEAL steps to help it really sink in. Taking in the good could substantially improve a person's gains from human resources training, psychotherapy, mindfulness training, coaching, or the psychological aspects of health care treatments.

- Take in rewarding experiences related to the behaviors you want to encourage in yourself. For problematic desires such as addictions, you could help yourself increasingly choose a greater happiness over a lesser one.

- When you look for key experiences, be resourceful and kind to yourself. Even if you can't have the whole pie you long for, take in as much as you can.

- It's normal to be affected by the past due to painful events or shortfalls of important psychological "supplies." You can use key experiences to fill this hole in your heart.

- If you are addressing depressed mood or trauma, you can intensify the benefits of standard interventions through taking in the good.

- In relationships, appreciating and internalizing what is actually good in them will usually make each person feel better and strengthen the bond between them.
- In both formal and informal ways, you can use the HEAL steps to help others, including children.
- It's common for blocks to arise related to taking in the good. These blocks are a chance to learn more about yourself. You can also handle them in effective ways.
- When you're faced with a challenge, experiences of key strengths will help you meet it in a responsive way. As you experience these strengths again and again, you'll be able to stay in the green zone with increasingly intense challenges.

Chapter 10

21 Jewels

This chapter is a collection of practices for growing key strengths inside yourself. I think of these as twenty-one jewels for the treasure chest of the heart. They include a sense of protection, relaxation, pleasure, enthusiasm, self-compassion, feeling like a good person—and of course the hallmarks of the responsive brain: peace, contentment, and love. These are the foundational inner strengths that I've seen change my own life and the lives of others. Look for opportunities to experience these strengths in everyday life, plus use the guided practices below to weave them into your brain whenever you want.

How to Use This Chapter

The key strengths are organized in terms of your three core needs, for safety, satisfaction, and connection, with seven strengths for each one. Each practice begins with an introduction and then guides you through the four HEAL steps of taking in the good. Because you already know these steps, my suggestions will be brief and direct. Since each practice stands on its own, there will be some unavoidable repetition of suggestions. Feel free to adapt these to your own needs. For instance, you may find that the way I talk about absorbing one strength can be applied to absorbing a different one, too.

Remember, the fourth step in these practices is optional. If you're going to include this step, before beginning one of the guided practices, see if you can identify a neutral trigger that's become associated with the negative material. But often there is no clear neutral trigger; if you can't think of one, it's all right, and you can still do the other parts of the fourth step.

A Single Issue or Want

If you're grappling with a particular situation, relationship, or state of mind, such as a draining but necessary slog at work, a teenager with attitude, or a blue mood, then you could find the strength that would give you the specific help you need, and just focus on that one for a while. For instance, the strength of refuge (page 183) would help with feeling drained, compassionate assertiveness (page 215) with a difficult relationship, and gratitude and gladness (page 192) with the blues. For strengths that are well matched to specific challenges, see the table "Matching Some Antidote Experiences to Negative Material" in chapter 8 (page 137).

Focusing on One Core Need

Or perhaps you'd like to develop all seven strengths related to one of your core needs. If anxiety or anger are concerns, take in the strengths in the section titled "Safety" on page 177. Issues of disappointment, frustration, loss, drivenness, or addiction would be served by having more of the strengths in the "Satisfaction" section that follows. And for loneliness, hurt, shame, envy, low self-worth, or ill will, go to the final section, "Connection." If you like, focus on a new strength each day of the week and see how you feel at its end. Or you can simply keep all seven strengths in mind and draw on whichever one would help you the most in a particular situation. You can also use the "Hardwiring Your Happiness" checklist in the previous chapter to track the strengths you cultivated each day.

The Top Ten

All of the strengths listed in this chapter are valuable. But if I had to pick just ten, they'd be refuge, feeling all right right now, and peace (for safety); enthusiasm, feeling the fullness of this moment, and contentment (for satisfaction); feeling cared about, feeling like a good person, and love (for connection); and an integrated sense of peace, contentment, and love merging together (see the practice at the end of chapter 7). And you are welcome to create your own top ten.

You can try a different strength daily, over ten days, or you can focus on two or three strengths each day. If you want a deep dive over three days, you can practice the three strengths for safety on day 1, the three for satisfaction on day 2, and the three for connection on day 3; also, in the morning and in the evening of each of these days, do the "One Minute for Good" practice in the box on page 176.

21 Days of Good

If you want to really go for it, how about taking just three weeks to really boost your mind, your brain, and your life? Pick a new strength each day, and feel it growing inside you.

You could explore the twenty-one strengths in their sequence here. Or you could engage them in three-day cycles, alternating among the needs (safety, satisfaction, and connection), with one addressed on each of three consecutive days. For fun you could take a popcorn approach and pick one strength at random each day, gradually crossing them off until there is only one left. If you like, you could replace one or more of the strengths below with a different one, such as curiosity or generosity.

To enrich this process, you can journal about it, do it with a friend or in your family, or weave it into your therapy, sobriety process, or spiritual practice. Think of this as a kind of retreat, or if that seems too Spartan, as a vacation in a luxurious spa in which you're bathing in luscious healing experiences rather than sulfurous mud. At the end of the three weeks, honor your sincere efforts and celebrate the results.

By setting aside twenty-one days in a row to enjoy and deepen these strengths, you can make sure that your core needs for safety, satisfaction, and connection are being more cared for, and you will rest with increasing stability in the green, responsive setting of your brain. Along the way, you'll be a good friend to yourself, building up momentum and making a habit of hardwiring happiness.

ONE MINUTE FOR GOOD

If these options seem too complicated, no problem. Just take a minute to do what I often do on first waking, just before bed, at the start of meditation, or before heading into a challenging situation:

For a breath or three, be aware of what's generally happening in your mind and body without trying to change it. Find an intimacy with yourself.

Start relaxing, letting your breathing soften and slow. Disengage from any worried thinking. Let go of any tension. Touch on a sense of strength and recognize protections such as friends nearby. Notice that you're all right right now. Rest in a growing peace.

Bring to mind one or more things you are grateful for or glad about. Think of something that makes you feel happy. Sense the fullness already present in this moment. Rest in a growing contentment.

Bring to mind one or more people (or a pet) who care about you. Let yourself feel appreciated, liked, or loved. Be aware of your own warmth and caring for others. Rest in a growing love.

Then get a sense of peace, contentment, and love woven together in your mind, three aspects of a single whole experience of ease and homecoming. Rest in the responsive mind. If you like, imagine moving through your day in this responsive way.

Finish up with another breath or two while you sense that peace, contentment, and love are sinking into you.

Safety

When you experience safety, your avoiding harms system goes green, into its responsive mode. You can build up both your capacity to *be* safe and your sense of *feeling* safe by regularly taking in *protection, strength, relaxation, refuge, seeing threats and resources clearly, feeling all right right now,* and *peace.* (Key experiences in the attaching system can also help you feel safe, and we'll explore these in "Connection.") This will help you feel increasingly at ease in life, with less and less need to struggle with or push away unpleasant experiences.

The avoiding system is rooted in ancient circuits in your brain stem and subcortex that are fast (good for survival) but rigid (not good for quality of life or for healing old pain). Unfortunately, these circuits are slow learners since the brain stem and subcortex generally have less neuroplasticity than the cortex does. In effect, these older parts of your brain need a *lot* of soothing to be at peace. So try to use lots of occasions to take in the key experiences below.

Besides their general benefits, the practices in this section should strengthen your *distress tolerance,* the capacity to stay open and centered and grounded in the responsive mode while having uncomfortable experiences. Distress tolerance is like a shock absorber helping you manage the unpleasant bumps of life without getting aversive and thus reactive toward them. They still hurt and they're surely not your preference, but you don't get upset about them or make a bad thing worse with overreactions. This is why many studies have shown that distress tolerance is a fundamental source of resilience, happiness, and achievement.

Protection

Protection decreases a person's sense of alarm. When you feel protected, there's less need for bracing, guarding, or anxiety. It's like watching a storm from inside a sturdy shelter: There could still be threats or problems outside, but they're not penetrating to harm you.

H *Notice any feeling of protection already present in the foreground or background of awareness. Perhaps a sense of strong walls around you, doors that are closed and locked, and other people nearby.*

Also, you can create a feeling of protection by thinking about resources inside you and in your life that could shield you, such as capabilities, virtues, credentials, friends, and family. You could also imagine protectors for yourself, such as people who care about you, even a whole group of protectors. Perhaps imagine a force field that nothing can penetrate to hurt you.

E *Open to the sense of protection. Explore what this experience is like. Let it fill your body and mind and become more intense. Stay with it, help it last. Open to relief or ease inside as you feel protected. You could add to this experience by embodying it; for example, look at pictures of people that you know care about you, or run your fingers over the lock on a door, or lean against a wall while feeling its solidity.*

A *Sense and intend that this experience of protection is sinking into you as you sink into it. Know that it is becoming part of you, a resource you can take with you wherever you go. As protection sinks in, feel a lessening of any need for resisting or bracing against anything inside you or out in the world. Any sense of alarm or threat is falling away. With protection sifting into you, you can let go of guarding, vigilance, and anxiety.*

L *Be aware of both the sense of protection and feelings of fear or vulnerability. Keep the positive experience of protection more prominent in awareness, and if you get hijacked by the negative material, drop it. Sense that feeling protected is soothing you and going into scared or vulnerable places inside. Perhaps there's an image of a nurturing protector successfully shielding fragile or young parts of you from danger. The feeling of protection is sinking into scared parts of you, reassuring them, helping these parts feel better. Then, when you want, let go of any negative material and just stay with this sense of protection. A few times over the next hour, for a dozen or more seconds at a time, be aware of only neutral or positive material—such as a sense of protection—while also bringing to mind a neutral trigger (e.g., people, situations, ideas) of feeling anxious or vulnerable.*

Strength

Fear comes from the perceived gap between internal strengths and external challenges. As your sense of genuine strength grows, this gap will shrink, even to nothing. Strength does not mean getting puffed up or aggressive. Determination, tenacity, bending but not breaking, and integrity are forms of strength. So are enduring hard times and surviving terrible ones.

H *Notice any sense of strength already present in the foreground or background of awareness, such as an ongoing aliveness in the body, the heart sturdily beating, or a steadfast caring for others.*

Awareness itself is strong, able to hold every bit of your experience.

Also create a feeling of strength. In recent events or in your past, look for times when you were strong. Perhaps you called on your body to keep standing during a long day at work or to continue running during a workout. Perhaps you stuck up for yourself, or for someone else. Maybe you got something done even though you wanted to quit. Let the ideas of these times become a felt sense of strength.

E *Open to the sense of strength. Explore what this experience is like. Let it fill your body and mind and become more intense. Stay with it, help it last, make a sanctuary for it in your mind. Return to this experience if your attention wanders. Become calmer and more confident as you feel stronger. Know that you can deal with what life brings. Find things that are fresh about the experience of strength. See what it's like to feel strong without any anger. Recall a time you were firm, grave, or assertive without getting aggressive or irritated. You can embody strength in various ways: perhaps tense different muscles to feel their power, or straighten up, or put a determined expression on your face and see what it looks like in a mirror. Be aware of how strength is important to you personally, why it matters; recognize its relevance to you.*

A *Intend that this experience of strength is sinking into you as you sink into it. Sense strength coming into you like fuel, like invigorating energy. Let yourself be changed a bit, let yourself become stronger. Know that strength is sinking in, weaving itself into you, becoming a resource inside that you can take with* *you wherever you go—both potent and portable. As strength sinks in, you feel a releasing of any struggle with anything inside you or out in the world. There's no need to resist anyone or anything.*

L *Be aware of both the sense of strength and feelings of weakness. Keep the positive experience of strength more prominent in awareness, and if you get hijacked by the negative material, drop it. Strength is supporting and soaking into places inside that have felt pushed around or overwhelmed, perhaps when you were a child. Now you are feeling strong, like a deeply rooted, mighty tree; the winds of life and other people are blowing by, and you are still standing tall after they pass. When you want, let go of any negative material and just stay with the sense of strength. A few times over the next hour, for a dozen or more seconds at a time, be aware of only neutral or positive material—such as a sense of strength—while also bringing to mind a neutral trigger of feeling weak or overwhelmed.*

Relaxation

As you relax, your parasympathetic nervous system gets more active, which calms down the fight-or-flight sympathetic nervous system. Tension drains out of your body, your heart rate and breathing slow down, and digestion eases—all of which turns down the dial on internal signals of threat, helping you relax even further.

H *Notice any sense of relaxation already present in your awareness. For example, in your breathing or in parts of your body* *that are still, there could be some ease and letting go. Also, you can create a feeling of relaxation. Take several breaths in which the exhalation is about twice as long as the inhalation. Relax key points, such as the jaw muscles, tongue, mouth, and eyes. Breathe into your diaphragm, just beneath your rib cage. Sense the tension draining out of your body. Imagine being in relaxing settings, such as on the beach under a warm sun. You can also progressively relax parts of your body, moving from your feet to your head.*

E *Open to relaxation, and feel what it's like. Let it fill you, becoming more intense. Stay with it, help it last. Let go more and more as you relax. Give yourself over to a delicious sense of calm. Notice different aspects of this experience, keeping it fresh for you. Feel a growing tranquility. Embody relaxation by lying down, rocking gently back and forth, or letting your face go completely slack. Think of one way that being more relaxed at home or work could help you.*

A *Sense that relaxation is sinking into you, becoming a part of you. As you become more relaxed, you can feel any tension or resistance falling away.*

L *Be aware of both relaxation and tension. Keep relaxation more prominent in awareness; if you get hijacked by the negative material, drop it. Relaxation is sinking into and easing places inside you that have been tight or contracted. Tension is easing as relaxation settles down into it like a gentle rain. When you want, let go of any negative material and just stay with the sense of relaxation. A few times over the next hour, be aware of only neutral or positive material—such as a sense of* *relaxation—while also bringing to mind a neutral trigger of feeling tense.*

Refuge

A refuge is anything that gives you a sense of sanctuary, refueling, uplift, or sacredness. You can rest and recharge in a refuge even as pain or difficulty swirls around you.

H *Notice any sense of refuge that's already present in your mind. Perhaps you're at home in bed, or in the bathtub, or cuddling with your mate. Or you're standing under trees and stars. Or at peace in meditation or prayer. You can also create a feeling of refuge by remembering being in a place you love, such as a cabin on a lake that your family stayed in each summer. Other potential refuges include teachers, teachings, and communities of the taught. You could find refuge in simply plugging away, in being scrappy and not giving up. Or in your capacity to see what's true, to tell the difference between the donut and the hole, or between people who treat you well and those who don't. You could take refuge in reason, in the process of figuring things out. Or in spirituality or religion, or in whatever you experience as God.*

E *Explore the qualities of particular refuges, such as a place or person. Then open to a general sense of refuge. What's it like to feel that you're in a safe haven? That you're grounded in things that are trustworthy and nurturing? Let this experience fill you, becoming more intense. Stay with it, help it last. You could embody or enact the sense of refuge by going to personal sanctuaries ranging from a familiar cozy chair in your living room to a church or temple; or you could bring something personally meaningful or sacred into your bedroom.*

A *Sense that the experience of refuge is becoming a part of you. Explore the feeling of refuge as being something you come from rather than being something you go to. As you feel more and more settled in refuge, release any struggle with anything.*

L *Be aware of both the experience of refuge and any sense of being pushed or drained. Stay centered in refuge as these challenges pass by, while you remain sheltered and nurtured. Let the knowing sink in that difficulties and pains can come and go without overwhelming you. Perhaps sense that feelings of refuge are connecting with young feelings of being invaded or unsafe. When you want, let go of any negative material and just stay with the sense of refuge. A few times over the next hour, be aware of only neutral or positive material—such as a sense of refuge—while also bringing to mind a neutral trigger of feeling pushed or drained.*

Seeing Threats and Resources Clearly

Due to "paper tiger paranoia" (chapter 2), your brain tends to overestimate the threats coming at you while underestimating your resources for dealing with them. When you see through these distortions, you can take in new, more accurate, and more reassuring and useful perspectives.

H *Notice it when you realize that a worry was overblown or that you overlooked available resources. Notice when others*

*could be building up your fears, perhaps for their own advan-
tage. Also, deliberately consider your beliefs about dangers in
the world and weaknesses in yourself, and look for the evidence
that these are not true. Perhaps talk about these beliefs and
the evidence for and against them with others, or just evalu-
ate them inside your own mind. For example, you could list
three or more reasons why a fearful or self-doubting belief is not
true.*

E *Open to a more realistic view of threats in your life and
your resources for handling them. Let this view, this perspective, expand in your mind and keep coming back to it. Open to
related feelings of settling down, confidence, or calm. You could
embody this experience by saying out loud or writing down your
realistic viewpoint about threats and resources.*

A *Sense that this realistic view is becoming a part of you. Let
the conviction form that it is true. Get a sense of coming from
this perspective from now on and how this would feel. As you
see threats and resources clearly, without distortion, feelings of
unease and anxiety fall away as you know in your heart that
you can deal with things. There's no need for fear.*

L *Be aware of your realistic view* as well as *any inaccurate beliefs that overestimate threats or underestimate resources. Keep
regenerating your sense of conviction in the realistic view, and
your knowing that the inaccurate beliefs are wrong. Perhaps
imagine a strong, smart person inside who represents the realistic view and is arguing with another person inside (maybe
exaggerated and silly) who represents the inaccurate beliefs—*

and make sure that the realistic view wins. When you want, let go of any negative material and just stay with the realistic view. A few times over the next hour, be aware of only neutral or positive material—such as a sense of conviction in the realistic view—while also bringing to mind a neutral trigger of the inaccurate beliefs.

Feeling All Right Right Now

Most of the inputs into your brain come from inside your body rather than from your external environment. This is because your brain needs to know, moment by moment, how your internal organs are doing to make sure you're okay. Much of this information flows through the hypothalamus, and if there is the least sign of anything wrong, it sounds an alarm that triggers the reactive, red setting of your brain. Even small shifts in your sense of breathing, heart rate, digestion, or facial expression can produce large changes in your thoughts and feelings.

This tight linkage between mind and body gives you a powerful way to rest in a growing sense of calm and ease, since most of the time your body is pretty much doing fine. Its messages up to your brain are usually like the reassuring calls of a night watchman: "All is well, all is well." You may not have been all right in the past and you may not be all right in the future, but you are basically all right right now.

Unfortunately, this good news is often hard to "hear" due to the negativity bias, which produces an ongoing background murmuring of anxiety to keep us always a little nervous and vigilant in order to survive. Most of the time, these messages of fear are false alarms. When you take advantage of the "all is well" signals coming up into your brain from your body by deliberately focusing on the fact that you are actually all right, almost every single moment of your life offers a wonderful opportunity to step out of fear and anger and into peace. And over time, this practice and related ones, such as taking in relaxation, can quiet the murmuring of needless anxiety.

H *Tune into signals from your body that all is well. Notice that there's plenty of air, that breathing is going just fine. Feel your pulse at your neck and know that your heart is beating okay. Sense your body in its entirety and recognize its fundamental vitality—even if there are also aches and pains and illness. Focus on parts of your body that are doing all right even if other parts aren't. Scan your immediate environment and know that in this instant you are not being attacked, that you are not about to die. Observe that awareness itself is fine and never hurt by what it holds; know that you can witness discomfort without being overwhelmed by it. Again and again register that you are all right in this moment.*

E *Open to feeling that you're all right right now. Keep renewing this feeling, moment after moment, in spite of any anxiety. Also open to related feelings of ease, relief, calm, and relaxation. Give your mind over to feeling all right, entirely all right, now. Notice the constant background sense of the body, and that it keeps going on being with a trustworthy continuity. Know what it's like to feel all right. You could embody this experience by exhaling with a kind of "Whew, safe at last." Do little things to feel more comfortable, such as putting on a shawl if you're chilled, and let in the resulting wave of feeling okay.*

A *Sense that feeling all right is becoming a part of you. Being fundamentally okay in your core, there's no need to push anything away, no basis for fear. Any struggle with life, any resisting or craving, falls away.*

L *Be aware of the experience of being all right alongside any upset or anxiety. Help the sense of being okay in your core seep into upset or anxiety, soothing and easing it, and putting it in perspective. Know that you will still be all right even if you've got to deal with hard things. When you want, let go of any negative material and stay with the sense of being all right right now. A few times over the next hour, be aware of only neutral or positive material—such as feeling all right right now—while also bringing to mind a neutral trigger of feeling upset or anxious.*

Peace

Peace is a global sense of serenity and ease, with no need to struggle with anything. You may be aware of dangers or challenges, but no fleeing or fighting is present in your mind, no fear or anger. Feeling at peace inside, you are peaceable with others.

H *Notice any sense of peace already present in your body or mind. Awareness itself is peaceful, as is the rhythm of breathing, the effortless appearance of sights, and the reassuring stability of a chair or table. Also create peacefulness by bringing to mind anything that helps you feel calm, undisturbed, or tranquil. Perhaps an image of a baby sleeping, the sound of waves on a warm beach, the felt remembrance of a time you were completely at peace, or a sense of the untroubled vastness of the universe. You could also activate a sense of peace by drawing on one or more of the key experiences above, such as relaxation or feeling all right right now.*

E *Once you find a sense of peace, open to it, give over to it, and let it fill your heart. Help the feeling of peace be as strong and lasting as possible. Explore the nuances of related feelings such as calm, tranquility, ease, and serenity. Be wholly at peace. If you like, meditate on peace; let it be your object of attention and absorption. Embody peace in how you walk, gaze at others, reach for objects, and speak.*

A *Sense that peace is sinking into you as you sink into it, becoming a part of you. Feel yourself peacefully breathing, breathing peace, being peace. There's no basis for any kind of resistance toward anything inside you or out in the world.*

L *Be mindful of peace in the foreground of awareness as well as any kind of unease in the background. Sense peace radiating outward in waves, connecting with and soothing and quieting whatever is unsettled. Peace is sinking into young parts of you that felt frightened or angry. Then, when you want, let go of any negative material and just stay with peace. A few times over the next hour, be aware of only neutral or positive material— such as a sense of peace—while also bringing to mind a neutral trigger of feeling uneasy.*

Satisfaction

When you experience satisfaction, your approaching rewards system enters its responsive setting. You can build up both your capacity to *be* satisfied and your sense of *feeling* satisfied by regularly taking in *pleasure, gratitude and gladness, positive emotion, accomplishment and agency, enthusiasm, the fullness of this moment,* and *contentment.* If you do this regularly, both in everyday life and in the guided practices below, you'll feel increasingly thankful, fulfilled, and successful instead of disappointed, sad, frustrated, or driven. You'll feel already full, with no reason to chase after or grab on to pleasant experiences.

Pleasure

Enjoying the taste of toasted raisin bread or the humor in a cartoon may not seem like much, but simple pleasures like these ease emotional upsets, lift your mood, and enrich your life. They also provide health benefits, by releasing endorphins and natural opioids that shift you out of stressful, draining reactive states and into happier responsive ones. As a bonus, some pleasures—such as dancing, sex, your team winning a game of pick-up basketball, or laughing with friends—come with energizing feelings of vitality or passion that enhance long-term health. Opportunities for pleasure are all around you, especially if you include things like the rainbow glitter of the tiny grains of sand in a sidewalk, the sound of water falling into a tub, the sense of connection in talking with a friend, or the reassurance that comes from the stove working when you need to make dinner.

Your brain tries to hold on to things that are pleasant, but this actually feels stressful since experiences are inherently fleeting and insubstantial. In this practice, you get the best of both worlds: You enjoy pleasures without holding on to them, which actually heightens the pleasure. Plus, you'll be learning how to let pleasant experiences flow through your mind without any reactive grasping after them.

H *Notice any sense of pleasure that's already present. Scan the senses of sight, sound, taste, touch, and smell for pleasures in the background or foreground of awareness. In your mind, see if there's anything funny, interesting, or aesthetically pleasing. Also create pleasure by being nice to your body, looking for beauty, joking around, using your hands in a craft, taking beautiful photographs, or doing a favorite activity. Spend a minute or a day looking for things that give you pleasure. Explore your favorite pleasures in depth, slowing down and really focusing on the experience.*

E *Open to a pleasure, and help it last. Keep returning attention to it, and release any thought that you're not allowed to feel this pleasure. Relish it, much as you might take half a minute to let a bite of chocolate truffle slowly melt in your mouth. Receive the pleasure fully and let it flow through you without trying to hang on to it. Embody this experience by moving toward or into the sources of pleasure, or by murmuring in pleasure. Reflect briefly on how pleasure is relevant to you, how it is important in your life.*

A *Sense and intend that pleasure is sinking into you as you sink into it. Like water seeping into soil, pleasure is becoming part of you, a resource you can take with you wherever you go.*

Feel how pleasure is settling into you without you trying to hold on to it. Let yourself feel that in this moment there is enough, and no need for wanting more.

L   *Be aware of pleasure* and *any pain, and keep the positive experience of pleasure more prominent in awareness. Sense that these feelings of pleasure are soothing and going into any pains inside. When you want, let go of any negative material and just stay with the sense of pleasure. A few times over the next hour, a dozen or more seconds at a time, be aware of only neutral or positive material—such as a sense of pleasure—while also bringing to mind a neutral trigger (e.g., people, situations, ideas) of feeling pained.*

Gratitude and Gladness

Gratitude is a feeling of thankfulness about something you have been given. Gladness is a more general sense of feeling pleased, rewarded, delighted, or happy about something, without it necessarily being a gift. Much of the time these two sweet feelings form a blend, so we'll explore them together here. Gratitude, gladness, and related feelings like appreciation may seem so homey and Hallmark card–ish that they're easy to dismiss, but studies in fact show that cultivating them has lasting and important benefits, including lifting your mood, increasing satisfaction with life, and building resilience.

H   *Notice feelings of gratitude or gladness that are already present in your mind. Perhaps there is a background sense of being glad about where you live, or you're pleased that your child is in a good mood today. As you go about your day, be particularly attentive to any feelings of gratitude or gladness that naturally arise. Also create an experience of gratitude or gladness by looking for things to feel grateful for or glad about. They could be seemingly small or simple. Perhaps something nice happened recently, or you have enough food, or you have a friend who likes you. You could feel grateful for a pet, flowers blooming, good fortune, helping hands, or the gift of life itself. Reflect in similar ways about your past and future. Find things to feel grateful for or glad about in the lives of others. Help the knowing of these facts become experiences of gratitude and gladness.*

E *Open to gratitude and gladness. Explore what these experiences are like, and keep them going. Gently help them become as rich and intense as possible, filling your whole body. Open to related feelings such as joy, ease, or fulfillment. Embody gratitude and gladness by smiling, bouncing up and down in delight, softening your face, or reaching your arms out to the world.*

A *Let gratitude and gladness sink into you. As you give your mind to gratitude and gladness, let yourself feel content, that there is already plenty for you in this moment, and that you don't need to chase after or hold on to anything more.*

L *Be aware of gratitude and gladness* and *feelings of disappointment or loss. Keep making gratitude and gladness more prominent, and if you get carried away by the negative material, drop it from awareness. Sense that gratitude and gladness are connecting with any disappointment or loss. Imagine that some of the many things you feel grateful for or glad about are showering down into and gradually filling any emptiness* *inside. Perhaps gratitude and gladness are touching young parts of you that felt unhappy. Then, when you want, let go of any negative material and stay with the sense of gratitude and glad-ness. A few times over the next hour, a dozen or more seconds at a time, be aware of only neutral or positive material—such as a sense of gratitude and gladness—while also bringing to mind a neutral trigger of disappointment or loss.*

Positive Emotion

Any positive emotion is an opportunity to enjoy living and to feel satisfied here and now. Positive emotions also have many physical health benefits, including boosting your immune system, protecting your cardiovascular system, and increasing the odds of a long life.

It's wonderful that there are so many good feelings that you can explore and enjoy, as you would the many rides in a vast amusement park. For example, the approaching system includes interest, eagerness, inspiration, success, abundance, cheerful-ness, exhilaration, carefreeness, bliss, lightheartedness, awe, joy, and feeling fortunate or blessed. There are other positive feelings in the avoiding and attaching systems, such as peacefulness and love. Because there are so many different positive emotions, in the practice below I'll just use "good feeling"—you can replace it with any word you like—and my suggestions will be simple and open-ended.

H *Notice when there's any good feeling in the foreground or background of your awareness, or create one using the methods in chapter 6. For example, think of something in your life these days or in your past that makes you happy.*

E *Open to the good feeling. Let it fill you and become more intense. Stay with it, help it last, make room for it in your mind. Find ways to embody it, such as letting an appropriate expression come over your face or shifting your posture or body language to match the feeling. Be aware of how this good feeling could be relevant to you.*

A *Help the good feeling sink into you, like the warmth from a mug of hot tea spreading into your hands. Let the good feeling encourage a sense of satisfaction, of fulfillment, so there's no basis for grasping for anything more.*

L *Be aware of both the good feeling* and *a related bad feeling. For example, you could be aware of both cheerfulness and glumness, confidence and self-doubt, happiness and sadness, or abundance and scarcity. Focus on the good feeling, with the bad feeling off in the wings of awareness. Imagine or sense that the good feeling is connecting with the bad one, perhaps seeping into it like a soothing balm, gradually easing and replacing it. When you want, let go of the bad feeling and experience only the good one. A few times over the next hour, be aware of only neutral or positive material—such as a good feeling—while also bringing to mind a neutral trigger of a bad feeling.*

Accomplishment and Agency

Accomplishment is the feeling of attaining a goal, and agency is the sense of being able to make something happen. These experiences usually occur together, so we'll explore both of them here.

You accomplish many things every day, most of them

relatively small and easy to overlook, such as getting the kids off to school, finishing a shift at work, buying groceries, or returning a phone call. You also accomplish things through restraint, such as letting others have their say, and endurance (e.g., getting through a bout of back pain). Each of these accomplishments is a chance to experience gratification and success rather than frustration and failure.

Agency—being able to make things happen—is the opposite of helplessness. You might know what it's like to feel trapped, immobilized, defeated, or despairing. This experience of futility, that there is nothing you can do, can easily become a *learned helplessness* that is both hard to change and a major risk for depression. To prevent this attitude or to help undo it, repeatedly take in experiences of agency, of feeling like a hammer instead of a nail.

H *Notice when you are already feeling good about having attained a goal. Also pay attention when you make choices or initiate actions, especially little ones like deciding what you think about something, shifting into a more comfortable position, or reaching for the saltshaker.*

Also create a sense of accomplishment or agency by paying special attention to things you get done over the course of a day. Reflect on a major achievement, including the many little achievements that led up to it. Look back over your life at the things you got through and can put behind you, from learning to walk to finishing high school. Consider how you've added value in situations or to other people. Recall ways you've influenced others or played a leadership role. Be aware of choices you've made. Let knowing these facts become an experience of accomplishment or agency.

E *When you find an experience of accomplishment or agency, open to it and let it fill you. Help it last and become more intense. Help conviction grow inside that you have made things happen, that you are competent and effective, and that you will continue to be so. See if there are any related feelings, such as dignity, potency, pride, self-respect, or freedom. Notice any resistance to a sense of success or worth and focus instead on making room in your mind for the good feelings. Replay and savor past achievements or awards. Explore the sense that you've arrived and can take a breath and look back at the ground you've already covered.*

A *Feel this sense of accomplishment or agency sinking into you, a resource you'll have inside wherever you go. Imagine what it would be like to feel already accomplished and potent, and see if you can shift into a sense of this. Let it sink in that you can build on a foundation of what you've already done. Let ease spread through your body and mind, and release any pressure or drivenness.*

L *Be aware of accomplishment or agency in the foreground of awareness with also some sense of frustration or failure in the background—perhaps just the idea of frustration or failure known in passing, or a sense of how these feel in your body, or a memory of being thwarted or falling short. Imagine or sense that accomplishment or agency plus related feelings of success and worth are connecting with frustration or failure, soaking into them, like good news reaching and satisfying a longing inside. You could imagine that younger parts or layers of yourself are receiving the truth of the many things you've accomplished or caused to come into being. Perhaps there's an image of a* *nurturing person who is holding you as a child, reassuring you that you will reach goals and get things done and make a difference. Then let go of any negative material and spend some seconds or more with only the positive experience. A few times over the next hour, be aware of only neutral or positive material—such as a sense of accomplishment or agency—while also bringing to mind a neutral trigger of frustration or failure.*

Enthusiasm

I think the sweet spot in life is to pursue your dreams and take care of others with your whole heart while not getting fixated on or stressed out about the results. In this place, you live with purpose and passion but without losing your balance and falling into a sense of pressure, strain, or depletion. This sweet spot is very valuable, so take it in whenever you experience it. I'll refer to its various aspects with the umbrella term "enthusiasm" in the practice below.

H *Notice when you are already enthusiastic, energized toward a goal without stressing about it. You could be looking forward to seeing a friend, having a good time with your kids over breakfast, motivated to finish a workout, eager to get to the bottom of what's been worrying your mate, fiercely committed to protecting your child from a bully, vigorously engaged with getting a project done at work, making music with gusto, or having a lively sense of teamwork with others. Also, you can create enthusiasm by recalling the sense of it in past activities. As you go through your day, look for opportunities to allow and encourage more of a sense of energy or passion in famil-*

iar, perhaps seemingly humdrum activities. Notice any inner inhibitions about being vibrant, thrilled, jazzed up, loud, or intense—perhaps a fear of being "too much" for others—and see if you can let these inhibitions go and instead ignite your enthusiasm.

E *Open to enthusiasm, explore what it feels like, and keep it going. Help it become intense, and feel it in your body. Enjoy it. See how you can care about a goal without getting driven or upset about it. Explore the sense that you can work hard for something while also being at peace that you've done all you could whatever the outcome may be. Embody your enthusiasm by revealing it to others, letting your face light up, or moving and speaking more quickly.*

A *Intend and sense that enthusiasm is soaking into you, that you are naturally becoming more enthusiastic as a person. Really register the feeling of the sweet spot, that combination of being energized toward a goal without stressing about the results. Take in the sense of being enthusiastically engaged in the present without clutching at a future result. Let yourself become both contented and lively.*

L *Be aware of enthusiasm and the blahs (or related feelings of apathy, depression, boredom, or numbness). (At another time, you could be aware of both enthusiasm and drivenness, or related feelings of pressure, worry about reaching a goal, or compulsion.) Keep making enthusiasm a stronger feeling. Sense that enthusiasm is bringing life to the blahs, perhaps connecting with and energizing parts of you that felt numb or suppressed.*

Feel enthusiasm spreading within you, becoming more and more your way of being. Then, when you want, let go of any blahs and feel only enthusiasm. A few times over the next hour, be aware of only neutral or positive material—such as a sense of enthusiasm—while also bringing to mind a neutral trigger of the blahs.

Feeling the Fullness of This Moment

Your brain is continually flooded by stimulation coming from your body and environment, and from within the brain itself. A tiny fraction of this flood enters awareness, but there's still so much stimulation that attention spotlights only a small portion and we largely ignore the rest. This natural process gives you a great opportunity, available anytime you like, to widen your attention to include all the contents of awareness. When you open to all the sounds, sights, tastes, touches, smells, thoughts, feelings, and desires in your mind at any moment, there's an almost overwhelming sense of fullness and enoughness. With so much here, who could want for anything more?

For me, doing this practice is like looking down at a glass of soda water. Awareness is like the surface of the water, and all the little bubbles pop-pop-popping away are the various contents of experience emerging into consciousness. If you could watch these bubbles in slow motion, you'd see that some are coming into being while others are passing away, much as sounds and feelings overlap one another in your mind. Then, shifting your perspective to look at the side of the clear glass, you'd see bubbles rising to breach the surface, like coalitions of synapses taking a few tenths of a second to form the neural basis of a sound or feeling coming into awareness. We experience life entirely on the surface of the water, on the surface of this moment of consciousness, and can only imagine the neural activity that underlies it. Still, the incredible richness of these bubbles right now is thrilling and deeply satisfying all by itself.

It helps at first to do this practice in a quiet place, perhaps with your eyes closed, so you don't feel too bombarded by stimuli. Then you can try it out in everyday life.

H *Relax and become more aware of your body. Explore the many sensations of breathing, including how it feels in your stomach and hips, chest, upper lip and nose, throat, shoulders, and neck. Notice how sensations continually pass away as new ones appear in the mind. Let it be okay that sensations keep changing. You can feel comfortable with letting go of your experiences because they are endlessly renewed. Next, instead of attention skipping from one sensation of breathing to another one, see if you can perceive all the sensations of breathing at the same time, as if you are widening the spotlight of attention to include the whole stage of awareness. This widening is aided by relaxing and softening, and by letting sensations come to you rather than reaching for them. In the beginning it's normal to get a sense of the whole body breathing for just a second or two before attention refocuses on one sensation or another, but with practice you'll be able to sustain a sense of the whole for longer periods.*

When you like, open attention even wider to include more and more of the stream of consciousness: sounds, sights (the shadings or textures if your eyes are closed), tastes, smells, and touches, as well as thoughts and feelings, images and desires.

There's no need to keep track of all these little bubbles of experience fizzing into awareness, no need to label them or make sense of them or connect them with one another. Just let every bit of experience come and go—as if your awareness were a net through which the river of time flows, the contents of this moment of experience being what's streaming this instant through the net.

E *Become increasingly aware of the* arriving *of this stream, the many little things landing in awareness each moment, filling you, giving to you. Open to feeling almost overwhelmed by everything appearing in awareness. Get a sense of fullness in your mind, a sense of enoughness. See if you can find a sense of being so full you couldn't possibly want more. Be aware of any feelings of satisfaction or contentment. Open to this experience of fullness, let it fill your mind. Keep giving over to it, helping it last.*

A *Let the sense of fullness sink into you. Imagine approaching life from feeling already full, and help the experience of this become a part of you. When you are fed by fullness, there's no need to hold on to anything or grasp for anything more.*

L *Be aware of fullness and any sense of shortage or lack. Keep renewing the sense of fullness, keeping it more prominent than shortage or lack. Know or sense that fullness is connecting with shortage or lack, like waves of fullness washing down into hollowed out or hungry places inside, soothing and filling them. Any sense of wanting or needing or insisting is falling away, replaced by fullness. When you like, let go of any sense of short-*

age or lack and stay with only fullness. A few times over the next hour, be aware of only neutral or positive material—such as a sense of fullness—while also bringing to mind a neutral trigger of a sense of shortage or lack.

Contentment

Contentment is a global sense of well-being combined with no wish whatsoever for this moment to be anything other than what it is. Pleasant experiences pass through awareness with no need to hold on to them. You feel fulfilled in your core, with no drivenness, greed, or possessiveness. Feeling full inside, you are generous with others.

H *Notice any sense of contentment already present in the foreground or background of your awareness. In many ordinary moments—brushing teeth, stepping onto a bus, holding a child, reading a book, looking out a window—there's already a sense of well-being, with no desire for anything else. Create contentment by thinking of things in the past or present that made you feel happy or fulfilled. Or directly call up the sense that your body has plenty of air and food, and your mind plenty of enjoyments; there's no need for anything more. You could also create a sense of contentment by drawing on one or more of the key experiences in this section, "Satisfaction," such as gladness and gratitude, or the fullness of this moment.*

E *Once you find contentment, open to it, giving over to it and letting it fill you. Help the feeling of contentment to be as strong and lasting as possible. Be wholly contented. If you like,* *meditate on contentment; let it be your object of attention and absorption. See what it's like to breathe, sit, walk, look, reach, speak, or act with contentment.*

A *Intend and sense that contentment is becoming a part of you. Imagine living in contentment, and let the sense of this sink into you. As you become contentment, contentment is becoming you. There's no basis for any kind of drivenness toward anything inside you or out in the world.*

L *Be mindful of contentment in the foreground of awareness as well as discontent (or related feelings such as disappointment, frustration, or loss) in the background. Let contentment connect with and nourish any parts inside you—including young ones—that are hungry or rattled. Then, when you want, let go of any negative material and just stay with contentment. A few times over the next hour, be aware of only neutral or positive material—such as a sense of contentment—while also bringing to mind a neutral trigger of feeling discontented.*

Connection

When you experience connection, your attaching to others system goes green, into its responsive mode. You can build up both your capacity to *be* connected and your sense of *feeling* connected by regularly taking in a sense of *feeling cared about, feeling valued, compassion and kindness, self-compassion, compassionate assertiveness, feeling like a good person,* and *love.*

These attaching type experiences will have bonus benefits for your avoiding and approaching systems. First, they will help you feel safe. As our ancestors evolved in dangerous conditions, being physically and emotionally close to others in their group kept them alive; on the Serengeti plains, exile was a death sentence. Today, feeling cared about sends soothing, calming oxytocin into your brain's alarm bell, the amygdala; it also increases cortisol receptors in your hippocampus, so this part of your brain now more quickly recognizes that there is plenty of cortisol, and it signals your hypothalamus more rapidly to quit calling for stress hormones. Second, feeling connected is satisfying. For example, social contact, play, and loving touch all release rewarding opioids in your brain. Love is a universal medicine.

In some senses, the psyche can be divided into three parts: a core self, an inner nurturer, and an inner critic. (This idea is adapted from transactional analysis and more recent work on trauma.) The inner nurturer is caring, protective, guiding, and encouraging, while the inner critic is judging, belittling, doubting, fault-finding, and shaming. A little bit of the inner critic is helpful, but during both childhood and adulthood, many of us acquire a loud and scathing inner critic and a relatively quiet and feeble inner nurturer. The core self can feel beleaguered, getting yelled at by a big inner critic while the inner nurturer murmurs kindly but helplessly in the corner. We all need a strong inner nurturer both to keep the inner critic in check and to give us the support life demands. You can grow this inner nurturer each time you take in the key experiences below.

Feeling Cared About

By *feeling cared about,* I mean feeling included, seen, liked, or loved. Even if the form of the caring has problems with it, try to sense the good wishes for you in the other person's heart. My mother loved me dearly, but she often expressed it by telling me what I could do better, which became pretty irritating. Finally I realized that I could look past her surface personality to the love behind it, like seeing a warm fire through a screen of vines, leaves, and thorns. I did this because it was good for *me*, but it also nurtured more peace between us.

H *Notice any ways you already feel included, seen, liked, or loved. Perhaps there's a background sense of being part of a couple, a family, or a team at work. Or create a feeling of being cared about. Recall a time you belonged to a group, felt understood, or were loved. Bring to mind one or more beings who care about you. You could think of a person, a group of people, a pet, or a spiritual being or force. The relationship does not need to be perfect, but in at least one slice of the relationship pie, you know you are cared about. If sadness or related feelings about not being cared about come up, be with them some, and then try to return your attention to ways that you have been truly cared about.*

E *Open to feeling cared about. Let this fill your mind and heart and become as intense as possible. Stay with it, help it last, make a sanctuary for it in your mind. Explore different aspects of this experience, such as how feeling included is different from feeling loved. What's it like to feel that you matter to someone or that you are cherished? You could embody this experience by placing a hand on your heart or on your cheek; you might imagine that a loving being is touching you gently. Reflect for a moment on how being cared about is important or relevant to you.*

A *Sense and intend that feeling cared about is sinking into you. Notice any difficulty with letting in a particular aspect of being cared about, such as feeling liked or loved, and then try to become more open to it. As you feel more cared about deep down inside, see if there can be a letting go of any clinging in your relationships.*

L *Be aware of feeling cared about and feeling not cared about. Keep the positive experience stronger in awareness. Get a sense that feeling cared about is touching places inside that have felt excluded, unseen, disliked, or unloved, and it is soothing them or filling them up. Feeling cared about does not change the facts of whatever has happened, but it can ease the pain of the past. Old feelings of hurt, including any from childhood, are being gradually replaced by a sense that others care about you. When you want, let go of any negative material and just stay with feeling cared about. A few times over the next hour, for a dozen or more seconds at a time, be aware of only neutral or positive material—such as a sense of feeling cared about—while also bringing to mind a neutral trigger (e.g., people, situations, ideas) of feeling not cared about.*

Feeling Valued

As social animals, we all have powerful needs to feel valued rather than dismissed, shunned, humiliated, disrespected, scorned, disdained. As a child, you needed to feel cherished by your parents, praised by your teachers, and wanted by your peers. An adult benefits from feeling sought after by potential mates, appreciated by his or her partner, respected by colleagues and managers, and not taken for granted by family. When these normal needs aren't met, it's natural to develop feelings of inadequacy mingled with hurt and anger, and tendencies in relationships toward extremes of clinging or distance. On the other hand, when your needs are met through experiences of feeling valued, you develop a healthy sense of worth, which paradoxically promotes humility and a giving heart.

H *Notice when there is already a sense of worth or being recognized in your mind, and notice when others stir up these feelings in you, such as with praise or respect. Create experiences of feeling valued by remembering a time you were complimented or acknowledged; a time you knew you were appreciated, perhaps after some contribution or generosity; a time you were wanted, sought after, or chosen. Consider that you value others but don't always show it; in the same way, others value you but don't always show it. Consequently, put in a correction factor in which you intuit more of the valuing that others do have for you. Expand your notion of being valued to include a sense of people thinking any one of these things about you:* You made a difference; you helped me; I'm glad you're in my life; you're good at this; you're interesting and talented; the team is better with you on it; you contribute; you're special; I respect you. *Look for little ways that others appreciate you.*

E *When you feel valued, open to it. Explore different aspects of this experience. Help it last and become more intense. Perhaps imagine a cheering squad of friends and family rooting for you, clapping and praising you. Imagine talking to yourself in a caring way, as you would speak with a friend who was feeling unwanted or second-rate or a loser; imagine telling yourself firmly how you make a difference for others and what your particularly good qualities are. Embody a sense of worth by sitting as if you respect yourself, or by walking across a room with dignity, like someone who adds value.*

A *Feel a sense of worth sinking into you, spreading through your mind like a golden mist. Let a sense of having value grow inside you. Imagine what it would be like to be at work with this sense of being valuable, or at home, or in an important relationship; let yourself move into this sense of being, and let it move into you. As the sense of worth sinks ever more deeply into you, any need to impress others or to prove yourself falls away.*

L *Be aware of feeling valued as well as any feelings of inadequacy (or related feelings of smallness, worthlessness, or shame). Keep refocusing on feeling valued, wanted, worthy. Sense that feeling valued, appreciated, respected, even treasured, is connecting with feelings of inadequacy, easing any old pain, reassuring you deep down, and gradually replacing inadequacy with feelings of worth. Let feeling valued touch parts of yourself that have felt devalued, dismissed, disdained, unwanted. Then let go of any negative material and focus only on feelings of worth. A few times over the next hour, for a dozen or more seconds at a time, be aware of only neutral or positive material—such as a sense of worth—while also bringing to mind a neutral trigger of feeling inadequate.*

Compassion and Kindness

Compassion is the wish that a living being not suffer, and is usually combined with feelings of sympathetic concern. Kindness is the wish that a being be happy, usually with feelings of warmth. In everyday life, the two often meld together—with related feelings of helpfulness, friendliness, and support—so we'll consider them together here. While compassion can feel softly sad—which is of course perfectly appropriate and fine—the cultivation of it through a practice like the one just below can also activate reward centers in your brain to give you a greater sense of its sweetness and beauty.

H *Notice when you already feel compassion or kindness. Also create this experience by calling to mind a person, a group of people, or a pet you care about. Perhaps offer good wishes to them, such as by saying to yourself "May you be at peace."*

E *Open to compassion and kindness. Let these feelings fill your mind and body, becoming more intense. Give yourself over to them and help them last. Sense into your chest near your heart and imagine warmth spreading there. Bring a friend to mind and send compassion and kindness to him or her, perhaps by saying things to yourself such as "May you be safe, healthy, happy, and live with ease." Try this with other sorts of people, including those you really appreciate, those you feel neutral about, such as strangers on the street, and perhaps even those who have mistreated you. You can extend your warmth and good wishes to people you will never know, letting your compassion and kindness radiate out to include the whole world. See what it feels like to send your good wishes out to all living beings, including animals and plants. Embody compassion or kindness by murmuring comfort as you might when seeing a friend in pain or, as appropriate, by extending your arms out as if you were cradling or hugging someone.*

A *Let compassion and kindness sink into you, like the sun's warmth into your skin. Make room in yourself for these feelings. Let yourself shift into becoming kinder and more compassionate, and as this happens, let any anger or ill will toward others fall away.*

L *Be aware of compassion and kindness as well as any indifference or ill will toward others (and related feelings such as jealousy, envy, anger, resentment, or vengeance). Keep renewing your warmheartedness, sensing it connecting with and gradually infusing any indifference or ill will. Let compassion and kindness touch any anger inside you. Feel what it's like to see another person clearly, while also having compassion and kindness toward him or her. See what it's like to know that someone has mistreated you and to want justice, while at the same time wishing that he or she not suffer and instead be truly happy. Feel compassion and kindness sinking into any places inside that have felt pinched or cold toward others, loosening and filling and warming them. Then let go of any negative material and feel only compassion and kindness. A few times over the next hour, be aware of only neutral or positive material—such as a sense of compassion and kindness—while also bringing to mind a neutral trigger of indifference or ill will.*

Self-Compassion

This is simply the application of compassion toward yourself, often with related feelings, such as a sense that many others have difficulties and pains like your own. Studies have shown that self-compassion lowers stress and self-criticism while increasing resilience and self-worth. Self-compassion is not feeling sorry for yourself or wallowing helplessly; if anything, it makes you stronger. Yet many people who find it easy to be compassionate toward others find it hard to be compassionate toward themselves. Before opening to self-compassion, it could help to prime the pump with the practice of feeling cared about found at the beginning of this section, "Connection."

H *Notice when you already have feelings of warmth, support, or compassion toward yourself. Also, create a sense of self-compassion by deliberately extending warmth and good wishes to yourself. Recognize some of the ways that you are hurting, burdened, or stressed, including over small matters. How would you feel toward a friend experiencing similar things? You'd probably feel sympathetic and caring, and wish that your friend did not suffer, no matter how subtly. Can you feel this way toward yourself?*

E *Open to self-compassion and let it fill you. Help it last and become more intense. Notice any resistance to self-compassion and try to make room in your heart for it. In your mind or out loud, say compassionate things to yourself, such as "I wish I felt better. May this pain pass." You can be specific, such as saying to yourself "May I find work soon" or "I will be loved again" or "I hope this chemotherapy goes well." Keep returning to self-compassion, not letting yourself get hijacked by upsets or pain. Embody this experience by placing a hand on your heart or cheek, or by patting your arm gently as you would that of a friend in need.*

A *Feel self-compassion sinking into you, becoming a part of you, a resource inside wherever you go. Sense inside a grow-*

ing warmth toward yourself and a sweetness, caring, and strength on your own behalf. As self-compassion sifts down into you, see if you can feel a growing ease and peace in your relationships.

L *Be aware of self-compassion alongside self-criticism (or other stress or pain, such as a headache, grievance, or loss). Imagine or sense that self-compassion is connecting with self-criticism, gently putting whatever happened in perspective, softening any harsh inner voices. Let knowing that many other people also have your faults ease any shame. Imagine that younger parts of you are receiving compassion, are taking in tender sympathetic concern. Then let go of any negative material and just feel self-compassion. A few times over the next hour, be aware of only neutral or positive material—such as self-compassion—while also bringing to mind a neutral trigger of self-criticism.*

Feeling Like a Good Person

Everyone has good qualities, such as patience, determination, fairness, forgiveness, honesty, kindness, and love (see page 97 in chapter 6). Recognizing these qualities in yourself is simply seeing reality with clear eyes, like recognizing good food in your cupboard or goodness in another person. Even if you, like me, have done things worthy of remorse, they do not wipe out your good qualities; you are still a fundamentally good person. Unfortunately, many people have a hard time feeling this. But if you repeatedly take in the sense of being a good person, you'll feel more reassured about it inside and more confident when dealing with others.

H *Notice any underlying sense of being a good person that's already present, such as a background knowing of your basic decency. Or create this experience. Pick a good character quality that you know you have—it could be persistence, a desire for justice, or a warm heart—and think of one or more examples of it. Be aware of any blocks to recognizing the fact of this good quality, such as remembering exceptions to it; let them go, and then come back to the ways this good quality is actually true about you. Get a sense of any feelings or sensations related to the good quality. Consider how this part of you benefits others. Let yourself feel glad about having this good quality.*

Repeat this for a few other good qualities you have. Then as you go through your day, notice some of your good wishes toward others and your good qualities in action. Let this recognition of specific good intentions and actions become a more general sense of the goodness inside you, and a growing conviction that you are indeed a good person.

E *Open to a sense of the goodness inside you, your true and natural kindness, decency, fairness, responsibility, perseverance, and other honorable qualities. What do these qualities feel like? Stay with the experience of your goodness. Protect it, make a sanctuary for it in your mind. Know that you don't have to be special to be a good person. Soften inside, with perhaps relief or joy at feeling like a good person. Let a sense of goodness fill you. Embody this experience by letting goodness show in your face. Sit, stand, walk, and talk while feeling like a good person. Register it when you do good things for others.*

A *Feel goodness spreading inside you like warmth or light, becoming a part of you. Sense the conviction growing in your* *mind that you are a good person. Imagine yourself in challenging situations or relationships while having a strong sense of your goodness, and then let this way of being sink in. Feeling and knowing the good that is in you, there's no need to act from guilt or shame, or to cling to reassurance from others.*

L *Be aware of both your goodness and any shame (or related feelings of being tainted, damaged goods, unlovable, defective, doomed, or a bad person). Keep reestablishing a strong sense of your goodness, including aspects of it such as caring, decency, and good intentions. Know that whatever is good in you can be obscured but never lost. Sense that the good in you is touching shame and related feelings, bringing light and warmth into them like the rising sun reaching into the darkest shadows. Feel the goodness in you while also being aware of and caring toward any parts inside that feel dirty or bad. When you want, let go of the negative material and simply rest in feelings of goodness, such as wishing others well. A few times over the next hour, be aware of only neutral or positive material—such as a sense of being a good person—while also bringing to mind a neutral trigger of shame or related feelings.*

Compassionate Assertiveness

It's natural to have needs and wants in our relationships. If we don't speak up for them, they're less likely to be met. But if we push for them without taking the other person into account, they're also less likely to be met, especially over time. Compassionate assertiveness is where heart and strength come together, the twin pillars of healthy relationships. Then you act with integrity and wish others well while also taking care of yourself.

You maintain your boundaries and say what you need to say and if need be say it again. You can communicate with dignity and gravity without getting sucked into pointless quarreling. You are loving, while not waiving your rights or getting exploited. Each time you register the *combination* of compassion and assertiveness, it deepens your capacity to be direct, revealed, and free with others. And as you feel stronger, more independent and autonomous, you'll feel even more comfortable in the depths of intimacy.

H *Notice any ways you already feel assertive. As you go through your day, be aware of times when you are clear, firm, persuasive, or fully expressed. Notice how this feels, especially when it feels good. Notice that others are usually fine with your assertiveness. In particular, notice when goodwill and strength are both present in your heart, and how this feels, and what the results are in your relationships. Also create the combination of compassion and assertiveness. Recall a time you felt both kind and strong. Or imagine being this way in a relationship and how it would feel. You could think of someone you like and respect who is loving while still being very much his or her own person, and then imagine how it would feel to be a little more like this person.*

E *Stay with feeling caring and assertive. Let the sense of this fill your arms and chest and face. Breathe deeply. Help this feeling grow inside. In your own mind, stand up for your right to stand up. Know that you have rights of your own, and that whether others are happy or not is primarily in their hands, not yours. Remember or imagine the sense of being both loving with someone and comfortable expressing yourself fully. Embody this*

*experience by letting dignity and authority come into your face
and voice while also being caring and kind.*

A *Let feeling compassionately assertive sink into you. Let yourself reshape around this new way of being. As you feel more
relaxed and independent in your relationships, and also more
compassionate in them, let yourself feel more at peace with
others, more centered and balanced. Let any feelings of needi-
ness or quarreling fall away.*

L *Be aware of both compassionate assertiveness and any
sense of being weak in relationships (or related feelings of being squelched, dominated, silenced, or pushed to the margins).
Keep the combination of strength and caring in the foreground
of your awareness, gradually connecting with any sense of weakness in the background of awareness. Let nurturing strength
reach for and touch places inside, including young ones, that
have felt weak or overrun. When you want, let go of any negative material and stay with feeling compassionately assertive.
A few times over the next hour, be aware of only neutral or
positive material—such as feeling compassionately assertive—
while also bringing to mind a neutral trigger of feeling weak in
relationships.*

Love

Love is a deep, powerful, often intense feeling of affection, caring, sweetness, and commitment. It is usually applied to others,
though it is possible to feel love for the natural world, humanity
as a whole, God (in whatever way you experience or imagine
this), and oneself. Whether you feel loved or feel loving, love

is love, whether it's coming in or going out. When you're resting in love, any knots of longing or clinging can loosen and fall away.

H *Find any sense already present in your awareness of being connected to others who like you, who wish you well. There could be a feeling in your mind that someone loves you. Also find the warmth that is already inside you, the good wishes for others in the foreground or background of your awareness. Be aware of any sense, already present, of nurturance, protection, providing, or caring. Perhaps someone is on your mind and there is love in the mix of thoughts and feelings about this person.*

Also create a sense of being loved by bringing to mind someone who loves you, or has loved you. Recall or imagine being with this person. See his or her face. Be aware of the love for you in his or her heart. Let yourself experience being loved. Consider other people who have loved you over the years, or who love you in your life today, and let it land again and again that you are loved. (Include pets or spiritual beings, if you like.) Bring to mind a wider range of relationships, soaking in the fact that many people have included, liked, or been grateful to you. Even more broadly, explore the sense of being connected to humanity and nature and the universe, recognizing and feeling both your own place and your belonging within a greater whole.

Try to find a sense of feeling loved enough already. It is fine to wish for more love while also letting yourself feel loved enough. Then you don't have to chase love, or try to influence what is happening in the minds of others so that they will think you're great or want to be with you or love you. Any sense of stress or worry about love is falling away, any pain or loss or longing.

Create a sense of being loving by bringing to mind someone you love. Think of those you love, like, or appreciate. Think of people for whom you feel compassion. Think of people you feel happy to see. Nurture the feeling of love itself. Get a sense of love flowing outward from you.

E *Open to feeling loved, help it last and grow and become fuller in you. Open to feeling loving, with warmth and caring and good wishes radiating from you. Let feeling loved and feeling loving come together into a single sense of love. Love washing into and out of you. Abiding simply as love. If you like, meditate on love; make it your object of attention and absorption. See what it's like to breathe, sit, walk, look, reach, speak, or act with love.*

A *Feel and know that love is spreading inside you. Let your mind rest on and take the shape of love. Imagine living from love, and let the sense of this sink in. As you become love, and love is becoming you, there's no basis for any clinging or other disturbance in your relationships.*

L *Feel love in the foreground of awareness as well as any hurt (or related feelings, such as anger) in the background. Let love touch and soothe the hurt. Inhaling love, exhaling love, feel your love reaching down into parts of yourself that haven't felt properly loved. See if you can get a sense of these parts receiving love and softening around it. When you want, let go of any negative material and stay with love. A few times over the next*

hour, be aware of only neutral or positive material—such as a
sense of love—while also bringing to mind a neutral trigger of
feeling hurt.

Then, in the days to come, trust in love. Remarkably, more than any other kind of experience, love brings you home. Home to the resting state of your brain, home to inner strength and peace, home to your own good nature. As you love in ways large and small, the effects will ripple outward to touch others both known and unknown, helping to bring both them and you home to happiness.

Afterword

As I hope you've found, taking in the good can be very powerful for a person. Additionally, this practice has implications that move beyond the individual to the wider world.

The reactive mode of the brain has worked very well for survival for most of human history, but today it is stressing our whole planet. For more than 99 percent of the past 60 million years, our human and primate ancestors lived in small hunter-gatherer groups in which staying alive required identifying with "us" and mistrusting and often attacking "them." Now these reactive tendencies fuel conflicts between political, ethnic, and religious groups, and tension and aggression between nations. It's no less alarming for becoming a cliché: We've armed a Stone Age brain with nuclear weapons. Meanwhile, the fearful, greedy, and self-centered reactive setting of the brain promotes a kind of gorging of the earth's limited resources that is causing deforestation, mass extinctions, and global warming.

The objective conditions in the lives of our primate and human ancestors routinely forced their brains to go red, into the reactive setting. There was no way they could consistently, reliably meet their basic needs for safety, satisfaction, and connection. But the human species now actually does have the resources and know-how to protect, feed, and care about every single person. We could do this if we chose to do it. This possibility has never happened before, and it is taking a while for this new reality to sink in. How we manage this unprecedented opportunity will be the central story line of the next hundred if not thousand years.

To fulfill this opportunity, we can't just improve external conditions such as access to clean water or to education, as important as these are. It's been possible for at least a generation to meet every person's fundamental needs, yet this hasn't been done, and much poverty and injustice persists around the world. Even in developed countries such as the United States, much fear, frustration, and heartache persist in daily life. Given the brain's bias toward going red, we must improve internal conditions as well, inside the mind, through building up inner strengths and the bone-deep ongoing sense that core needs are already met. Then we won't be so vulnerable to the commercial and political manipulations that work only when we have an underlying sense of deficit or disturbance.

Imagine a world in which a critical mass of human brains— 100 million? a billion? more?—spend most if not all of each day in the responsive mode. Eventually there would come a tipping point, a qualitative alteration in the course of human history. People would still lock their doors at night, still reach for a profit, and still disagree and compete with one another. They would still need to be guided by values and virtues. But the ancient internal fires of fear, frustration, and heartache would be banked low or extinguished for lack of fuel. Remember how you feel, yourself, when you are resting in a basic sense of peace, contentment, and love. Remember what it's like to be with others who are also rested in this state of being. Imagine what your family would be like, your workplace and your community, too, if most everyone in it were centered in the responsive mode, the green setting, of the brain. Take it a step further and imagine how businesses would treat the people working in them, how governments would operate, and how nations might treat one another.

This is not a utopian vision. The responsive mode of the brain is our home base. For our sake and our children's children's sake, I hope we come home soon.

Reference Notes

Acknowledgments

xvii **practices such as gratitude:** Robert Emmons, *Thanks! How the Science of Gratitude Can Make You Happier* (New York: Houghton Mifflin Harcourt, 2007).

xvii **and forgiveness:** Frederic Luskin et al., "A Controlled Pilot Study of Stress Management Training of Elderly Patients with Congestive Heart Failure," *Preventive Cardiology* 5 (2002): 168–174.

xvii **research on savoring by Fred Bryant:** Fred B. Bryant et al., "Understanding the Processes That Regulate Positive Emotional Experience: Unsolved Problems and Future Directions for Theory and Research on Savoring," *International Journal of Wellbeing* 1, no. 1 (2011): 107–126; Bryant et al., "Using the Past to Enhance the Present: Boosting Happiness Through Positive Reminiscence," *Journal of Happiness Studies* 6 (2005): 227–260; Bryant, "A Four-Factor Model of Perceived Control: Avoiding, Coping, Obtaining, and Savoring," *Journal of Personality* 57, no. 4 (1989): 773–797.

xvii **Nancy Fagley:** Nancy S. Fagley, "Appreciation Uniquely Predicts Life Satisfaction Above Demographics, the Big 5 Personality Factors, and Gratitude," *Personality and Individual Differences* 53 (2012): 59–63.

xvii **Joseph Veroff:** Fred Bryant and Joseph Veroff, *Savoring: A New Model of Positive Experience* (Mahwah, N.J.: Lawrence Erlbaum Associates, Inc., 2007).

xvii **Jordi Quoidbach:** Jordi Quoidbach et al., "Positive Emotion Regulation and Well-Being: Comparing the Impact of Eight Savoring and Dampening Strategies," *Personality and Individual Differences* 49, no. 5 (2010): 368–373.

xvii **Erica Chadwick:** Bryant et al., "Understanding the Processes that Regulate Positive Emotional Experience."

xvii **the work on coherence therapy:** Brian Toomey and Bruce Ecker, "Competing Visions of the Implications of Neuroscience for Psychotherapy," *Journal of Constructivist Psychology* 22 (2009): 95–140; Ecker and Toomey, "Depotentiation of Symptom-Producing Implicit Memory in Coherence Therapy," *Journal of Constructivist Psychology* 21, no. 2 (2008): 87–150; Ecker and L. Hulley, *Depth Oriented Brief Therapy: How to Be Brief When You Were Trained to Be Deep, and Vice Versa* (San Francisco: Jossey-Bass, 1996).

xvii **sources that include Abraham Maslow:** Abraham Maslow, *The Farther Reaches of Human Nature* (New York: Penguin, 1993).

xvii **Roger Walsh:** Roger Walsh, "Lifestyle and Mental Health," *American Psychologist* 66 (2011): 579–592; Walsh, "The Meeting of Meditative Disciplines and Western Psychology," *American Psychologist* 61 (2006): 227–239.

xvii **Martin Seligman:** Martin Seligman, *Flourish: A Visionary New Understanding of Happiness and Well-Being* (New York: Free Press, 2011); Seligman, *Learned Optimism: How to Change Your Mind and Your Life* (New York: Vintage, 2006).

xvii **Chris Peterson:** Christopher Peterson et al., "Strengths of Character, Orientations to Happiness, and Life Satisfaction," *The Journal of Positive Psychology* 2, no. 3 (2007): 149–156.

xvii **Nansook Park:** Nansook Park, "Character Strengths: Research and Practice," *Journal of College & Character* 10, no. 4 (2009): 1–10.

xvii **Shauna Shapiro:** Shauna Shapiro, "Mindfulness and Psychotherapy," *Journal of Clinical Psychology* 65 (2009): 1–6.

xvii **Barbara Fredrickson:** Barbara Fredrickson, *Positivity: Top-Notch Research Reveals the 3 to 1 Ratio That Will Change Your Life* (New York: Three Rivers Press, 2009).

xvii **Sonja Lyubomirsky:** Sonja Lyubomirsky, *The How of Happiness: A New Approach to Getting the Life You Want* (New York: Penguin Press, 2008).

xvii **Michele Tugade:** Michele Tugade, *Positive Emotions and Coping: Examining Dual-Process Models of Resilience*, in S. Folkman (ed.), *Oxford Handbook of Stress, Health, and Coping* (New York: Oxford University Press, 2011), pp. 186–199.

xvii **Todd Kashdan:** Todd Kashdan, *Curious? Discover the Missing Ingredient to a Fulfilling Life* (New York: William Morrow, 2009).

xvii **Dacher Keltner:** Dacher Keltner, *Born to Be Good: The Science of a Meaningful Life* (New York: W.W. Norton & Company, Inc., 2009).

xvii **Robert Emmons:** Emmons, *Thanks!* (New York: Houghton Mifflin Harcourt, 2007).

xvii **Michael McCullough:** Michael McCullough et al., "Is Gratitude a Moral Affect?" *Psychological Bulletin* 127, no. 2 (2001): 249–266.

xvii **and Wil Cunningham:** William A. Cunningham and Tobias Brosch, "Motivational Salience: Amygdala Tuning from Traits, Needs, Values, and Goals," *Current Directions in Psychological Science* 21, no. 1 (2012): 54–59.

Chapter 1: Growing Good

INNER STRENGTHS

4 **Researchers have identified other strengths:** Steven M. Southwick and Dennis S. Charney, "The Science of Resilience: Implications for the Prevention and Treatment of Depression," *Science* 338 (2012): 79–82.

5 **A well-known idea in medicine:** I have adapted the "stress-diathesis" model that is used in health care and in research on stress and its consequences.

6 **just one strength, positive emotions:** Michael A. Cohn et al., "Happiness Unpacked: Positive Emotions Increase Life Satisfaction by Building Resilience," *Emotion* 9 (2009): 361–368; Greg C. Feldman et al., "Responses to Positive Affect: A Self-Report Measure of Rumination and Dampening," *Cognitive Therapy and Research* 32, no. 4 (2008): 507–525; Tugade and Fredrickson, "Regulation of Positive Emotions: Emotion Regulation Strategies That Promote Resilience," *Journal of Happiness Studies* 8 (2007): 311–333.

6 **Positive emotions encourage:** Lyubomirsky et al., "Pursuing Happiness: The Architecture of Sustainable Change," *Review of General Psychology* 9, no. 2 (2005): 111–131.

6 **They also strengthen your immune system:** Ed Diener and Micaela Y. Chan, "Happy People Live Longer: Subjective Well-Being Contributes to Health and Longevity," *Applied Psychophysiology* 3, no. 1 (2011): 1–43; Fredrickson et al., "Open Hearts Build Lives: Positive Emotions, Induced Through Loving-Kindness Meditation, Build Consequential Personal Resources," *Journal of Personality and Social Psychology* 95, no. 5 (2008): 1045–1062; Y. Chida and A. Steptoe, "Positive Psychological Well-Being and Mortality: A Quantitative Review of Prospective Observational Studies," *Psychosomatic Medicine* 70, no.7 (2008): 741–756;

S. Pressman and S. Cohen, "Does Positive Affect Influence Health?" *Psychological Bulletin* 131 (2005): 925–971.

6 **On average, about a third:** This is a ballpark estimate. For background, see these papers: Tena Vukasovic et al., "Genetic Contribution to the Individual Differences in Subjective Well-Being: A Meta-Analysis," *Journal for General Social Issues* 21 (2012): 1–17; Southwick and Charney, "The Science of Resilience."

IN THE GARDEN

6 **manage your mind in three primary:** There is a fourth option—transcend the mind—in which you step outside the frame of mind and brain altogether, connected to something divine, spiritual, or unconditioned, if this is meaningful to you (it is to me). Of course, by definition, this is not a way to *manage* the mind itself, so I'll bow to this possibility and then stay inside the framework of the natural world in this book.

EXPERIENCE-DEPENDENT NEUROPLASTICITY

10 **slowly but surely sculpting neural structure:** Eric R. Kandel, *In Search of Memory: The Emergence of a New Science of Mind* (New York: W. W. Norton & Company, 2007); Joseph E. LeDoux, *Synaptic Self: How Our Brains Become Who We Are* (New York: Penguin Books, 2003).

10 **genes inside neurons turn on or off:** Victoria Ho et al., "The Cell Biology of Synaptic Plasticity," *Science* 334 (2011): 623–628; D. Feldman, "Synaptic Mechanisms for Plasticity in Neocortex," *Annual Review of Neuroscience* 32 (2009): 33–55; Gianluigi Mongillo et al., "Synaptic Theory of Working Memory" *Science* 319 (2008): 1543–1546.

10 **All mental activity:** Glen O. Gabbard, "A Neurobiologically Informed Perspective on Psychotherapy," *British Journal of Psychiatry* 177 (2000): 117–122; Kandel, *In Search of Memory.*

10 **But intense, prolonged, or repeated:** Kandel, "A New Intellectual Framework for Psychiatry," *American Journal of Psychiatry* 155 (1998): 457–469.

10 **London taxi drivers:** Eleanor Maguire et al., "Navigation-Related Structural Change in the Hippocampi of Taxi Drivers," *National Academy of Sciences* 87 (2000): 4398–4403.

11 **Moving from the cab:** Above the brain stem, while there is just one hypothalamus and pituitary gland, most parts of the brain come in pairs, one on the left side and one on the right, including the hippocampus and insula. Unfortunately, the confusing convention in neuroscience is to refer to these paired parts in the singular (e.g., the hippocampus), and I'll follow this convention, too.

11 **behind the forehead that control attention:** Eileen Luders et al., "The Underlying Anatomical Correlates of Long-Term Meditation: Larger Hippocampal and Frontal Volumes of Gray Matter," *NeuroImage* 45 (2009): 672–678; Sara Lazar et al., "Meditation Experience Is Associated with Increased Cortical Thickness," *Neuroreport* 16 (2005): 1893–1897.

11 **the *insula*:** Britta Holzel et al., "Investigation of Mindfulness Meditation Practitioners with Voxel-Based Morphometry," *Social Cognitive and Affective Neuroscience* 3 (2008): 55–61; Lazar et al., "Meditation Experience."

11 **the hippocampus:** Luders et al., "Anatomical Correlates of Long-Term Meditation"; Holzel et al., "Investigation of Mindfulness Meditation."

11 **genes that calm down stress reactions:** Jeffery Dusek et al., "Genomic Counter-Stress Changes Induced by the Relaxation Response," *PLoS One* 3 (2008): e2576.

THE EXPERIENCES THAT SERVE YOU MOST

13 **Negative experiences might have value:** Southwick and Charney, "The Science of Resilience."

Chapter 2: Velcro for the Bad

THE EVOLVING BRAIN

18 **The Evolving Brain:** The dates in this section are approximate.

18 **Every human being shares:** Scott W. Emmons, "The Mood of a Worm," *Science* 338 (2012): 475–476.

18 **Multicelled creatures emerged:** Elizabeth Pennisi, "Nervous System May Have Evolved Twice," *Science* 339 (2013): 391.

18 **Mammals arose:** There are some scholarly disagreements about this dating, depending on how one categorizes mammals and primates.

18 **By 2.5 million years ago:** Shannon McPherron et al., "Evidence for Stone-Tool Assisted Consumption of Animal Tissues before 3.39 Million Years Ago at Dikika, Ethiopia," *Nature* 446 (2010): 857–860; Semaw et al., "2.5-Million-Year-Old Stone Tools from Gona, Ethiopia," *Nature* 385 (1997): 333–336.

18 **and our own species—*Homo sapiens*:** Michael Balter, "New Light on Revolutions That Weren't," *Science* 336 (2012): 530–561.

18 **Over the last 600 million years:** This is a broad point. For a sampling of research that supports it, see Pierre-Yves Placais and Thomas Preat, "To Favor Survival Under Food Shortage, the Brain Disables Costly Memory," *Science* 339 (2013): 440–442; Linda Palmer and Gary Lynch, "A Kantian View of Space," *Science* 328 (2010): 1487–1488; Tobias Esch and George B. Stefano, "The Neurobiology of Stress Management," *Neuroendocrinology Letters* 31, no.1 (2010): 19–39.

19 **Our hominid and human predecessors:** Pontus Skoglund et al., "Origins and Genetic Legacy of Neolithic Farmers and Hunter-Gatherers in Europe," *Science* 336 (2012): 466–469.

19 **While some bands interacted peacefully:** Jung-Kyoo Choi and Samuel Bowles, "The Coevolution of Parochial Altruism and War," *Science* 318 (2007): 636–640.

BAD IS STRONGER THAN GOOD

19 **Bad Is Stronger Than Good:** The title of this section is taken from the paper by Roy Baumeister et al., "Bad Is Stronger Than Good," *Review of General Psychology* 5 (2001): 323–370.

20 **For starters, your brain is always:** Eldad Yechiam and Guy Hochman, "Losses as Modulators of Attention: Review and Analysis of the Unique Effects of Losses Over Gains," *Psychological Bulletin* 139, no.2 (2013): 497–518.

21 **Then when the least little thing:** Baumeister et al., "Bad Is Stronger Than Good"; Paul Rozin and Edward Royzman, "Negativity Bias, Negativity Dominance, and Contagion," *Personality & Social Psychology Review* 5 (2001): 296–320.

21 **Negative stimuli are perceived more rapidly:** Baumeister et al., "Bad Is Stronger Than Good"; Rozin and Royzman, "Negativity Bias."

21 **We recognize angry faces more quickly:** J. S. Morris et al., "A Differential Neural Response in the Human Amygdala to Fearful and Happy Facial Expressions," *Nature* 383 (1996): 812–815.

21 **in fact, the brain will react:** J. S. Morris et al. "Conscious and Unconscious Emotional Learning in the Human Amygdala" *Nature* 393 (1998): 467–470.

21 **The psychologist Daniel Kahnemann:** Daniel Kahneman and Amos Tversky, "Prospect Theory: An Analysis of Decision Under Risk," *Econometrica* 47, no. 2 (1979): 163–292; Yechiam and Hochman, "Losses as Modulators of Attention."

21 **Lasting intimate relationships:** John Gottman, *Why Marriages Succeed or Fail: And How You Can Make Yours Last* (New York: Simon & Schuster, 1995).

21 **People really begin to thrive:** Fredrickson, *Positivity*.

21 **Negative contaminates positive more than positive:** Rozin and Royzman, "Negativity Bias."

21 **a misdeed will harm a hero's:** Rozin and Royzman, "Negativity Bias."

21 **The extra impact of the bad:** Baumeister et al., "Bad Is Stronger Than Good."

22 **almond-sized amygdala:** Cunningham and Brosch, "Motivational Salience"; Israel Liberzon et al., "Extended Amygdala and Emotional Salience: A PET Activation Study of Positive and Negative Affect," *Neuropsychopharmacology* 28, no. 4 (2003): 726–733; Stephan B. Hamann et al., "Ecstasy and Agony: Activation of the Human Amygdala in Positive and Negative Emotion," *Psychological Science* 13, no. 2 (2002): 135–141; Hugh Garavan et al., "Amygdala Response to Both Positively and Negatively Valenced Stimuli," *Neuroreport* 12, no. 12 (2001): 2779–2783.

22 **in most people it is activated more:** Cunningham et al., "Neural Correlates of Evaluation Associated with Promotion and Prevention Regulatory Focus," *Cognitive, Affective, and Behavioral Neuroscience* 5 no. 2 (2005): 202–211; Andrew J. Calder et al., "Neuropsychology of Fear and Loathing," *Nature* 2 (2001): 353–363.

22 **other person's anger activated your amygdala:** Hugo D. Critchley, "Neural Mechanisms of Autonomic, Affective, and Cognitive Integration," *Journal of Comparative Neurology* 493 (2005): 154–166.

22 **hippocampus formed an initial neural trace:** Guestavo Morrone Parfitt et al., "Moderate Stress Enhances Memory Persistence: Are Adrenergic Mechanisms Involved?" *Behavioral Neuroscience* 126, no. 5 (2012): 729–730.

22 **even marking new baby neurons:** E. D. Kirby et al., "Basolateral Amygdala Regulation of Adult Hippocampal Neurogenesis and Fear-Related Activation of Newborn Neurons," *Molecular Psychiatry* 17 (2012): 527–536.

VICIOUS CIRCLES

22 **This snowballing effect occurs:** Bruce McEwen and Peter Gianaros, "Stress- and Allostasis-Induced Brain Plasticity," *Annual Review of Medicine* 62 (2011): 431–435.

23 **in a one-two punch:** McEwen and Gianaros, "Stress- and Allostasis-Induced Brain Plasticity"; Poul Videbech and Barbaba Ravnkilde, "Hippocampal Volume and Depression: A Meta-Analysis of MRI Studies," *American Journal of Psychiatry* 161, no. 11 (2004): 1957–1966; Stephanie Campbell et al., "Lower Hippocampal Volume in Patients Suffering from Depression: A Meta-Analysis," *American Journal of Psychiatry* 161, no. 4 (2001): 598–607.

23 **This is a problem:** McEwen and Gianaros, "Stress- and Allostasis-Induced Brain Plasticity."

PAPER TIGER PARANOIA

23 **still make the second mistake:** Tali Sharot, *The Optimism Bias: A Tour of the Irrationally Positive Brain* (New York: Vintage, 2011).

24 **But in general, the default setting:** Deborah Kermer et al., "Loss Aversion Is an Affective Forecasting Error," *Psychological Science* 17, no. 8 (2006): 649–653; Baumeister et al., "Bad Is Stronger Than Good"; Rozin and Royzman, "Negativity Bias."

24 **There are even regions:** Nadine Gogolla et al., "Perineuronal Nets Protect Fear Memories from Erasure," *Science* 325 (2009): 1258–1261.

VELCRO AND TEFLON

25 **recollections tend to be positively biased:** Daniel L. Schachter, *The Seven Sins of Memory: How the Mind Forgets and Remembers* (New York: Houghton Mifflin Harcourt Books, 2002).

26 **holding most of your inner strengths:** The inner strengths as well as the feelings of inadequacy, etc., that are not based on learning and memory—in other words, they are not *acquired*—are based on *innate*, genetically determined characteristics and tendencies.

26 **Unfortunately, the formation of implicit memory:** For references for the statements made in this paragraph, see Baumeister et al., "Bad Is Stronger Than Good"; Rozin and Royzman, "Negativity Bias."

26 **a sense of helplessness:** Seligman, *Learned Optimism.*

26 **a major factor in depression:** Seligman, *Learned Optimism.*

WASTED EFFORTS

28 **This is the central weakness:** Some psychotherapies are noteworthy exceptions. These include focusing (Eugene T. Gendlin, *Focusing* [New York: Random House, 1982]), EMDR (Deborah L. Korn and Andrew M. Leeds, "Preliminary Evidence of Efficacy for EMDR Resource De-

velopment and Installation in the Stabilization Phase of Treatment of Complex Posttraumatic Stress Disorder," *Journal of Clinical Psychology* 58, no. 12 [2002]: 1465–1487); coherence therapy (Toomey and Ecker, "Competing Visions"; Ecker and Toomey, "Depotentiation of Symptom-Producing Implicit Memory in Coherence Therapy"); and broad minded affective coping (Nicholas Terrier, "Broad Minded Affective Coping [BMAC]: A 'Positive' CBT Approach to Facilitating Positive Emotions," *International Journal of Cognitive Therapy* 31, no. 1 [2010]: 65–78.)

Chapter 3: Green Brain, Red Brain

THREE OPERATING SYSTEMS

34   **the influential work of Paul MacLean:** Paul D. MacLean, *The Triune Brain in Evolution: Role in Paleocerebral Functions* (New York: Springer, 1990).

34   **Jaak Panksepp:** Jaak Panksepp, *Affective Neuroscience: The Foundations of Human and Animal Emotions* (New York: Oxford University Press, 1998); Panksepp, "Affective Consciousness: Core Emotional Feelings in Animals and Humans," *Consciousness & Cognition* 14, no. 1 (2005): 30-80; Jeffrey Burgdorf and Panksepp, "The Neurobiology of Positive Emotions," *Neuroscience and Biobehavioral Reviews* 30 (2006): 173–187.

34   **Stephen Porges:** Stephen W. Porges, *The Polyvagal Theory: Neurophysiological Foundations of Emotions, Attachment, Communication, and Self-Regulation* (New York: W.W. Norton & Company, 2011).

34   **Paul Gilbert:** Paul Gilbert, "Introducing Compassion-Focused Therapy," *Advances in Psychiatric Treatment* 14 (2009): 199–208.

34   **E. Tory Higgins:** E. Tory Higgins, "Beyond Pleasure and Pain," *American Psychologist* 52, no. 12 (1997): 1280–1300.

THE RESPONSIVE MODE

39   **when your brain is not *disturbed*:** Porges, *The Polyvagal Theory.*

39   **Neurochemical systems involving *oxytocin*:** Waguih William IsHak et al., "Oxytocin's Role in Enhancing Well-Being: A Literature Review," *Journal of Affective Disorders* 130, no. 1 (2011): 1–9; Inga D. Neumann, "Brain Oxytocin: A Key Regulator of Emotional and Social Behaviours in Both Females and Males," *Journal of Neuroendocrinology* 20 (2008): 858–865.

39   **natural *opioids*:** Pawel K. Olszewski et al., "Oxytocin as Feeding Inhibitor: Maintaining Homestasis in Consummatory Behavior," *Pharmacology Biochemistry and Behavior* 97 (2010): 47–54; Esch and Stefano, "The Neurobiology of Stress Management."

39   **regions such as the *subgenual cingulate*:** Hugo D. Critchley and Yoko Nagai, " How Emotions Are Shaped by Bodily States," *Emotion Review* 4, no. 2 (2012): 163–168.

39   **and neural networks:** Critchley, "Neural Mechanisms."

39   **In it, you'll often feel:** Critchley, "Neural Mechanisms."

39   **Mammals, including us, become friendly:** Panksepp, *Affective Neuroscience.*

IT'S GOOD TO BE HOME

40   **Our ancestors evolved this setting:** Ilia Karatsoreos and Bruce McEwen, "Psychobiological Allostasis: Resistance, Resilience, and Vulnerability," *Trends in Cognitive Sciences* 15, no. 12 (2011): 576–584; Porges, *The Polyvagal Theory*; Esch and Stefano, "The Neurobiology of Stress Management"; Panksepp, "Affective Consciousness"; Panksepp, *Affective Neuroscience.*

41   **For example, the *endorphins*:** Esch and Stefano, "The Neurobiology of Stress Management."

41   **Unlike pathogenic processes:** Craig M. Becker et al., "Salutogenesis 30 Years Later: Where Do We Go From Here?" *International Electronic Journal Health Education* 13 (2010): 25–32.

41   **Responsive type experiences prepare your mind:** Critchley, "Neural Mechanisms."

41   **your hypothalamus becomes less active:** Olszewski et al., "Oxytocin as Feeding Inhibitor"; Panksepp, *Affective Neuroscience.*

41   **are gradually extinguished:** Resting in the responsive mode with a deeply internalized felt sense of your core needs already being met is not itself enlightenment. For that, I believe that one also needs profound insight, virtue, love, and perhaps grace. But the de-fueling of the neuropsychological "fires" of hatred and greed (to use Buddhist terms), and heartache—in the avoiding, approaching, and attaching systems—both supports and clears the way for very deep engagement with religious or spiritual practice and the upper reaches of human potential.

42   **Challenges are faced, competition and confrontations:** Douglas P. Fry, "Life Without War," *Science* 336 (2012): 879–884.

VELCRO FOR THE GOOD

42   **Its messages guide the *executive control*:** William W. Seeley et al., "Dissociable Intrinsic Connectivity Networks for Salience Processing and Executive Control," *Journal of Neuroscience* 27 (2007): 2356–2349.

43   **Less amygdala reactivity to the bad:** Wil Cunningham and Tabitha Kirkland, "The Joyful, Yet Balanced Amygdala: Moderated Responses to Positive But Not Negative Stimuli in Trait Happiness," *Social Cognitive and Affective Neuroscience* (2013 April 5, e-pub ahead of print).

43   **You need what Wil Cunningham:** Cunningham and Kirkland, "Joyful Amygdala."

43   **In terms of amygdala activation:** Cunningham and Brosch, "Motivational Salience"; Cunningham and Kirkland, "Joyful Amygdala."

43   **the ones with a joyful amygdala:** Cunningham et al. "Neural Correlates of Evaluation."

44   **an "approach orientation":** Daniel J. Siegel, *The Mindful Brain* (New York: W.W. Norton & Company, 2007).

44   **These people also have relatively high positive:** Cunningham and Kirkland, "Joyful Amygdala."

44   **In fact, these happier individuals:** Cunningham and Kirkland, "Joyful Amygdala."

44   **prolong dopamine inputs to your amygdala:** Douglas Roberts-Wolfe et al., "Mindfulness Training Alters Emotional Memory Recall Compared to Active Controls: Support for an Emotional Information Processing Model of Mindfulness," *Frontiers in Human Neuroscience* 6 (2012): 1–13.

THE REACTIVE MODE

45   **the other setting of your brain:** I'm referring to the responsive and reactive modes of the brain in a dichotomous way, consistent with the categorical distinctions made by scholars in reference to homeostatic/allostatic and sympathetic/parasympathetic activations. In the complex and messy biology of real animals, including us, these distinctions get blurry in that at any time there can be a mix of homeostatic-responsive and allostatic-reactive processes. But in general, these categories used by scholars are accurate and helpful. In the language of systems theory, the responsive and reactive modes are global "strange attractors."

45   **bodily resources are depleted:** Bruce McEwen and Peter Gianaros, "Central Role of the Brain in Stress and Adaptation: Links to Socioeconomic Status, Health, and Disease," *Annals of the New York Academy of Sciences* 1186 (2010): 190–222.

46   **The natural, biologically based rhythm:** McEwen and Gianaros, "Central Role of the Brain in Stress and Adaptation"; Robert Sapolsky, *Why Zebras Don't Get Ulcers* (New York: Holt Paperbacks, 2004).

46   **Just entering the red zone:** Esch and Stefano, "The Neurobiology of Stress Management."

46   **Even though reactive experiences feel bad:** McEwen and Gianaros, "Stress- and Allostasis-Induced Brain Plasticity."

48   **All this puts the brain:** McEwen and Gianaros, "Central Role of the Brain in Stress and Adaptation"; Critchley, "Neural Mechanisms."

48   **As a result, while the reactive:** Esch and Stefano, "The Neurobiology of Stress Management."

48   **Going red feels bad emotionally:** Esch and Stefano, "The Neurobiology of Stress Management."

49   **they are risk factors for depression:** Byung Kook Lim et al., "Anhedonia Requires MC4R-Mediated Synaptic Adaptations in Nucleus Accumbens," *Nature* 487 (2012): 183–189.

49   **Many psychological disorders involve reactive extremes:** While depression is often a reaction to loss (e.g., bankruptcy), and one of its most common features is lack of pleasure in things that were once enjoyable—both of which are related to the approaching rewards system—depression also appears after trauma (avoiding system) and after rejection or shaming (attaching system). Therefore, I think of depression as potentially involving all three operating systems, sometimes one more than the others.

49   **In your body, the gradually accumulating:** McEwen and Gianaros, "Central Role of the Brain in Stress and Adaptation."

49   **which increases inflammation:** Esch and Stefano, "The Neurobiology of Stress Management"; Paul H. Black, "The Inflammatory Response is an Integral Part of the Stress Response: Implications for Atherosclerosis, Insulin Resistance, Type II Diabetes, and Metabolic Syndrome X," *Brain, Behavior, & Immunity* 17 (2003): 350–364; Black, "Stress and the Inflammatory Response: A Review of Neurogenic Inflammation," *Brain, Behavior, & Immunity* 16 (2002): 622–653.

49   **weakens your immune system:** McEwen, "Stress Adaptation, and Disease: Allostasis and Allostatic Load," *Annals of the New York Academy of Sciences* 840 (1998): 33–44.

49   **and wears on your cardiovascular system:** McEwen and Gianaros, "Central Role of the Brain in Stress and Adaptation."

49   **In your brain, allostatic load causes:** Agnieszka Mika et al., "Chronic Stress Impairs Prefrontal Cortex–Dependent Response Inhibition and

Spatial Working Memory," *Behavioral Neuroscience* 126, no. 5 (2012): 605–619; Ronald S. Duman and George K. Aghajanian, "Synaptic Dysfunction in Depression: Potential Therapeutic Targets," *Science* 338 (2012): 68–72; Daniel J. Christoffel et al., "Structural and Synaptic Plasticity in Stress-Related Disorders," *Reviews in Neurosciences* 22, no. 5 (2011): 535–549; McEwen, "Protective and Damaging Effects of Stress Mediators: Central Role of the Brain," *Dialogues in Clinical Neuroscience* 8, no. 4 (2006): 367–381.

49   **It impairs *myelination*:** M. P. Leussis and S. L. Andersen, "Is Adolescence a Sensitive Period for Depression? Behavioral and Neuroanatomical Findings from a Social Stress Model," *Synapse* 62, no. 1 (2007): 22–30; Q. Wang et al., "Alterations of Myelin Basic Protein and Ultrastructure in the Limbic System at the Early Stage of Trauma-Related Stress Disorder in Dogs," *Journal of Trauma* 56, no. 3 (2004): 604–610.

49   **reduces the *neurotrophin*, BDNF:** McEwen and Gianaros, "Central Role of the Brain in Stress and Adaptation"; Esch and Stefano, "The Neurobiology of Stress Management."

49   **we need to protect neurons:** E. L. van Donkelaar, "Stress-Mediated Decreases in Brain-Derived Neurotropic Factor as Potential Confounding Factor for Acute Tryptophan Depletion–Induced Neurochemical Effects," *Journal of the European College of Neuropsychopharmacology* 11 (2009): 812–821.

50   **Simply regarding others as "them":** Jennifer N. Gutsell and Michael Inzlicht, "Empathy Constrained: Prejudice Predicts Reduced Mental Simulation of Actions During Observation of Outgroups," *Journal of Experimental Social Psychology* 46 (2010): 841–845; Xiaojin Xu et al., "Do You Feel My Pain? Racial Group Membership Modulates Empathic Neural Responses," *Journal of Neuroscience* 9, no. 26 (2009): 8525–8529; Lasana T. Harris and Susan T. Fiske, "Social Groups That Elicit Disgust Are Differentially Processed in mPFC," *Social Cognitive and Affective Neuroscience* 2 (2007): 45–51.

49   **our tendency to dehumanize and devalue:** Charles Efferson et al., "The Coevolution of Cultural Groups and Ingroup Favoritism," *Science* 321 (2008): 1844–1849.

49   **Compared to other animals:** Christopher Boehm, "Ancestral Hierarchy and Conflict," *Science* 336 (2012): 844–847.

DEVELOPING A RESPONSIVITY BIAS

53   **recover more quickly from negative experiences:** Fredrickson et al., "What Good Are Positive Emotions in Crisis? A Prospective Study of Resilience and Emotions Following the Terrorist Attacks on the U.S. on

9/11/01," *Journal of Personality and Social Psychology* 84, no. 2 (2003): 365–376; Fredrickson and Robert Levenson, "Positive Emotions Speed Recovery from the Cardiovascular Sequelae of Negative Emotions," *Psychology Press* 12 (1998): 191–220.

Chapter 4: HEAL Yourself

GETTING GOOD AT TAKING IN THE GOOD

64 **Your family background could also play:** Bryant et al., "Understanding the Processes that Regulate Positive Emotional Experience."

65 **And by taking in the good:** Fredrickson et al., "What Good Are Positive Emotions in Crisis?"; Fredrickson and Levenson, "Positive Emotions Speed Recovery."

EVERYDAY JEWELS

71 **five minutes at most:** Of course, you can do this practice more often.

74 *If you take care of the:* This is a Tibetan proverb.

Chapter 5: Take Notice

THE MUSIC OF EXPERIENCE

79 **the benefits of cognitive therapy:** Fidelma Hanrahan et al., "A Meta-Analysis of Cognitive Therapy for Worry in Generalized Anxiety Disorder," *Clinical Psychology Review* 33, no. 1 (2013): 120–132; Bunmi O. Olatunji et al., "Cognitive-Behavioral Therapy for Obsessive-Compulsive Disorder: A Meta-Analysis of Treatment Outcome and Moderators," *Journal of Psychiatric Research* 47, no. 1 (2013): 33–41; Rebecca Gould et al., "Cognitive Behavioral Therapy for Depression in Older People: A Meta-Analysis and Meta-Regression of Randomized Controlled Trails," *Journal of the American Geriatrics Society* 60, no. 10 (2012): 1817–1830; Stefan G. Hofmann et al., "The Efficacy of Cognitive Behavioral Therapy: A Review of Meta-Analyses," *Cognitive Therapy and Research* 36, no.5 (2012): 427–440.

80 **Besides being enjoyable:** Esch and Stefano, "The Neurobiology of Stress Management."

81 **like pleasure, relaxation dials down stress:** Elizabeth Broadbent et al., "A Brief Relaxation Intervention Reduces Stress and Improves Surgical Wound Healing Response: A Randomished Trial," *Brain, Behavior, & Immunity* 26, no. 2 (2012): 212–217; Herbert Benson, *The Relaxation Response* (New York: HarperTorch, 2000).

81 **It also strengthens the immune system:** Benson, *The Relaxation Response*.

81 **increases resilience:** Brian Rees, "Overview of Outcome Data of Potential Mediation Training for Soldier Resilience," *Military Medicine* 176, no. 11 (2011): 1232–1242; Dusek et al., "Genomic Counter-Stress"; Mary Karapetian Alvord and Judy Johnson Grados, "Enhancing Resilence in Children: A Proactive Approach," *Professional Psychology: Research and Practice* 36, no. 3 (2005): 238–245.

81 **lowers anxiety:** Benson, *The Relaxation Response*.

LIKING AND WANTING

87 **separate circuits handle liking and wanting:** Kent C. Berridge et al., "The Tempted Brain Eats: Pleasure and Desire Circuits in Obesity and Eating Disorders," *ScienceDirect* 1350 (2010): 43–64; Berridge, "Wanting and Liking: Observations from the Neuroscience and Psychology Laboratory," *Inquiry* 52, no. 4 (2009): 378–398; S. Pecina and Berridge, "Hedonic Hot Spot in Nucleus Accumbens Shell: Where Do Mu-Opioids Cause Increased Impact of Sweetness?" *Journal of Neuroscience* 25, no. 50 (2005): 11777–11786; Berridge, "Food Reward: Brain Substrates of Wanting and Liking," *Neuroscience Biobehavioral Review* 20, no. 1 (1996): 1–25.

Chapter 6: Creating Positive Experiences

RECENT EVENTS

94 **Finding positive meaning in ordinary events:** Tugade and Federickson, "Regulation of Positive Emotions."

THE FUTURE

100 **time travel draws on midline networks:** Ylva Ostby et al., "Mental Time Travel and Default-Mode Network Functional Connectivity in the Developing Brain," *Proceedings of the National Academy of Sciences* 109, no. 42 (2012): 16800–16804.

SHARING GOOD WITH OTHERS

100 **talking about good things with others:** Shelly L. Gable et al., "What Do You Do When Things Go Right? The Intrapersonal and Interpersonal Benefits of Sharing Positive Events," *Journal of Personality and Social Psychology* 87, no. 2 (2004): 228–245; Christopher A. Langston, "Capitalizing On and Coping with Daily-Life Events: Expressive Responses to Positive Events," *Journal of Personality and Social Psychology* 67 (1994): 1112–1125.

100 **highly developed neural networks for empathy:** Jean Decety and Philip L. Jackson, "The Functional Architecture of Human Empathy," *Behavorial and Cognitive Neuroscience Reviews* 3 (2004): 71–100.

FINDING THE GOOD IN THE BAD

101 **finding positive meaning in negative events:** Susan Folkman and Judith Moskowitz, "Positive Affect and the Other Side of Coping," *American Psychologist* 55 (2000): 647–654.

CARING ABOUT OTHERS

102 **reward centers in the brain activated:** Jorge Moll et al., "Human Fronto-Mesolimbic Networks Guide Decisions About Charitable Donation," *Proceedings of the National Academy of Sciences* 103 (2006): 15623–15628.

SEEING GOOD IN THE LIVES OF OTHERS

103 **Our ancestors lived in small bands:** Eric Alden Smith, "Communication and Collective Action: The Role of Language in Human Cooperation," *Evolution and Human Behavior* 31, no. 4 (2010): 231–245; Martin A. Nowak and Karl Sigmund, "Evolution of Indirect Reciprocity," *Nature* 437 (2005): 1291–1298; Ernst Fehr and Bettina Rockenbach, "Human Altruism: Economic, Neural, and Evolutionary Perspectives," *Current Opinion in Neurobiology* 14, no.6 (2004): 784–790; Fehr, "Human Behaviour: Don't Lose Your Reputation," *Nature* 432 (2004): 449–450.

IMAGINING GOOD FACTS

104 **The midline cortical networks:** Schachter, "Adaptive Constructive Processes and the Future of Memory," *American Psychologist* 67, no. 8 (2012): 603–613.

105 **Deep down in the emotional memory:** Schachter, "Adaptive Constructive Processes."

Chapter 7: Brain Building

ENRICHING AN EXPERIENCE

113 **It's a little like ice skating:** Thanks to Sally Clough Armstrong for this metaphor.

114 **rewarding than your brain initially expected:** Wulfram Gerstner et al., "Theory and Simulation in Neuroscience," *Science* 338 (2012): 60–65.

115 **Subcortical control centers:** Panksepp, *Affective Neuroscience.*

115 **Through this loop:** Critchley and Nagai, "How Emotions Are Shaped by Bodily States."

115 **studies show that leaning toward:** Tom F. Price et al., "Embodying Approach Motivation: Body Posture Influences Startle Eyeblink and Event-Related Potential Responses to Appetitive Stimuli," *Biological Psychology* 90 (2012): 211–217.

115 **your facial expressions, posture:** Price et al., "The Emotive Neuroscience of Embodiment," *Motivation and Emotion* 36, no. 1 (2012): 27–37; Paula Niedenthal, "Embodying Emotion," *Science* 316 (2007): 1002–1005.

116 **Consequently, you can enrich an experience:** Critchley and Nagai, "How Emotions Are Shaped by Bodily States."

116 **the more actively and bodily:** Seligman and Tracy A. Steen, "Positive Psychotherapy Progress: Empirical Validation of Interventions," *American Psychologist* 60, no. 5 (2005): 410–421.

NOVELTY

117 **Look for unexpected rewards:** Gerstner et al., "Theory and Simulation in Neuroscience."

118 **The survival of these baby neurons:** Gretchen Vogel, "Can We Make Our Brains More Plastic?" *Science* 338 (2012): 36–39.

Chapter 8: Flowers Pulling Weeds

HOW NEGATIVE MATERIAL WORKS IN YOUR BRAIN

127 ***reconstructed* from underlying seeds:** Schachter, "Adaptive Constructive Processes"; Karim Nader, "Memory Traces Unbound," *Trends in Neurosciences* 26, no. 2 (2003): 65–70; Nader et al., "The Labile Nature of Consolidation Theory," *Nature* 1, no. 3 (2000): 216–219.

127 *coalition* that represents the conscious experience: Evan Thompson, *Mind in Life: Biology, Phenomenology, and the Sciences of Mind* (Cambridge, Mass.: Harvard University Press, 2007).

127 Then when the negative material: Nader et al., "The Labile Nature of Consolidation Theory."

127 Little molecular machines need at least: Nader, "Memory Traces Unbound."

TWO METHODS FOR CHANGING NEGATIVE MATERIAL

129 "overwrite" the negative material: Mark E. Bouton, "Context and Behavioral Processes in Extinction," *Learning & Memory* 11 (2004): 485–494.

129 it might return with a vengeance: Pizzorusso Tommaso, "Erasing Fear Memories," *Science* 325 (2009): 1214–1215.

129 easier to reacquire down the road: Toomey and Ecker, "Competing Vision,"; Ecker and Toomey, "Depotentiation of Symptom-Producing."

130 for at least an hour: The exact duration of the window of reconsolidation is unknown, but it seems clearly to be less than six hours.

130 disrupt the reconsolidation of the negative: Yan-Xue Xue et al., "A Memory Retrieval-Extinction Procedure to Prevent Drug Craving and Relapse," *Science* 336 (2012): 241–245; Amy L. Milton and Barry J. Everitt, "Wiping Drug Memories," *Science* 336 (2012): 167–168; Daniela Schiller et al., "Preventing the Return of Fear in Humans Using Reconcolidation Update Mechanisms," *Nature* 463 (2010): 49–53; Marie-H. Monfils et al., "Extinction-Reconsolidation Boundaries: Key to Persistent Attenuation of Fear Memories," *Science* 324 (2009): 951–955.

130 reducing amygdala activation: Thomas Agren et al., "Disruption of Reconsolidation Erases a Fear Memory Trace in the Human Amygdala," *Science* 337 (2012): 1550–1552.

POWERFUL POSSIBILITIES

132 coherence therapy, developed by Bruce Ecker: Toomey and Ecker, "Competing Visions"; Ecker and Toomey, "Depotentiation of Symptom-Producing."

Chapter 9: Good Uses

WANTING WHAT'S GOOD FOR YOU

148   **grit your teeth and exercise willpower:** Kelly McGonigal, *The Willpower Instinct: How Self-Control Works, Why It Matters, and What You Can Do to Get More* (New York: Avery, 2011).

148   **a genetic variation that produces less:** Cornelia Kegel et al., "Differential Susceptibility in Early Literacy Instruction Through Computer Games: The Role of the Dopamine D4 Receptor Gene (DRD4)," *Mind, Brain, and Education* 5: 71–78.

148   **rewarding experiences related to the wants:** Schachter, "Adaptive Constructive Processes"; G. Elliott Wimmer and Dapha Shohamy, "Preference by Association: How Memory Mechanisms in the Hippocampus Bias Decisions," *Science* 338 (2012): 270–273.

LIFTING A BLUE MOOD

154   **not be used with severe depression:** Also, if you have bipolar disorder, be careful about intense and long-lasting positive emotions, since they might kindle a manic episode. See June Gruber, "Can Feeling Too Good Be Bad? Positive Emotion Persistence (PEP) in Bipolar Disorder," *Current Directions in Psychological Science* 20, no. 4 (2011): 217–221.

RECOVERING FROM TRAUMA

156   **see the work of Judith Herman:** Judith Herman, *Trauma and Recovery: The Aftermath of Violence—from Domestic Abuse to Political Terror* (New York: Basic Books, 1997).

156   **Peter Levine:** Peter A. Levine, *In an Unspoken Voice: How the Body Releases Trauma and Restores Goodness* (Berkeley: North Atlantic Books, 2010).

156   **Pat Ogden:** Pat Ogden, *Trauma and the Body: A Sensorimotor Approach to Psychotherapy* (New York: W. W. Norton & Company, 2006).

156   **Bessel van der Kolk:** Bessel A. van der Kolk, *Traumatic Stress: The Effects of Overwhelming Experience on Mind, Body, and Society* (New York: The Guilford Press, 2006).

HEALING CHILDREN

162   **produces less effective dopamine receptors:** Kegel et al., "Differential Susceptibility in Early Literacy."

HANDLING BLOCKS

164 **Overanalyzing, pulling out:** Bryant et al., "Understanding the Processes that Regulate Positive Emotional Experience."

164 **seeking to feel good is selfish:** Feldman et al., "Responses to Positive Affect"; Joanne V. Wood et al., "Savoring Versus Dampening: Self-Esteem Differences in Regulating Positive Affect," *Journal of Personality and Social Psychology* 85 (2003): 566–580.

166 **there's no point in feeling good:** Bryant and Veroff, *Savoring*.

DEALING WITH CHALLENGES IN A RESPONSIVE WAY

168 **be appropriately cautious:** If there has been any actual or threatened violence in the relationship, be careful and seek professional help before taking action.

168 **This is called *mental rehearsal*:** Schachter, "Adaptive Constructive Processes."

Chapter 10: 21 Jewels

SAFETY

177 **Key experiences in the attaching system:** Paul Gilbert, *The Compassionate Mind: A New Approach to Life's Challenges* (Oakland, Calif.: New Harbinger Publications, Inc., 2010).

177 **The avoiding system is rooted:** Hamann et al., "Ecstasy and Agony; Sergio Paradiso, "Cerebral Blood Flow Changes Associated with Attribution of Emotional Valence to Pleasant, Unpleasant, and Neutral Visual Stimuli in a PET Study of Normal Subjects," *American Journal of Psychiatry* 156, no. 10 (1999): 1618–1629.

177 **distress tolerance is a fundamental source:** Teresa M. Leyro, "Distress Tolerance and Psychopathological Symptoms and Disorders: A Review of the Empirical Literature among Adults," *Psychological Bulletin* 136, no. 4 (2010): 576–600.

186 **it sounds an alarm:** Critchley, "Neural Mechanisms."

186 **Even small shifts in your sense:** Critchley and Nagai, "How Emotions Are Shaped by Bodily States"; Porges, *The Polyvagal Theory*.

189 **peacefully breathing, breathing peace, being peace:** See Thich Nhat Hanh's beautiful book *Being Peace* (Berkeley: Parallax Press, 2005).

SATISFACTION

190 **pleasures like these ease emotional upsets:** Panksepp, "Affective Consciousness."

190 **by releasing endorphins and natural opioids:** Panksepp, "Affective Consciousness"; Panksepp, *Affective Neuroscience.*

190 **energizing feelings of vitality or passion:** Pressman and Cohen, "Does Positive Affect Influence Health?"

192 **Gratitude, gladness, and related feelings:** Fagley, "Appreciation Uniquely Predicts Life Satisfaction"; Michael G. Adler and Fagley, "Appreciation: Individual Differences in Finding Value and Meaning as a Unique Predictor of Subjective Well-Being," *Journal of Personality* 73 (2005): 79–114; Emmons, *Thanks!*; Emmons and McCullough, "Counting Blessings Versus Burdens: An Experimental Investigation of Gratitude and Subjective Well-Being in Daily Life," *Journal of Personality and Social Psychology* 84, no. 2 (2003): 377–389.

CONNECTION

204 **they will help you feel safe:** Gilbert, *The Compassionate Mind.*

205 **oxytocin into your brain's alarm bell:** Andreas Meyer-Lindenberg, "Impact of Prosocial Neuropeptides on Human Brain Function," *Progress in Brain Research* 170 (2008): 463–470; Daniele Viviani and Ron Stoop, "Opposite Effects of Oxytocin and Vasopressin on the Emotional Expression of the Fear Response," *Progress in Brain Research* 170 (2008): 207–218.

205 **increases cortisol receptors in your hippocampus:** Markus Heinrichs et al., "Social Support and Oxytocin Interact to Suppress Cortisol and Subjective Responses to Psychosocial Stress," *Biological Psychiatry* 54 (2003): 1389–1398.

205 **social contact:** Decety and Margarita Svetlova, "Putting Together Phylogenetic and Ontogenetic Perspectives on Empathy," *Developmental Cognitive Neuroscience* 2 no. 1 (2011): 1–24.

205 **play:** E. B. Keverne et al., "Beta-Endorphin Concentrations in Cerebrospinal Fluid of Monkeys Are Influenced by Grooming Relationships," *Psychoneuroendocrinology* 14 (1989): 155–161.

205 **loving touch:** Panksepp, "Affective Consciousness."

210 **While compassion can feel softly sad:** Olga M. Klimecki et al., "Functional Neural Plasticity and Associated Changes in Positive Affect after Compassion Training," *Cerebral Cortex* 6 (2012), doi: 10.1093/cercor/bhs142 PII: bhs142.

211 **the application of compassion toward yourself:** Kristin D. Neff, "Self-Compassion, Self-Esteem, and Well-Being," *Social and Personality Psychology Compass* 5, no. 1 (2011): 1–12; Neff, "Self-Compassion: An Alternative Conceptualization of a Healthy Attitude Toward Onself," *Self and Identity* 2, no. 2 (2003): 85–101.

211 **Studies have shown that self-compassion:** Neff, "Self-Compassion, Self-Esteem, and Well-Being"; Mark R. Leary et al., "Self-Compassion and Reactions to Unpleasant Self-Relevant Events: The Implications of Treating Oneself Kindly," *Journal of Personality* 92 (2007): 887–904; Christopher Germer, *The Mindful Path to Self-Compassion: Freeing Yourself from Destructive Thoughts and Emotions* (New York: The Guilford Press, 2009).

Afterword

221 **staying alive required identifying with "us":** Samuel Bowles, "Warriors, Levelers, and the Role of Conflict in Human Social Evolution," *Science* 336 (2012): 876–878; Bowles, "Did Warfare among Ancestral Hunter-Gatherers Affect the Evolution of Human Social Behaviors?" *Science* 324 (2009): 1293–1298; Choi and Bowles, "The Coevolution of Parochial Altruism and War."

Bibliography

Adler, Michael G., and Nancy Fagley. "Appreciation: Individual Differences in Finding Value and Meaning as a Unique Predictor of Subjective Well-Being." *Journal of Personality* 73 (2005): 79–114.

Agren, Thomas, Jonas Engman, Andreas Frick, Johannes Björkstrand, Elna-Marie Larsson, Tomas Furmark, and Mats Fredrikson. "Disruption of Reconsolidation Erases a Fear Memory Trace in the Human Amydala." *Science* 337 (2012): 1550–1552.

Alvord, Mary Karapetian, and Judy Johnson Grados. "Enhancing Resilence in Children: A Proactive Approach." *Professional Psychology: Research and Practice* 36, no. 3 (2005): 238–245.

Balter, Michael. "New Light on Revolutions That Weren't." *Science* 336 (2012): 530–561.

Baumeister, Roy, Ellen Bratlavsky, Catrin Finkenauer, and Kathleen Vohs. "Bad Is Stronger Than Good." *Review of General Psychology* 5 (2001): 323–370.

Becker, Craig M., Mary Alice Glascoff, and W. Michael Felts. "Salutogenesis 30 Years Later: Where Do We Go From Here?" *International Electronic Journal of Health Education* 13 (2010): 25–32.

Benson, Herbert. *The Relaxation Response.* New York: HarperTorch, 2000.

Berridge, Kent C. "Food Reward: Brain Substrates of Wanting and Liking." *Neuroscience Biobehavioral Review* 20, no. 1 (1996): 1–25.

———. "Wanting and Liking: Observations from the Neuroscience and Psychology Laboratory." *Inquiry* 52, no. 4 (2009): 378–398.

Berridge, Kent C., Chao-Yi Ho, Jocelyn M. Richard, and Alexandra G. DiFeliceantonio. "The Tempted Brain Eats: Pleasure and Desire Circuits in Obesity and Eating Disorders." *ScienceDirect* 1350 (2010): 43–64.

Black, Paul H. "The Inflammatory Response Is an Integral Part of the Stress Response: Implications for Atherosclerosis, Insulin Resistance, Type II Diabetes, and Metabolic Syndrome X." *Brain, Behavior, & Immunity* 17 (2003): 350–364.

———. "Stress and the Inflammatory Response: A Review of Neurogenic Inflammation." *Brain, Behavior, & Immunity* 16 (2002): 622–653.

Boehm, Christopher. "Ancestral Hierarchy and Conflict." *Science* 336 (2012): 844–847.

Bouton, Mark E. "Context and Behavioral Processes in Extinction." *Learning & Memory* 11 (2004): 485–494.

Bowles, Samuel. "Did Warfare Among Ancestral Hunter-Gatherers Affect the Evolution of Human Social Behaviors?" *Science* 324 (2009): 1293–1298.

———. "Warriors, Levelers, and the Role of Conflict in Human Social Evolution." *Science* 336 (2012): 876–878.

Broadbent, Elizabeth, Arman Kahokehr, Roger J. Booth, Janine Thomas, John A. Windsor, Christina M. Buchanan, Benjamin R. L. Wheeler, Tarik Sammour, and Andrew G. Hill. "A Brief Relaxation Intervention Reduces Stress and Improves Surgical Wound Healing Response: A Randomished Trial." *Brain, Behavior, & Immunity* 26, no. 2 (2012): 212–217.

Bryant, Fred B. "A Four-Factor Model of Perceived Control: Avoiding, Coping, Obtaining, and Savoring." *Journal of Personality* 57, no. 4 (1989): 773–797.

Bryant, Fred B., Erica D. Chadwick, and Katharina Kluwe. "Understanding the Processes That Regulate Positive Emotional Experience: Unsolved Problems and Future Directions for Theory and Research on Savoring." *International Journal of Wellbeing* 1, no. 1 (2011): 107–126.

Bryant, Fred. B., Colette M. Smart, and Scott P. King. "Using the Past to Enhance the Present: Boosting Happiness Through Positive Reminiscence." *Journal of Happiness Studies* 6 (2005): 227–260.

Bryant, Fred B., and Joseph Veroff. *Savoring: A New Model of Positive Experience*. Mahwah, New Jersey: Lawrence Erlbaum Associates, Inc., 2007.

Burgdorf, Jeffery, and Jaak Panksepp. "The Neurobiology of Positive Emotions." *Neuroscience and Biobehavioral Reviews* 30 (2006): 173–187.

Calder, Andrew J., Andrew D. Lawrence, and Andrew W. Young. "Neuropsychology of Fear and Loathing," *Nature* 2 (2001): 353–363.

Campbell, Stephanie, Michael Marriott, Claude Nahmias, and Glenda M. MacQueen. "Lower Hippocampal Volume in Patients Suffering from Depression: A Meta-Analysis." *American Journal of Psychiatry* 161, no. 4 (2001): 598–607.

Chida, Yoichi, and Andrew Steptoe. "Positive Psychological Well-Being and Mortality: A Quantitative Review of Prospective Observational Studies." *Psychosomatic Medicine* 70, no.7 (2008): 741–756.

Choi, Jung-Kyoo, and Bowles, Samuel. "The Coevolution of Parochial Altruism and War." *Science* 318 (2007): 636–640.

Christoffel, Daniel J., Sam A. Golden, and Scott J. Russo. "Structural and Synaptic Plasticity in Stress-Related Disorders." *Reviews in Neurosciences* 22, no. 5 (2011): 535–549.

Cohn, Michael A., Barabara L. Fredrickson, Stephanie L. Brown, Joseph A. Mikels, and Anne M. Conway. "Happiness Unpacked: Positive Emotions Increase Life Satisfaction by Building Resilience." *Emotion* 9 (2009): 361–368.

Critchley, Hugo D. "Neural Mechanisms of Autonomic, Affective, and Cognitive Integration." *Journal of Comparative Neurology* 493 (2005): 154–166.

Critchley, Hugo D., and Yoko Nagai. "How Emotions Are Shaped by Bodily States." *Emotion Review* 4, no. 2 (2012): 163–168.

Cunningham, William A., and Tobias Brosch. "Motivational Salience: Amygdala Tuning from Traits, Needs, Values, and Goals." *Current Directions in Psychological Science* 21, no. 1 (2012): 54–59.

Cunningham, William A., and Tabitha Kirkland. "The Joyful, Yet Balanced Amygdala: Moderated Responses to Positive But Not Negative Stimuli in Trait Happiness." *Social Cognitive and Affective Neuroscience* (April 5, 2013; e-pub ahead of print).

Cunningham, William A., Carol L. Raye, and Macia K. Johnson. "Neural Correlates of Evaluation Associated with Promotion and Prevention Regulatory Focus." *Cognitive, Affective, and Behavioral Neuroscience* 5, no. 2 (2005): 202–211.

Decety, Jean, and Philip L. Jackson. "The Functional Architecture of Human Empathy." *Behaviorial and Cognitive Neuroscience Reviews* 3 (2004): 71–100.

Decety, Jean, and Margarita Svetlova. "Putting Together Phylogenetic and Ontogenetic Perspectives on Empathy." *Developmental Cognitive Neuroscience* 2, no. 1 (2011): 1–24.

Diener, Ed, and Micaela Y. Chan. "Happy People Live Longer: Subjective Well-Being Contributes to Health and Longevity." *Applied Psychophysiology* 3, no. 1 (2011): 1–43.

Duman, Ronald S., and George K. Aghajanian. "Synaptic Dysfunction in Depression: Potential Therapeutic Targets." *Science* 338 (2012): 68–72.

Dusek, Jeffery A., Hasan H. Out., Ann L. Wohlhueter, Manoj Bhasin, Luiz F. Zerbini, Marie G. Joseph, Herbert Benson, and Towia A. Libermann. "Genomic Counter-Stress Changes Induced by the Relaxation Response." *PLoS One* 3 (2008): e2576.

Ecker, Bruce, and L. Hulley. *Depth Oriented Brief Therapy: How to Be Brief When You Were Trained to Be Deep, and Vice Versa.* San Francisco: Jossey-Bass, 1996.

Ecker, Bruce, and Brian Toomey. "Depotentiation of Symptom-Producing Implicit Memory in Coherence Therapy." *Journal of Constructivist Psychology* 21, no. 2 (2008): 87–150.

Efferson, Charles, Rafael Lalive, and Ernst Fehr. "The Coevolution of Cultural Groups and Ingroup Favoritism." *Science* 321 (2008): 1844–1849.

Emmons, Robert. *Thanks! How the Science of Gratitude Can Make You Happier.* New York: Houghton Mifflin Harcourt, 2007.

Emmons, Robert A., and Michael McCullough. "Counting Blessings Versus Burdens: An Experimental Investigation of Gratitude and Subjective Well-Being in Daily Life." *Journal of Personality and Social Psychology* 84, no. 2 (2003): 377–389.

Emmons, Scott W. "The Mood of a Worm." *Science* 338 (2012): 475–476.

Esch, Tobias, and George B. Stefano. "The Neurobiology of Stress Management." *Neuroendocrinology Letters* 31, no.1 (2010): 19–39.

Fagley, Nancy. "Appreciation Uniquely Predicts Life Satisfaction Above Demographics, the Big 5 Personality Factors, and Gratitude." *Personality and Individual Differences* 53 (2012): 59–63.

Fehr, Ernst. "Human Behaviour: Don't Lose Your Reputation." *Nature* 432 (2004): 449–450.

Fehr, Ernst, and Bettina Rockenbach. "Human Altruism: Economic, Neural, and Evolutionary Perspectives." *Current Opinion in Neurobiology* 14, no.6 (2004): 784–790.

Feldman, Daniel. "Synaptic Mechanisms for Plasticity in Neocortex." *Annual Review of Neuroscience* 32 (2009): 33–55.

Feldman, Greg C., Jutta Joormann, and Sheri L. Johnson. "Responses to Positive Affect: A Self-Report Measure of Rumination and Dampening." *Cognitive Therapy and Research* 32, no. 4 (2008): 507–525.

Folkman, Susan, and Judith Moskowitz. "Positive Affect and the Other Side of Coping." *American Psychologist* 55 (2000): 647–654.

Fredrickson, Barbara. *Positivity: Top-Notch Research Reveals the 3 to 1 Ratio That Will Change Your Life.* New York: Three Rivers Press, 2009.

Fredrickson, Barbara L., Michael A. Cohn, Kimberly A. Coffey, Jolynn Pek, and Sandra M. Finkel. "Open Hearts Build Lives: Positive Emotions, Induced Through Loving-Kindness Meditation, Build Consequential Personal Resources." *Journal of Personality and Social Psychology* 95, no. 5 (2008): 1045–1062.

Fredrickson, Barbara, and Robert Levenson. "Positive Emotions Speed Recovery from the Cardiovascular Sequelae of Negative Emotions." *Psychology Press* 12 (1998): 191–220.

Fredrickson, Barbara L., Michele M. Tugade, Christian E. Waugh, and Gregory R. Larkin. "What Good Are Positive Emotions in Crisis? A Prospective Study of Resilience and Emotions Following the Terrorist Attacks on the U.S. on 9/11/01." *Journal of Personality and Social Psychology* 84, no. 2 (2003): 365–376.

Fry, Douglas P. "Life Without War." *Science* 336 (2012): 879–884.

Gabbard, Glen O. "A Neurobiologically Informed Perspective on Psychotherapy." *British Journal of Psychiatry* 177 (2000): 117–122.

Gable, Shelly L., Harry T. Reis, Emily A. Impett, and Evan R. Asher. "What Do You Do When Things Go Right? The Intrapersonal and Interpersonal Benefits of Sharing Positive Events." *Journal of Personality and Social Psychology* 87, no. 2 (2004): 228–245.

Garavan, Hugh, Cara J. Pendergrass, Thomas Ross, Elliot A. Stein, and Robert Risinger. "Amygdala Response to Both Positively and Negatively Valenced Stimuli." *Neuroreport* 12, no. 12 (2001): 2779–2783.

Gendlin, Eugene T. *Focusing.* New York: Random House, 1982.

Germer, Christopher. *The Mindful Path to Self-Compassion: Freeing Yourself from Destructive Thoughts and Emotions.* New York: The Guilford Press, 2009.

Gerstner, Wulfram, Henning Sprekeler, and Gustavo Deco. "Theory and Simulation in Neuroscience." *Science* 338 (2012): 60–65.

Gilbert, Paul. *The Compassionate Mind: A New Approach to Life's Challenges.* Oakland, Calif.: New Harbinger Publications, Inc., 2010.

———. "Introducing Compassion-Focused Therapy." *Advances in Psychiatric Treatment* 14 (2009): 199–208.

Gogolla, Nadine, P. Caroni, A. Lüthi, and C. Herry. "Perineuronal Nets Protect Fear Memories from Erasure." *Science* 325 (2009): 1258–1261.

Gottman, John. *Why Marriages Succeed or Fail: And How You Can Make Yours Last.* New York: Simon & Schuster, 1995.

Gould, Rebecca L., Mark C. Couson, and Robert J. Howard. "Cognitive Behavioral Therapy for Depression in Older People: A Meta-Analysis and Meta-Regression of Randomized Controlled Trails." *Journal of the American Geriatrics Society* 60, no. 10 (2012): 1817–1830.

Gruber, June. "Can Feeling Too Good Be Bad? Positive Emotion Persistence (PEP) in Bipolar Disorder." *Current Directions in Psychological Science* 20, no. 4 (2011): 217–221.

Gutsell, Jennifer N., and Michael Inzlicht. "Empathy Constrained: Prejudice Predicts Reduced Mental Simulation of Actions During Observation of Outgroups." *Journal of Experimental Social Psychology* 46 (2010): 841–845.

Hamann, Stephan B., Timothy D. Ely, John M. Hoffman, and Clinton D. Kilts. "Ecstasy and Agony: Activation of the Human Amygdala in Positive and Negative Emotion." *Psychological Science* 13, no. 2 (2002): 135–141.

Hanh, Thich Nhat. *Being Peace.* Berkeley: Parallax Press, 2005.

Hanrahan, Fidelma, Andy P. Field, Fergal W. Jones, and Graham C. L. Davey. "A Meta-Analysis of Cognitive Therapy for Worry in Generalized Anxiety Disorder." *Clinical Psychology Review* 33, no. 1 (2013): 120–132.

Harris, Lasana T., and Susan T. Fiske. "Social Groups That Elicit Disgust Are Differentially Processed in mPFC." *Social Cognitive and Affective Neuroscience* 2 (2007): 45–51.

Heinrichs, Markus, Thomas Baumgartner, Clemens Kirschbaum, and Ulrike Ehlert. "Social Support and Oxytocin Interact to Suppress Cortisol and Subjective Responses to Psychosocial Stress." *Biological Psychiatry* 54 (2003): 1389–1398.

Herman, Judith. *Trauma and Recovery: The Aftermath of Violence—from Domestic Abuse to Political Terror.* New York: BasicBooks, 1997.

Higgins, E. Tory. "Beyond Pleasure and Pain." *American Psychologist* 52, no. 12 (1997): 1280–1300.

Ho, Victoria M., Ji-Anne Lee, and Kelsey C. Martin. "The Cell Biology of Synaptic Plasticity." *Science* 334 (2011): 623–628.

Hofmann, Stefan G., Anu Asnaani, Imke J. J. Vonk, Alice T. Sawyer, and Angela Fang. "The Efficacy of Cognitive Behavioral Therapy: A Review of Meta-Analyses." *Cognitive Therapy and Research* 36, no.5 (2012): 427–440.

Holzel, Britta K., Ulrich Ott, Tim Gard, Hannes Hempel, Martin Weygandt, Katrin Morgen, and Dieter Vaitl. "Investigation of Mindfulness Meditation Practitioners with Voxel-Based Morphometry." *Social Cognitive and Affective Neuroscience* 3 (2008): 55–61.

IsHak, Waguih William, Maria Kahloond, and Hala Fakhrye. "Oxytocin's Role in Enhancing Well-Being: A Literature Review." *Journal of Affective Disorders* 130, no. 1 (2011): 1–9.

Kahneman, Daniel, and Amos Tversky. "Prospect Theory: An Analysis of Decision Under Risk." *Econometrica* 47, no. 2 (1979): 163–292.

Kandel, Eric R. *In Search of Memory: The Emergence of a New Science of Mind.* New York: W. W. Norton & Company, 2007.

———. "A New Intellectual Framework for Psychiatry." *American Journal of Psychiatry* 155 (1998): 457–469.

Karatsoreos, Inga N., and Bruce S. McEwen. "Psychobiological Allostasis: Resistance, Resilience, and Vulnerability." *Trends in Cognitive Sciences* 15, no. 12 (2011): 576–584.

Kashdan, Todd. *Curious? Discover the Missing Ingredient to a Fulfilling Life.* New York: William Morrow, 2009.

Kegel, Cornelia A. T., Adriana G. Bus, and Marinus H. van Ijzendoorn. "Differential Susceptibility in Early Literacy Instruction Through Computer Games: The Role of the Dopamine D4 Receptor Gene (DRD4)." *Mind, Brain, and Education* 5: 71–78.

Keltner, Dacher. *Born to Be Good: The Science of a Meaningful Life.* New York: W.W. Norton & Company, Inc., 2009.

Kermer, Deborah A., Erin Driver-Linn, Timothy D. Wilson, and Daniel T. Gilbert. "Loss Aversion Is an Affective Forecasting Error." *Psychological Science* 17, no. 8 (2006): 649–653.

Keverne, Eric B., Nicholas D. Martensz, and Bernadette Tuite. "Beta-Endorphin Concentrations in Cerebrospinal Fluid of Monkeys Are Influenced by Grooming Relationships." *Psychoneuroendocrinology* 14 (1989): 155–161.

Kirby, E. D., A. R. Friedman, D. Covarrubias, C. Ying, W. G. Sun, K. A. Goosens, R. M. Sapolsky, and D. Kaufer. "Basolateral Amygdala Regulation of Adult Hippocampal Neurogenesis and Fear-Related Activation of Newborn Neurons." *Molecular Psychiatry* 17 (2012): 527–536.

Klimecki, Olga M., Susanne Leiberg, Claus Lamm, and Tania Singer. "Functional Neural Plasticity and Associated Changes in Positive Affect After Compassion Training." *Cerebral Cortex* 6 (2012), doi: 10.1093/cercor/bhs142 PII: bhs142.

Korn, Deborah L., and Andrew M. Leeds. "Preliminary Evidence of Efficacy for EMDR Resource Development and Installation in the Stabilization Phase of Treatment of Complex Posttraumatic Stress Disorder." *Journal of Clinical Psychology* 58, no. 12 (2002): 1465–1487.

Langston, Christopher A. "Capitalizing on and Coping with Daily-Life Events: Expressive Responses to Positive Events." *Journal of Personality and Social Psychology* 67 (1994): 1112–1125.

Lazar, Sara W., Catherine E. Kerr, Rachel H. Wasserman, Jeremy R. Gray, Douglas N. Greve, Micheal T. Treadway, Metta McGarvey, Brian T. Quinn, Jeffery A. Dusek, Herbert Benson, Scott L. Rauch, Christopher I. Moore, and Bruce Fisch. "Meditation Experience Is Associated with Increased Cortical Thickness." *Neuroreport* 16 (2005): 1893–1897.

Leary, Mark R., Eleanor B. Tate, Claire E. Adams, Ashley Batts, and Allen Jessica Hancock. "Self-Compassion and Reactions to Unpleasant Self-Relevant Events: The Implications of Treating Oneself Kindly." *Journal of Personality* 92 (2007): 887–904.

LeDoux, Joseph E. *Synaptic Self: How Our Brains Become Who We Are.* New York: Penguin Books, 2003.

Leussis, M. P., and S. L. Andersen. "Is Adolescence a Sensitive Period for Depression? Behavioral and Neuroanatomical Findings from a Social Stress Model." *Synapse* 62, no. 1 (2007): 22–30.

Levine, Peter A. *In an Unspoken Voice: How the Body Releases Trauma and Restores Goodness.* Berkeley: North Atlantic Books, 2010.

Leyro, Teresa M. "Distress Tolerance and Psychopathological Symptoms and Disorders: A Review of the Empirical Literature Among Adults." *Psychological Bulletin* 136, no. 4 (2010): 576–600.

Liberzon, Israel, K., Luan Phan, Laura R. Decker, and Stephan F. Taylor. "Extended Amygdala and Emotional Salience: A PET Activation Study of Positive and Negative Affect." *Neuropsychopharmacology* 28, no. 4 (2003): 726–733.

Lim, Byung Kook, Kee Wui Huang, Brad A. Grueter, Patrick E. Rothwell, and Robert C. Malenka. "Anhedonia Requires MC4R-Mediated Synaptic Adaptations in Nucleus Accumbens." *Nature* 487 (2012): 183–189.

Luders, Eileen, Arthur W. Toga, Natasha Lepore, and Christian Gaser. "The Underlying Anatomical Correlates of Long-Term Meditation: Larger Hippocampal and Frontal Volumes of Gray Matter." *NeuroImage* 45 (2009): 672–678.

Luskin, Frederic, Megan Reitz, Kathryn Newell, Thomas Gregory Quinn, and William Haskell. "A Controlled Pilot Study of Stress Management Training of Elderly Patients with Congestive Heart Failure." *Preventive Cardiology* 5 (2002): 168–174.

Lyubomirsky, Sonja. *The How of Happiness: A New Approach to Getting the Life You Want.* New York: Penguin Press, 2008.

Lyubomirsky, Sonja, Kennon M. Sheldon, and David Schkade. "Pursuing Happiness: The Architecture of Sustainable Change." *Review of General Psychology* 9, no. 2 (2005): 111–131.

MacLean, Paul D. *The Triune Brain in Evolution: Role in Paleocerebral Functions.* New York: Springer, 1990.

Maguire, Eleanor, David Gadian, Ingrid Johnsrude, Catriona Good, John Ashburner, Richard Frackowiak, and Christopher Frith. "Navigation-Related Structural Change in the Hippocampi of Taxi Drivers." *National Academy of Sciences* 87 (2000): 4398–4403.

Maslow, Abraham. *The Farther Reaches of Human Nature.* New York: Penguin, 1993.

McCullough, Michael, Shelley D. Kirkpatrick, Robert A. Emmons, and Davd B. Larson. "Is Gratitude a Moral Affect?" *Psychological Bulletin* 127, no. 2 (2001): 249–266.

McEwen, Bruce S. "Protective and Damaging Effects of Stress Mediators: Central Role of the Brain." *Dialogues in Clinical Neuroscience* 8, no. 4 (2006): 367–381.

———. "Stress, Adaptation, and Disease: Allostasis and Allostatic Load." *Annals of the New York Academy of Sciences* 840 (1998): 33–44.

McEwen, Bruce, and Peter Gianaros. "Central Role of the Brain in Stress and Adaptation: Links to Socioeconomic Status, Health, and Disease." *Annals of the New York Academy of Sciences* 1186 (2010): 190–222.

———. "Stress- and Allostasis-Induced Brain Plasticity." *Annual Review of Medicine* 62 (2011): 431–435.

McGonigal, Kelly. *The Willpower Instinct: How Self-Control Works, Why It Matters, and What You Can Do to Get More.* New York: Avery, 2011.

McPherron, Shannon P., Zeresenay Alemseged, Curtis W. Marean, Jonathan G. Wynn, Denné Reed, Denis Geraads, René Bobe, and Hamdallah A. Béarat. "Evidence for Stone-Tool Assisted Consumption of Animal Tissues Before 3.39 Million Years Ago at Dikika, Ethiopia." *Nature* 446 (2010): 857–860.

Meyer-Lindenberg, Andreas. "Impact of Prosocial Neuropeptides on Human Brain Function." *Progress in Brain Research* 170 (2008): 463–470.

Mika, Agnieszka, G. J. Mazur, A. N. Hoffman, J. S. Talboom, H. A. Bimonte-Nelson, F. Sanabria, and C. D. Conrad. "Chronic Stress Impairs Prefrontal Cortex-Dependent Response Inhibition and Spatial Working Memory." *Behavioral Neuroscience* 126, no. 5 (2012): 605–619.

Milton, Amy L., and Barry J. Everitt. "Wiping Drug Memories" *Science* 336 (2012): 167–168.

Moll, Jorge, Frank Krueger, Roland Zahn, Matteo Pardini, Ricardo de Oliveira-Souza, and Jordan Grafman. "Human Fronto-Mesolimbic Networks Guide Decisions About Charitable Donation." *Proceedings of the National Academy of Sciences* 103 (2006): 15623–15628.

Monfils, Marie-H., Kiriana K. Cowansage, Eric Klann, and Joseph E. LeDoux. "Extinction-Reconsolidation Boundaries: Key to Persistent Attenuation of Fear Memories." *Science* 324 (2009): 951–955.

Mongillo, Gianluigi, Omri Barak, and Misha Tsodyks. "Synaptic Theory of Working Memory." *Science* 319 (2008): 1543–1546.

Morris, J. S., K. J. Friston, C. Buchel, C. D. Frith, A. W. Young, A. J. Calder, and R. J. Dolan. "A Differential Neural Response in the Human Amygdala to Fearful and Happy Facial Expressions." *Nature* 383 (1996): 812–815.

Morris, J. S., A. Ohman, and R. J. Dolan. "Conscious and Unconscious Emotional Learning in the Human Amygdala." *Nature* 393 (1998): 467–470.

Nader, Karim. "Memory Traces Unbound." *Trends in Neurosciences* 26, no. 2 (2003): 65–70.

Nader, Karim, Glenn E. Schafe, and Joseph. E. LeDoux. "The Labile Nature of Consolidation Theory." *Nature* 1, no. 3 (2000): 216–219.

Neff, Kristin D. "Self-Compassion: An Alternative Conceptualization of a Healthy Attitude Toward Onself." *Self and Identity* 2, no. 2 (2003): 85–101.

———. "Self-Compassion, Self-Esteem, and Well-Being." *Social and Personality Psychology Compass* 5, no. 1 (2011): 1–12.

Neumann, Inga D. "Brain Oxytocin: A Key Regulator of Emotional and Social Behaviours in Both Females and Males." *Journal of Neuroendocrinology* 20 (2008): 858–865.

Niedenthal, Paula. "Embodying Emotion." *Science Magazine* 316 (2007): 1002–1005.

Nowak, Martin A., and Sigmund, Karl. "Evolution of Indirect Reciprocity." *Nature* 437 (2005): 1291–1298.

Ogden, Pat. *Trauma and the Body: A Sensorimotor Approach to Psychotherapy.* New York: W. W. Norton & Company, 2006.

Olatunji, Bunmi O., M. L. Davis, M. B. Powers and J. A. Smits. "Cognitive-Behavioral Therapy for Obsessive-Compulsive Disorder: A Meta-Analysis of Treatment Outcome and Moderators." *Journal of Psychiatric Research* 47, no. 1 (2013): 33–41.

Olszewski, Pawel K., Anica Klockars, Helgi B. Schiöth, and Allen S. Levine. "Oxytocin as Feeding Inhibitor: Maintaining Homestasis in Consummatory Behavior." *Pharmacology Biochemistry and Behavior* 97 (2010): 47–54.

Ostby, Ylva, Kristine B. Walhovda, Christian K. Tamnes, Håkon Grydeland, Lars Tjelta Westlye, and Anders M. Fjell. "Mental Time Travel and Default-Mode Network Functional Connectivity in the Developing Brain." *Proceedings of the National Academy of Sciences* 109, no. 42 (2012): 16800–16804.

Palmer, Linda, and Gary Lynch. "A Kantian View of Space." *Science* 328 (2010): 1487–1488.

Panksepp, Jaak. "Affective Consciousness: Core Emotional Feelings in Animals and Humans." *Consciousness & Cognition* 14, no. 1 (2005): 30–80.

———. *Affective Neuroscience: The Foundations of Human and Animal Emotions.* New York: Oxford University Press, 1998.

Paradiso, Sergio. "Cerebral Blood Flow Changes Associated with Attribution of Emotional Valence to Pleasant, Unpleasant, and Neutral Visual Stimuli in a PET Study of Normal Subjects." *American Journal of Psychiatry* 156, no. 10 (1999): 1618–1629.

Parfitt, Guestavo Morrone, Ândrea Kraemer Barbosa, Renan Costa Campos, André Peres Koth, and Daniela Martí Barros. "Moderate Stress Enhances Memory Persistence: Are Adrenergic Mechanisms Involved?" *Behavioral Neuroscience* 126, no. 5 (2012): 729–730.

Park, Nansook. "Character Strengths: Research and Practice." *Journal of College & Character* 10, no. 4 (2009): 1–10.

Pecina, S., and Kent C. Berridge. "Hedonic Hot Spot in Nucleus Accumbens Shell: Where Do Mu-Opiods Cause Increased Impact of Sweetness?" *Journal of Neuroscience* 25, no. 50 (2005): 11777–11786.

Pennisi, Elizabeth. "Nervous System May Have Evolved Twice." *Science* 339 (2013): 391.

Peterson, Christopher, Willibald Ruch, Ursula Beermann, Nansook Park, and Martin Seligman. "Strengths of Character, Orientations to Happiness, and Life Satisfaction." *Journal of Positive Psychology* 2, no. 3 (2007): 149–156.

Placais, Pierre-Yves, and Thomas Preat. "To Favor Survival Under Food Shortage, the Brain Disables Costly Memory." *Science* 339 (2013): 440–442.

Porges, Stephen W. *The Polyvagal Theory: Neurophysiological Foundations of Emotions, Attachment, Communication, and Self-Regulation.* New York: W.W. Norton & Company, 2011.

Pressman, S., and S. Cohen. "Does Positive Affect Influence Health?" *Psychological Bulletin* 131 (2005): 925–971.

Price, Tom F., L. W. Dieckman, and Eddie Harmon-Jones. "Embodying Approach Motivation: Body Posture Influences Startle Eyeblink and Event-Related Potential Responses to Apptitive Stimuli." *Biological Psychology* 90 (2012): 211–217.

Price, Tom F., Carly K. Peterson, and Eddie Harmon-Jones. "The Emotive Neuroscience of Embodiment." *Motivation and Emotion* 36, no. 1 (2012): 27–37.

Quoidbach, Jordi, Elizabeth V. Berry, Michel Hansenne, and Moïra Mikolajczak. "Positive Emotion Regulation and Well-Being: Comparing the Impact of Eight Savoring and Dampening Strategies." *Personality and Individual Differences* 49, no. 5 (2010): 368–373.

Rees, Brian. "Overview of Outcome Data of Potential Mediation Training for Soldier Resilience." *Military Medicine* 176, no. 11 (2011): 1232–1242.

Roberts-Wolfe, Douglas, Matthew D. Sacchet, Elizabeth Hastings, Harold Roth, and Willoughby Britton. "Mindfulness Training Alters Emotional Memory Recall Compared to Active Controls: Support for an Emotional Information Processing Model of Mindfulness." *Frontiers in Human Neuroscience* 6 (2012): 1–13.

Rozin, Paul, and Edward Royzman. "Negativity Bias, Negativity Dominance, and Contagion." *Personality & Social Psychology Review* 5 (2001): 296–320.

Sapolsky, Robert. *Why Zebras Don't Get Ulcers.* New York: Holt Paperbacks, 2004.

Schachter, Daniel L. "Adaptive Constructive Processes and the Future of Memory." *American Psychologist* 67, no. 8 (2012): 603–613.

———. *The Seven Sins of Memory: How the Mind Forgets and Remembers.* New York: Houghton Mifflin Harcourt Books, 2002.

Schiller, Daniela, Marie H. Monfils, Candace M. Raio, David C. Johnson, Joseph E. LeDoux, and Elizabeth A. Phelps. "Preventing the Return of Fear in Humans Using Reconsolidation Update Mechanisms." *Nature* 463 (2010): 49–53.

Seeley, William W., Vinod Menon, Alan F. Schatzberg, Jennifer Keller, Gary H. Glover, Heather Kenna, Allan L. Reiss, and Michael D. Greicius. "Dissociable Intrinsic Connectivity Networks for Salience Processing and Executive Control." *The Journal of Neuroscience* 27 (2007): 2356–2349.

Seligman, Martin. *Flourish: A Visionary New Understanding of Happiness and Well-Being.* New York: Free Press, 2011.

———. *Learned Optimism: How to Change Your Mind and Your Life.* New York: Vintage, 2006.

Seligman, Martin, and Tracy A. Steen. "Positive Psychotherapy Progress: Empirical Validation of Interventions." *American Psychologist* 60, no. 5 (2005): 410–421.

Semaw, Sileshi, P. Renne, J. W. K. Harris, C. S. Feibel, R. L. Bernor, N. Fesseha, and K. Mowbray. "2.5-Year-Old Stone Tools from Gona, Ethiopia." *Nature* 385 (1997): 333–336.

Shapiro, Shauna. "Mindfulness and Psychotherapy." *Journal of Clinical Psychology* 65 (2009): 1–6.

Sharot, Tali. *The Optimism Bias: A Tour of the Irrationally Positive Brain.* New York: Vintage, 2011.

Siegel, Daniel J. *The Mindful Brain.* New York: W.W. Norton & Company, 2007.

Skoglund, Pontus, Helena Malmström, Maanasa Raghavan, Jan Stora, Per Hall, Eske Willerslev, M. Thomas P. Gilbert, Anders Götherström, and Mattias Jakobsson. "Origins and Genetic Legacy of Neolithic Farmers and Hunter-Gatherers in Europe." *Science* 336 (2012): 466–469.

Smith, Eric Alden. "Communication and Collective Action: The Role of Language in Human Cooperation." *Evolution and Human Behavior* 31, no. 4 (2010): 231–245.

Southwick, Steven M., and Dennis S. Charney. "The Science of Resilience: Implications for the Prevention and Treatment of Depression." *Science* 338 (2012): 79–82.

Terrier, Nicholas. "Broad Minded Affective Coping (BMAC): A 'Positive' CBT Approach to Facilitating Positive Emotions." *International Journal of Cognitive Therapy* 31, no. 1 (2010): 65–78.

Thompson, Evan. *Mind in Life: Biology, Phenomenology, and the Sciences of Mind.* Cambridge, Mass.: Harvard University Press, 2007.

Tommaso, Pizzorusso. "Erasing Fear Memories." *Science* 325 (2009): 1214–1215.

Toomey, Brian, and Ecker, Bruce. "Competing Visions of the Implications of Neuroscience for Psychotherapy." *Journal of Constructivist Psychology* 22 (2009): 95–140.

Tugade, Michele. *Positive Emotions and Coping: Examining Dual-Process Models of Resilience.* In S. Folkman (ed.), *Oxford Handbook of Stress, Health, and Coping.* New York: Oxford University Press, 2011, pp. 186–199.

Tugade, Michele M., and Barbara L. Fredrickson. "Regulation of Positive Emotions: Emotion Regulation Strategies That Promote Resilience." *Journal of Happiness Studies* 8 (2007): 311–333.

Valente, Thomas W. "Network Interventions." *Science* 337 (2012): 49–53.

van der Kolk, Bessel A. *Traumatic Stress: The Effects of Overwhelming Experience on Mind, Body, and Society.* New York: The Guilford Press, 2006.

Videbech, Poul, and Barbaba Ravnkilde. "Hippocampal Volume and Depression: A Meta-Analysis of MRI Studies." *American Journal of Psychiatry* 161, no. 11 (2004): 1957–1966.

Viviani, Daniele, and Ron Stoop. "Opposite Effects of Oxytocin and Vasopressin on the Emotional Expression of the Fear Response." *Progress in Brain Research* 170 (2008): 207–218.

Vogel, Gretchen. "Can We Make Our Brains More Plastic?" *Science* 338 (2012): 36–39.

Vukasovic, Tena, Denis Bratko, and Ana Butkovic. "Genetic Contribution to the Individual Differences in Subjective Well-Being: A Meta-Analysis." *Journal for General Social Issues* 21 (2012): 1–17.

Walsh, Roger. "Lifestyle and Mental Health." *American Psychologist* 66 (2011): 579–592.

———. "The Meeting of Meditative Disciplines and Western Psychology." *American Psychologist* 61 (2006): 227–239.

Wang, Qingsong, Zhenggou Wang, Peifang Zhu, and Jianxin Jiang. "Alterations of Myelin Basic Protein and Ultrastructure in the Limbic System at the Early Stage of Trauma-Related Stress Disorder in Dogs." *The Journal of Trauma* 56, no. 3 (2004): 604–610.

Wimmer, G. Elliott, and Dapha Shohamy. "Preference by Association: How Memory Mechanisms in the Hippocampus Bias Decisions." *Science* 338 (2012): 270–273.

Wood, Joanne V., Sara A. Heimpel, John L. Michela. "Savoring Versus Dampening: Self-Esteem Differences in Regulating Positive Affect." *Journal of Personality and Social Psychology* 85 (2003): 566–580.

Xu, Xiaojin; Xiangyu Zuo, Xiaoying Wang, and Shihui Han. "Do You Feel My Pain? Racial Group Membership Modulates Empathic Neural Responses." *Journal of Neuroscience* 9, no. 26 (2009): 8525–8529.

Yan-Xue Xue, Yi-Xiao Luo, Ping Wu, Hai-Shui Shi, Li-Fen Xue, Chen Chen, Wei-Li Zhu, Zeng-Bo Ding, Yan-ping Bao, Jie Shi, David H. Epstein, Yavin Shaham, and Lin Lu. "A Memory Retrieval-Extinction Procedure to Prevent Drug Craving and Relapse." *Science* 336 (2012): 241–245.

Yechiam, Eldad, and Hochman, Guy. "Losses as Modulators of Attention: Review and Analysis of the Unique Effects of Losses Over Gains." *Psychological Bulletin* 139, no. 2 (2013): 497–518.

Index

Also available from Rider:

Super Brain
Unleash the explosive power of your mind

Deepak Chopra and Rudolph E. Tanzi

Two pioneers in health – Dr Deepak Chopra and Professor Rudolph E. Tanzi, one of the world's foremost experts on the causes of Alzheimer's – share a bold new understanding of the brain and a prescriptive plan for how we can use it to achieve physical, mental and spiritual well-being. They contend that by using techniques and skills such as mindfulness, intention and meditation, we can create new neural pathways in the brain. Thus, we can transform it into our most powerful tool for achieving health, happiness and enlightenment.

ISBN 9781846043673

Order direct from www.riderbooks.co.uk

Mindfulness
25 Ways to Live in the Moment through Art

Christophe André

Mindfulness is a uniquely beautiful work. Illustrated in full colour throughout, this bestselling book draws upon art as a source of inspiration. Expert practitioner Christophe André invites us to consider paintings while practising mindfulness techniques. With stunning simplicity and clarity, he sets out 25 lessons that could change your life – from understanding what it means to live mindfully, to useful tips for everyday situations.

Mindfulness offers an enduring source of quiet contemplation, enabling us to still our minds and become calmly aware of the present moment. From acceptance to freedom, from happiness to love, *Mindfulness* shows us how to approach our lives as living works of art.

ISBN 9781846044632

Order direct from www.riderbooks.co.uk

How to See Yourself As You Really Are
A Practical Guide to Self-Knowledge

His Holiness the Dalai Lama

How to See Yourself As You Really Are is based on the Buddhist belief that love and insight work together to bring about enlightenment like two wings of a bird. Here, His Holiness the Dalai Lama draws on wisdom and techniques – refined over centuries in Tibetan monasteries – to shed light on how we hurt ourselves through misguided and exaggerated notions of self, others, events and physical things. Adopting as its structure the traditional Buddhist steps of meditative reflection, *How to See Yourself As You Really Are* includes practical exercises and gives readers a clear path on which to assess their growth and personal development.

ISBN 9781846040405

Order direct from www.riderbooks.co.uk

The Miracle of Mindfulness

The Classic Guide to Meditation by the
World's Most Revered Master

Thich Nhat Hanh

In this beautifully written book, Buddhist monk and Nobel Peace Prize nominee Thich Nhat Hanh explains how to acquire the skills of mindfulness. Once we have these skills, we can slow our lives down and discover how to live in the moment – even simple acts like washing the dishes or drinking a cup of tea can be transformed into acts of meditation.

Thich Nhat Hanh's gentle anecdotes and practical exercises help us to arrive at greater self-understanding and peacefulness, whether we are beginners or advanced students. Irrespective of our particular religious beliefs, we can begin to reap the immense benefits that meditation has been proven to offer and experience the miracle of mindfulness for ourselves.

ISBN 9781846041068

Order direct from www.riderbooks.co.uk

ISBN 978-1-84604-106-8

Mind Whispering
How to break free from self-defeating emotional habits

Tara Bennett-Goleman
Author of *Emotional Alchemy*

Mind Whispering aims to transform us into more fully integrated human beings – mentally, emotionally and interpersonally. By using the practical techniques within it, our minds can be more free, our perceptions more true, our responses more artful, our connections more genuine – and our hearts happier.

Tara Bennett-Goleman's first book, *Emotional Alchemy,* was a *New York Times* bestseller and was translated into 25 languages. In her new work, *Mind Whispering,* the author draws on the very latest ideas in cognitive psychology, neuroscience and Eastern traditions to offer 'mind whispering' practices that will help us to become more positive and cultivate healing and beneficial states of being.

ISBN 9781846043390

Order direct from www.riderbooks.co.uk